Mastering Secured Transactions

Carolina Academic Press Mastering Series
Russell L. Weaver, Series Editor

Mastering Bankruptcy
George W. Kuney

Mastering Civil Procedure
David Charles Hricik

Mastering Corporations and Other Business Entities
Lee Harris

Mastering Criminal Law
Ellen S. Podgor, Peter J. Henning, Neil P. Cohen

Mastering Evidence
Ronald W. Eades

Mastering Intellectual Property
George W. Kuney, Donna C. Looper

Mastering Legal Analysis and Communication
David T. Ritchie

**Mastering Negotiable Instruments (UCC Articles 3 and 4)
and Other Payment Systems**
Michael D. Floyd

Mastering Products Liability
Ronald W. Eades

Mastering Professional Responsibility
Grace M. Giesel

Mastering Secured Transactions
Richard H. Nowka

Mastering Statutory Interpretation
Linda D. Jellum

Mastering Tort Law
Russell L. Weaver, John H. Bauman, Ronald W. Eades,
Andrew R. Klein, Edward C. Martin, Paul J. Zwier II

Mastering Secured Transactions

UCC Article 9

Richard H. Nowka

UNIVERSITY OF LOUISVILLE
LOUIS D. BRANDEIS SCHOOL OF LAW

CAROLINA ACADEMIC PRESS
Durham, North Carolina

Library of Congress Cataloging in Publication Data

Nowka, Richard H.
  Mastering secured transactions : UCC article 9 / Richard H. Nowka.
    p. cm.
  Includes index.
  ISBN 978-1-59460-362-4 (alk. paper)
  1. Security (Law)--United States. I. Title.

  KF1050.N69 2008
  346.7307'4--dc22

                              2008041486

Carolina Academic Press
700 Kent Street
Durham, NC 27701
Telephone (919) 489-7486
Fax (919) 493-5668
www.cap-press.com

Printed in the United States of America

Contents

Table of Statutes

Series Editor's Foreword

The Carolina Academic Press Mastering Series is designed to provide you with a tool that will enable you to easily and efficiently "master" the substance and content of law school courses. Throughout the series, the focus is on quality writing that makes legal concepts understandable. As a result, the series is designed to be easy to read and is not unduly cluttered with footnotes or cites to secondary sources.

In order to facilitate student mastery of topics, the Mastering Series includes a number of pedagogical features designed to improve learning and retention. At the beginning of each chapter, you will find a "Roadmap" that tells you about the chapter and provides you with a sense of the material that you will cover. A "Checkpoint" at the end of each chapter encourages you to stop and review the key concepts, reiterating what you have learned. Throughout the book, key terms are explained and emphasized. Finally, a "Master Checklist" at the end of each book reinforces what you have learned and helps you identify any areas that need review or further study.

We hope that you will enjoy studying with, and learning from, the Mastering Series.

Russell L. Weaver
Professor of Law & Distinguished University Scholar
University of Louisville, Louis D. Brandeis School of Law

Preface

Mastering Secured Transactions is a comprehensive resource for studying the sections and concepts of Article 9 of the Uniform Commercial Code. Because the book examines virtually all sections of Article 9, it will be useful as a study aid for a course on Secured Transactions or Commercial Law and for a bar examination.

As a teacher, I want to stress that the book is not a substitute for the statutory supplement your professor will require for the course. Mastering Secured Transactions explains the sections and concepts of Article 9 using text and examples, but you will want to read the Article 9 section and the official comment for each section you study.

Citations in the book to Article 9 are to the 1999 Official Text of Article 9, known as Revised Article 9, which includes subsequent amendments and modifications (mostly minor) adopted in 2000, 2001, 2003, and 2005. The 1999 Official Text is the most current version of Article 9. All states have adopted Revised Article 9, although each state has enacted minor variations, so as you study for a bar examination you should consult the Article 9 of the particular state.

Citations in the book to Article 1 are to the 2001 Official Text of Article 1, known as Revised Article 1. Thirty-four states have enacted Revised Article 1 as of November 2008. Citations to Article 2 are to the current Article 2, not the Amended Article 2 that no state has enacted as of this writing.

On the first day of my Secured Transactions course I always tell the students that Secured Transactions is my favorite course to teach, and I predict that it will be one of their favorite courses. Not surprising to me, many first-day skeptics agree with me by the end of the semester. I hope you will feel the same and I hope this book helps you make that discovery.

Richard H. Nowka
November 2008

Mastering Secured Transactions

Chapter 1

Secured Transactions That Article 9 Governs

Roadmap

- The meaning of "secured transaction"
- The meaning of "security interest"
- Security interests under other UCC Articles
- Agricultural liens
- Consignments
- Sales of receivables
- Leases of goods
- Transactions excluded from Article 9

A. Introduction

The American Law Institute and National Conference of Commissioners of Uniform State Laws began drafting the Uniform Commercial Code (UCC) in the mid 1940s. Their purpose was to provide uniform laws to govern commercial transactions. Those bodies adopted the first Official Draft of the UCC, the 1952 Official Draft, and submitted it to the state legislatures for enactment. Each Article of the UCC has been revised and amended since then. All states have enacted the UCC, although the UCC of each state contains variations, mostly minor, from the official text of the UCC.

Article 9 of the UCC creates a comprehensive scheme for regulating financing transactions where an interest in personal property or fixtures secures an obligation—a security interest. The short title of Article 9 is "Secured Transactions." A secured transaction is a transaction involving a security device, most frequently a security interest. The debtor grants a security interest to the creditor when the debtor owes an obligation to the creditor. Although granting a security interest is a voluntary act of the debtor, typically the creditor has superior bargaining power and requires the debtor to grant a security interest as a condition to making a loan or giving other value to the debtor. A security interest is the interest of the creditor in the debtor's personal property as collateral for the obligation the debtor owes and, if necessary, the right to take the property in payment of the obligation. A security interest maximizes the likelihood of payment of the obligation because if the debtor fails to pay the obligation, the creditor can use the property, for example sell it, to pay the debt. A creditor with a security interest has two sources of payment: the debtor and the property. The scope of Article 9 is over security interests in personal property and fixtures. Except for the limited situations noted in the next section, Article 9 does not govern transactions where an interest in real property secures an obligation.

Article 9 applies to some secured transactions that do not involve a debtor granting a security interest. It governs statutory agricultural liens, consignment transactions, sales of receivables, and security interests arising under other Articles of the UCC. Some of these transactions are included in the definition of "security interest," although they do not involve repayment of an obligation.

Before examining the transactions that Article 9 governs, it is helpful to define cursorily several recurring terms. They are examined more fully in subsequent chapters. *Attachment* and *attach* refer to the requirements for creating an enforceable security interest. *Perfection* of a security interest refers to the acts required to protect the security interest from claims of other persons to the collateral. *Priority* of a security interest refers to the superiority of the security interest against claims of other persons to the collateral.

B. General Scope of Article 9 — Section 9-109(a)

One of the more impressive features of Article 9 is the many types of transactions it governs. Section 9-109(a) declares that Article 9 governs any transaction, regardless of its title or form, "that creates a security interest in personal property or fixtures by contract." Section 1-201(b)(35) defines *security interest* to mean an interest in personal property or fixtures that secures payment or performance of an obligation. If the characteristics of a transaction include an interest in personal property as collateral for an obligation, it is a security interest regardless of the label the parties give the transaction.

Immediately, you realize that an interest in *real* property that secures an obligation, such as a real property mortgage, is not a "security interest in personal property" and not within the scope of Article 9. Section 9-109(d)(11) explicitly states that principle. However, the collateral for a security interest could be the debtor's right to receive payment, such as a promissory note, and the promissory note could be secured by an interest in real property. In that situation, section 9-203(g), discussed in Chapter 2, gives the secured party a security interest in the mortgage, as well as in the promissory note. The mortgage is collateral for the debt, just as the promissory note is collateral for the debt. For example, Owner borrows $5,000 from Lender, signs a promissory note for that amount, and secures her promissory note to Lender with a mortgage on her real property. Article 9 does not govern the mortgage transaction. Lender subsequently borrows $15,000 from Bank and grants Bank a security interest in the promissory note to secure its debt. Article 9 covers the Lender-Bank security interest in the promissory note. Consequently, Bank's security interest in the promissory note results in Bank having a security interest in the mortgage that secures the note. Bank does not have a mortgage, but rather a security interest in the mortgage.

Most security interests within the scope of Article 9 are the credit-in-exchange-for-collateral type: debtor borrows money and grants a security interest in its personal property or debtor buys personal property on credit and grants a security interest in the property purchased. However, Article 9 governs some transactions that do not have the typical characteristics of a security interest and excludes some transactions that are security interest-like transactions. The following sections examine those transactions.

1. Security Interests Arising under Articles 2 (Sales), 2A (Leases), 4 (Bank Deposits and Collections), and 5 (Letters of Credit)

Article 9 governs security interests arising under Articles 2, 2A, 4 and 5, although they are rarely a subject of law school study. These security interests arise from operation of the applicable UCC section, not from agreement between the parties. Consequently, Article 9 alters the normal attachment and perfection requirements for such security interests.

a. Security Interests Arising under Articles 2 and 2A

Articles 2 and 2A govern sales and leases of goods respectively. A security interest arises under Article 2 when: 1) the seller of goods reserves title to goods sold (Section 2-401); 2) the seller of goods procures a negotiable bill of lading to its own order, or a non-negotiable bill of lading to herself or her nominee (Section 2-505); or 3) the buyer of goods rightfully rejects tendered goods or justifiably revokes acceptance of goods (Section 2-711(3)). A security interest arises under Article 2A, section 2A-508(5), when the lessee of goods rightfully rejects tendered goods or justifiably revokes acceptance of goods. In the rejection and revocation situations, the buyer or the lessee is the secured party, just the opposite of the typical secured transaction where the seller is the secured party.

Article 9 postpones, until the debtor obtains possession of the goods, its attachment and perfection requirements for security interests arising under Articles 2 and 2A. Section 9-110 provides that these security interests are enforceable regardless of the secured party's compliance with the attachment requirements of section 9-203(b)(3). Consequently, these security interests automatically attach. Additionally, sections 9-110 and 9-309(6) establish automatic perfection for security interests arising under Articles 2 and 2A that continues until the debtor obtains possession of the goods.

However, the security interest created from the reservation of title by a seller presents a different situation — a situation where the seller typically relinquishes possession of the goods to the buyer before receiving full payment for them. That is the reason the seller reserves title. In that case, and in any other instance where the secured party contemplates relinquishing possession of goods, the secured party must satisfy Article 9's attachment and perfection requirements to have an enforceable, perfected security interest after relinquishing possession.

b. Security Interests Arising under Article 4

Article 4 governs bank deposits and collections. Section 4-210 establishes for a collecting bank a security interest in an item, typically a check, any accompanying documents, or the proceeds of either. Sections 9-109(a)(6) and 4-210(c) provide that Article 9 governs this security interest. Articles 9 and 4 combine to suspend Article 9's usual attachment and perfection requirements so long as the bank does not receive final settlement for the item or relinquish possession of it or any accompanying documents for purposes other than collection. Until one of these events occurs, section 4-210(3) provides that no security agreement is required, no filing of a financing statement is required, and the collecting bank's security interest has priority over conflicting perfected security interests in the item, accompanying documents, or proceeds of either. Sections 9-203(c) and 9-309(7) establish the same rules.

c. Security Interests Arising under Article 5

Article 5 governs letters of credit. A letter of credit is a three-party undertaking where the applicant for the letter requests the issuer of the letter, typically a bank, to promise the beneficiary of the letter that the issuer will pay an obligation that the applicant owes the beneficiary, regardless of the applicant's ability or willingness to pay. For example, suppose a foreign seller of goods to a New York buyer wants assurance that the buyer will pay the purchase price of the goods. To provide that assurance, the buyer requests its bank to issue a letter of credit to the seller whereby the bank promises to pay the seller the purchase price upon the seller's demand. The buyer is the applicant, the bank is the issuer, and the seller is the beneficiary.

Section 5-118 provides that an issuer of a letter of credit has a security interest in a document presented under a letter of credit to the extent it honors or gives value for the document. The *document presented under a letter of credit* frequently is a draft: an instrument consisting of an order of payment from the buyer to the seller. Sections 9-109(a)(6) and 5-118(b) provide that Article 9 governs this security interest. Articles 9 and 5 combine to suspend Article 9's usual attachment and perfection requirements provided the secured party has not been reimbursed or otherwise recovered the value given. Until either event occurs, section 5-118(b) provides that a security agreement is not required for attachment of the security interest. Sections 5-118(b)(2) and 9-309(8) additionally provide that if the document is presented in a medium other than a written or tangible medium (this allows for electronic documents), the security interest is perfected without additional action. If the document is presented in a written or tangible medium, and is not a certificated security, chattel paper, document of title, or letter of credit, sections 5-118(b)(3) and 9-309(8) perfect the security interest without additional action. These sections also grant the security interest priority over a conflicting security interest in the document, so long as the debtor does not have possession of it. If the document is a certificated security, chattel paper, document of title, or letter of credit, Official Comment 2 to section 5-118 notes that the Article 9 rules govern perfection and priority of the security interest.

2. Agricultural Liens — Section 9-109(a)(2)

Section 9-109(a)(2) brings agricultural liens on farm products within the scope of Article 9. Such liens are not security interests and are not created by agreement of the parties, but are created by statute in favor of a person who furnishes goods or services to a person engaged in farm operations. Typical agricultural liens include: a lien on livestock for the reasonable charges incurred by a person for keeping, caring for, feeding, and grazing the livestock; the licensed veterinarian's lien on an animal for professional services performed to the animal; and the landlord's lien for rent on the produce of premises that the landlord rented for farming.

An *agricultural lien* has three components under the definition in section 9-102(a)(5): 1) the lien secures payment or performance of an obligation for goods or services furnished in connection with the debtor's farming operation or payment of an obligation for rent on real property leased by debtor in connection with debtor's farming operations; 2) the lien is created by statute in favor of the person who furnished such goods or services in the ordinary course of its business, or created by statute in favor of a person that leased such real property to the debtor; and 3) the effectiveness of the lien does not depend on the lienholder's possession of the property subject to the lien. Article 9 governs only agricultural liens that fit Article 9's definition of an agricultural lien.

Section 9-102(a)(5) limits Article 9 governance of agricultural liens to liens on farm products. Section 9-102(a)(34) defines *farm products* as "crops grown, growing, or to be grown; ... livestock, born or unborn; ... supplies used or produced in a farming operation; or products of crops or livestock in their unmanufactured states" of a debtor engaged in a farming operation. *Farming operations*, defined in section 9-102(a)(35), means "raising, cultivating, propagating, fattening, grazing, or any other farming, livestock, or aquacultural operation." A person with a big garden is not engaged in farming operations. However, a dog breeder fits the "propagating" branch of the definition and could be considered a farmer. When farm products are in the possession of a person not engaged in farming operations, they are no longer farm products. For example, a rancher/debtor who raises cattle is engaged in farming operations. If the rancher sells the cattle to a beef processor, the cattle are inventory in the hands of the processor.

Article 9's governance of agricultural liens means that many Article 9 provisions applicable to security interests are applicable to an agricultural lien. The most important question is whether the holder of an agricultural lien must comply with Article 9's requirements for attachment and perfection. Article 9 is clear in applying its perfection requirements to an agricultural lien. Section 9-308(b) provides that: "An agricultural lien is perfected if it has become effective and all of the applicable requirements for perfection in Section 9-310 have been satisfied." Section 9-310(a) requires that a financing statement must be filed to perfect an agricultural lien.

Whether the lienholder must comply with Article 9's attachment requirements is not as clear. However, the relevant sections imply that the attachment requirements are not applicable. The attachment requirements established in sections 9-203(a) and (b) apply to a *security interest*. The definition of security interest in section 1-201(b)(35) does not include agricultural liens. Comparing the perfection requirements for security interests and agricultural liens provides further enlightenment. Section 9-308(a) states: "A security interest is perfected if it has attached and all of the applicable requirements for perfection in Sections 9-310 through 9-316 have been satisfied." Section 9-308(b) states: "An agricultural lien is perfected if it has become *effective* and all of the applicable requirements for perfection in Section 9-310 have been satisfied." It does not require attachment. Consequently, it appears the drafters did not intend Article 9's attachment requirements to apply to an agricultural lien.

3. Consignments — Sections 9-109(a)(4), 9-102(a)(20)

Section 9-109(a)(4) brings certain types of consignments within the scope of Article 9. You may have some familiarity with consignments from having either purchased or sold clothing or furniture at a consignment store. The consignment covered by Article 9 is similar, but with important differences. The following example illustrates the type of consignment that Article 9 governs. Suppose you have invented a new and improved mousetrap. Unfortunately, no merchant wants to buy them from you and risk being unable to resell them. You work a deal with your local hardware store where it agrees to sell the mousetraps in the store. You deliver 300 mousetraps to the store; it sells them for $5 each and remits the proceeds to you minus whatever amount you have agreed the store can retain. That transaction creates a consignment within the scope of Article 9. You are the consignor of the consigned goods. The hardware store is the consignee. The consignor has a security interest in the consigned goods under the section 1-201(b)(35) definition of a security interest. Governance of the consignment by Article 9 helps insure that other persons dealing with the consignee are on notice of the interest of the consignor because the consignor must satisfy Article 9's perfection requirements.

A working definition of a consignment is a transaction in which the owner of goods, the *consignor*, delivers them to a merchant, the *consignee*, for the purpose of sale. The owner retains title to the goods. When the merchant sells the consigned goods, it remits the proceeds, less its sales commission, to the consignor. Delivery of the goods from the consignor to the consignee is not a sale of the goods and the consignee is not obligated to purchase the consigned goods. Typically, the consignee returns all unsold goods. Goods are delivered under consignment for many purposes including price fixing, marketing distribution, and overcoming the unwillingness of a merchant to assume the risk of finding a market.

The Article 9 definition of *consignment* in section 9-109(a)(20) is much more detailed. A consignment consists of: 1) a transaction in which a consignor delivers goods to a merchant for the purpose of sale; 2) the merchant deals in goods of that kind under a name other than consignor, is not an auctioneer, and is not generally known by its creditors to be substantially engaged in selling the goods of others; 3) the aggregate value of each delivery of goods is $1000 or more at the time of delivery; 4) the goods are not consumer goods immediately before delivery; and 5) the transaction does not create a security interest that secures an obligation, meaning the consignment is not a disguised security interest. The *not consumer goods* requirement means that the consigned goods are not classified as consumer goods in the hands of the consignor. Consigned goods would be inventory to the consignee and could be consumer goods in the hands of the buyer from the consignee. But a transaction where a consignor consigns its consumer goods to the consignee is not a consignment within Article 9. For example, an owner might deliver her consumer-good motor vehicle valued at $5000 to a car dealer for the purpose of sale. Although the transaction is a consignment, it does not satisfy Article 9's definition and Article 9 does not govern the consignment because the consigned good is a consumer good immediately before delivery of it to the consignee.

Because a consignment that satisfies the Article 9 definition is a security interest, the consignor must comply with Article 9's requirements for attachment and perfection of a security interest. Although there is no obligation secured, the Article 9 definition labels the consignor the secured party, and the consignee the debtor. The attachment of a security interest, discussed in Chapter 2, requires that the consignor gives value to the consignee, the consignee has rights in the collateral, and the consignee has authenticated a security agreement. A typical consignment transaction will satisfy those requirements. First, the parties' consignment agreement (consignee sells goods and earns commission) satisfies the value requirement because the section 1-204 definition of value includes "any consideration sufficient to support a simple contract." Second, the consignee has rights in the consigned goods pursuant to the consignment agreement. Finally, the consignor and consignee would typically authenticate a record documenting the terms of the consignment, thus satisfying the authentication requirement.

The typical method of perfection of a consignment security interest is by filing of a financing statement. Additionally, section 9-103(d) makes the consignor's security interest in the consigned goods a *purchase-money security interest* in inventory. Purchase-money security interests receive greater protection under the Article 9 priority rules if the secured party satisfies specific requirements. Purchase-money security interests are discussed in Chapter 8.

a. Rights Acquired by Transferee of Consignee — Section 9-319

The questions most likely troubling the consignor (and perhaps the student) are: what are the rights of buyers of the consigned goods from the consignee, and what are the rights of creditors of the consignee in the consigned goods? Section 9-319 provides a logical, albeit somewhat knotted, answer. Except as otherwise provided in section 9-319(b), the consignee's rights in and title to the consigned goods are identical to those of the consignor as long as the goods are in the consignee's possession. This allows a consignee to transfer ownership in the consigned goods or use the goods as collateral as though the consignee were the owner or authorized to act by the owner. Section 9-319(a) gives a consignee those rights regardless of the fact that the transaction is a true consignment and a consignee would not normally have any rights in the consigned goods beyond the authority to possess and sell the goods. Consequently, a purchaser for value of the consigned goods or a creditor of the consignee may treat the goods as owned by the consignee and acquire the same rights it would obtain if the consignee were the owner. The buyer obtains title to the goods pursuant to section 9-319(a) regardless that the consignee does not own the goods. That result makes sense because one purpose of a consignment transaction is the sale of the goods.

However, a consignor is probably not as agreeable with the result when a creditor of the consignee claims the consigned goods. If the consignee has rights in the goods identical to those of the consignor, a creditor of the consignee can attach a security interest in the consigned goods regardless of whether the consignor authorized the consignee to create a security interest. For example, a creditor could secure a loan it makes to the consignee with a security interest in consignee's inventory. That inventory includes the consigned goods owned by the consignor because the consigned goods are inventory in the hands of the consignee. Protection of the consignor comes from section 9-319(b), which establishes an exception to section 9-319(a).

The exception of section 9-319(b) applies against creditors of the consignee and only if the consignor's security interest is perfected and would have priority over the rights of the consignee's creditor under the applicable Article 9 priority rules. A consignment security interest is perfected if the consignor files a financing statement. It has priority if the consignor perfects its security interest before the other creditor perfects or if the consignor satisfies the requirements for priority of a purchase-money security interest. The effect of satisfying those requirements is that the consignee's right and title to the consigned goods are not deemed identical to those of the consignor, but instead are determined by law other than Article 9. That means a creditor of the consignee would be unable to attach a security interest to the consigned goods because the consignee's rights typically would be only those of a bailee of goods who is not authorized to create a security interest in the goods. Consequently, the consignor's rights in the consigned goods are superior to the creditor of the consignee. However, if the consignor does not satisfy the conditions to the exception it does not operate, the consignee has the rights and title to the goods identical to those of consignor, and the consignee's creditor can attach those rights. Notice that the exception does not affect the rights of a purchaser for value from consignee.

4. Sales of Accounts, Chattel Paper, Payment Intangibles, and Promissory Notes—Sections 9-109(a)(3), 9-318, 1-201(b)(35)

A right to payment can be created in a variety of transactions. Goods and services can be sold on the recipient's oral or written promise to pay. Alternatively, that promise to pay could be memorialized by the recipient's signing of a promissory note. Goods can be sold pursuant to a written or electronic document wherein the buyer promises to pay and grants a security interest in the goods purchased. All of those transactions create a right to payment in favor of the supplier of the goods or services. These rights to payment, commonly known as *receivables*, are a valuable asset because the recipient of the goods or services is obligated to pay. (Official Comment 5 to section 9-102 discusses the various types of receivables.) However, the owner of the receivable may not want or be able to wait for its money. If you buy furniture on the "twelve months same as cash plan," you don't have to pay for twelve months, but the seller does not receive payment for twelve months. Consequently, the owner of the receivable might sell it so the owner can obtain payment earlier than the under the terms of the receivable.

You might find this discussion interesting, but are wondering how it connects to Article 9? The connection is that Article 9 governs a sale of a receivable. It is another type of transaction that is a security interest because the UCC says so. Section 1-201(b)(35) states that *security interest* "includes any interest of a ... buyer of accounts, chattel paper, a payment intangible, or a promissory note in a transaction that is subject to Article 9." Section 9-109(a)(3) provides that Article 9 applies to a sale of accounts, chattel paper, payment intangibles, or promissory notes. Consequently, Article 9 governs a transaction in such property that the parties intend as an outright sale. Article 9's definitions of secured party, debtor, and collateral, sections 9-102(a)(72), (28), and (12), respectively, label the buyer of such property a secured party, the seller a debtor, and the property sold the collateral. Of course, Article 9 governs the traditional security interest created when the owner of the receivable uses it as collateral to secure a loan.

Believe it or not, there is logic to UCC coverage. Official Comment 4 to section 9-109 declares: "[t]his approach [inclusion in Article 9] generally has been successful in avoiding difficult problems of distinguishing between transactions in which a receivable secures an obligation and those in which the receivable has been sold outright." More enlightening is the statement of the UCC's Permanent Editorial Board in PEB Commentary No. 14: "The reason for subjecting both sales and secured transactions to Article 9 was to inform third parties of existing interests in a debtor's receivables and to provide protection for all types of assignments of receivables." In plain language, the reason for including a sale of receivables as a transaction Article 9 governs is to protect persons who acquire an interest in the receivable from the owner *after* the owner sold it to the first buyer. The first buyer of such property must comply with Article 9's perfection requirements to have priority over subsequent creditors and purchasers of the receivable from the seller. If the first buyer complies with the perfection requirements, subsequent parties have notice of its interest. A buyer who does not comply risks subordination to subsequent buyers and creditors. Chapters 2, 3, and 5 discuss attachment and perfection of a security interest in receivables.

The problem avoided by Article 9's governance of sales of receivables starts with an unscrupulous receivable owner. Suppose the owner of an account sells it in order to obtain funds. In principle, no interest remains with the owner and consequently there is nothing to sell. However, because there is no easily verifiable method to determine whether the owner has sold an account, the owner sells it again. Now we have two buyers of the same account. Only one buyer will obtain satisfaction. The other buyer has only an action against the owner based on the owner's lack of title. Frequently the owner is now insolvent.

The buyer of a receivable might question why Article 9 should apply. It naturally believes it has purchased all rights and interests in the receivable so there is nothing left for the seller to sell or the seller's creditors to attach. The drafters of Article 9 indicate their concurrence with the buyer's contention in Official Comment 2 to section 9-318.

> The fact that a sale of an account or chattel paper gives rise to a "security interest" does not imply that the seller retains an interest in the property that has been sold. To the contrary, a seller of an account or chattel paper retains no interest whatsoever in the property to the extent that it has been sold.

Additionally, section 9-318(a) emphatically supports the buyer: "A debtor [the seller] that has sold an account, chattel paper, payment intangible, or promissory note does not retain a legal or equitable interest in the collateral sold." Section 9-318(b), however, adopts a rule that establishes the rights of creditors and purchasers for value of an *account or chattel paper* from a debtor that previously sold the account or chattel paper. Under section 9-318(b), the seller of accounts or chattel paper is deemed to have rights and title to the property identical to the rights and title it sold for as long as the buyer's "security interest" is unperfected. Consequently, the seller can sell or create a security interest in the receivable already sold if the initial buyer did not perfect the security interest created by the sale. If the initial buyer of the accounts or chattel paper perfects the "security interest" created by its purchase, the seller has no rights to sell or encumber and the subsequent buyer or creditor obtains nothing other than a cause of action against the seller. The rule of section 9-318(b) does not affect a sale of payment intangibles or promissory notes because such sales are perfected automatically upon attachment pursuant to sections 9-309(3) and (4).

An example helps illustrate section 9-318. Seller sells accounts to Buyer 1, and under section 9-318(a) Seller retains no interest in them. Because Article 9 deems the sale a security interest, the buyer must satisfy Article 9's attachment and perfection requirements to protect its rights. Buyer 1 does not perfect its security interest in the accounts. Seller sells the same accounts to Buyer 2, notwithstanding its lack of rights to sell. Nevertheless, for purposes of determining the rights of Buyer 2, section 9-318(b) states that Seller retains the rights it previously sold to Buyer 1. Consequently, Buyer 2 obtains rights in the accounts. If Buyer 2 perfects its security interest, it will be superior to the unperfected security interest of Buyer 1. If Buyer 1 had perfected its security interest in the accounts *before* Seller sold to Buyer 2, Seller would have had no rights to sell to Buyer 2. In that situation, Buyer 2 acquires only a cause of action against Seller. If Buyer 1 perfects its security interest in the accounts *after* Seller's sale to Buyer 2, Seller had rights to sell to Buyer 2. Priority between the two buyers is decided under the first-to-file-or-perfect rule of section 9-322, discussed in Chapter 6. These examples show how crucial it is that a buyer of accounts or chattel paper satisfy the perfection requirements of Article 9. A buyer that perfects its "security interest" protects itself against subsequent claimants of the receivable.

a. Definitions of Account, Chattel Paper, Payment Intangible, and Promissory Note—Sections 9-102(a)(2), (11), (61), (65)

Article 9 defines each type of receivable it covers. The definition of *account* in section 9-102(a)(2) is remarkably broad. It begins with a right to payment of a monetary obligation, whether or not earned by performance. The right to payment can arise from a variety of transactions: the sale, lease, license, assignment, or other disposition of property; services rendered or to be rendered; a policy of insurance issued or to be issued; a secondary obligation incurred or to be incurred; energy provided or to be provided; the use or hire of a vessel under a charter or other contract; the use of a credit card; winnings in a lottery or other state sponsored or licensed game of chance; and health care receivables. A typical account arises from a sale of goods on credit or providing services on credit. Suppose you buy goods and promise to pay for them in thirty days—that transaction creates an account; or you buy goods with a credit card—that transaction creates an account. A contract right to receive payment for services to be provided or goods to be sold is an account regardless that the right to payment is unearned when the account is sold. Some transactions are excluded from the definition of account. Account does not include a right to payment evidenced by chattel paper or an instrument, commercial tort claims, deposit accounts, investment property, letter-of-credit rights or letters of credit, or rights to payment for money or funds advance or sold, unless the right arises out of use of a credit card.

Chattel paper, defined in section 9-102(a)(11), generally means a record (allowing for both written and electronic chattel paper) that evidences both a monetary obligation and a security interest in or lease of goods, goods and software used in the goods, or goods and license of software used in the goods. The lease involved in chattel paper is a "true lease," not a transaction structured as a lease but in fact a security interest. Leases that are security interests are discussed later in this chapter. A typical chattel paper transaction arises with a purchase of goods under a retail installment sales agreement. That type of agreement requires that the buyer of goods pay the purchase price in installments (the monetary obligation) and grant the seller a security interest in the goods the buyer purchased. Often the seller of the goods sells the retail installment sales agreement in order to obtain funds for its business. That transaction is a sale of chattel paper. The buyer of the goods is the *account debtor*; the seller of the chattel paper is the *debtor*; the buyer of the chattel paper is the *secured party*; and the retail installment sales agreement is the chattel paper and also the *collateral*.

Payment intangible, defined in section 9-102(a)(61), is a general intangible under which the account debtor's principal obligation is a monetary obligation. A sale of a payment intangible arises in a situation where the creditor, such as a bank, in a loan transaction that is not evidenced by a promissory note or chattel paper, sells its right to receive payment. That is the typical situation where the lender of money sells its right to receive repayment of the loan.

Promissory note, defined in Section 9-102(a)(65), is an instrument that evidences a promise to pay a monetary obligation.

b. Exclusions from Article 9 — Section 9-109(d)

Article 9 excludes from its coverage certain transactions involving accounts, chattel paper, payment intangibles, and promissory notes. The exclusions cover sales and assignments that, according to Official Comment 12 to section 9-109, "by their nature, do not concern commercial financing transactions." The word *assignment*, a term Article 9 defines only in Official Comment 26 to section 9-102, means a *transfer of rights* and would include an outright sale and a security interest transfer.

Under Section 9-109(d)(4), Article 9 does not apply to a sale of accounts, chattel paper, payment intangibles, or promissory notes as part of a sale of the business out of which they arose. Consequently, if an owner of a business sells its entire business and the business assets include those types of receivables, Article 9 does not apply to the sale of such property. Section 9-109(d)(5) excludes assignments of receivables that are for the purpose of collection only. This exception covers the situation where the account owner assigns the account to a collection agency solely to facilitate collection of the debt. Article 9 excludes these assignments from its coverage although it does not seem that such assignments are either sale or security interest. A third exclusion, in section 9-109(d)(6), covers an assignment of a right to payment under a contract to a transferee who agrees to perform the obligations of the contract. In this situation, the owner transfers the entire contract, including the duty to perform and the right to receive payment. Finally, the assignment of a *single* account, payment intangible, or promissory note in full or partial satisfaction of a pre-existing debt is excluded by section 9-109(d)(7). In this situation, the owner of the receivable, already indebted to the transferee, transfers a single account, payment intangible, or promissory note in full or partial payment of the pre-existing debt. The transferee gives no new value for the assignment, other than relinquishing its claim on the debt.

5. Leases of Goods — Sections 9-109(a)(1), 9-505, 1-203

Leases of goods are a common commercial transaction. For example, a consumer might lease a car for three years or lease a washer and dryer for a year. A business might lease a fleet of cars, or copy machines, or a crane used in construction.

For reasons pertaining to federal tax law and principles of accounting, it can be advantageous for a person who wants to acquire the ownership of goods to structure the acquisition in the form of a lease of the goods. This transaction is a lease in name, labels, and format, but in substance it is a credit purchase of the goods coupled with a security interest. For our purposes, it does not matter how tax law or accounting principles would characterize such a transaction. But it does matter to Article 9 and Article 2A. Article 2A of the UCC establishes law that regulates *true* leases of goods, but expressly does not apply to security interests. The label *true* lease is not a label used in the UCC, but attorneys, judges, and law professors use it in distinguishing between leases governed by Article 2A, true leases, and leases that are security interests and governed by Article 9.

a. Determining Whether the Transaction Is a Security Interest— Section 1-203

Article 9 governs a transaction in the form of a lease of personal property that is a security interest. The difficulty lies in determining whether the transaction involved is a true lease or a security interest. The issue has produced a wealth of case law attempting to establish guidelines to aid in resolving the question. The UCC drafters offer their expertise in Article 1, section 1-203 by adopting factors whose inclusion in the transaction turn a purported lease into a security interest. You can judge how helpful section 1-203 is after you read and work with it.

The factors expressed in section 1-203 focus on the elements of the transaction, not the intent of the parties. In previous versions of the UCC, the definition of security interest declared that whether a lease was a security interest depended on whether the parties intended it as security. In the comment to section 1-203, the drafters state that the intent standard led to "unfortunate results." Consequently, they deleted all references to intent in section 1-203, and the intent of the parties is no longer a factor in determining whether the transaction is lease or security interest.

Section 1-203(a) declares that the facts of the case determine whether a transaction in the form of a lease creates a lease or security interest. That requires an examination of all aspects of the transaction to make the determination. Notwithstanding that declaration, subsection (b) provides factors whose presence in a lease transaction conclusively establishes the transaction as a security interest. Because the transaction is in the form of a lease, section 1-203 uses lease terminology to describe the factors and I will do the same.

The crucial factor in section 1-203(b) that turns a lease into a security interest is that the consideration paid by the lessee for its right to possess and use the goods (the rent) is an obligation for the term of the lease and is not subject to termination by the lessee. *Termination*, as defined in Article 2A, section 2A-103(1)(z), refers to either party using a power to end a contract for a reason other than default. Employing that definition in section 1-203(b) means that the lessee's rent is an obligation not subject to termination when the lease contract does not allow the lessee to discharge its liability for unpaid rent. This factor is present when the parties' agreement requires the lessee to pay the entire rent for the lease term regardless of whether the lessee possesses or uses the goods for the full lease term.

For example, suppose a two-year lease agreement with fixed monthly rent allows the lessee to return the goods to the lessor at any time, but the lessee nevertheless remains liable for the unpaid rent for the entire term of the lease. The section 1-203(b) factor is present because the lessee's obligation to pay the rent is not subject to termination. However, if the lease allows the lessee to return the goods at any time without any liability for future, unpaid rent, the lessee's obligation is subject to termination and the necessary factor is absent. In that case, the factor test of section 1-203(b) does not indicate the transaction is a security interest. Nevertheless, section 1-203(a) directs a court to examine all other facts of the transaction to determine whether it is a security interest.

However, section 1-203(b) does not make the transaction a security interest solely because the lessee cannot terminate the rent obligation. The transaction must include *one* of four other factors listed in section 1-203(b) before it is a security interest. The presence of any of the four factors, when coupled with a non-terminable obligation to pay the rent, conclusively establishes the transaction as a security interest under section 1-203(b).

The first factor is that the original term of the lease is equal to or greater than the remaining economic life of the goods. The *remaining economic life of the goods*, defined in section 1-203(e), is determined by referring to the facts and circumstances existing when the parties entered into the lease. This factor is established, for example, when there is a two-year lease of goods that have an economic life of only two years. In a true lease, the lessee purchases the possession and use of the goods for the period of the lease and at the expiration of the lease returns the goods, which have a residual economic value, to the lessor. If the lease term equals or exceeds the economic life of the goods, no residual value is returned to the lessor, and an essential element of a true lease is absent.

The second factor is that the lessee is obligated to either renew the lease for the remaining economic life of the goods or become the owner of the goods. This factor is established if the lease agreement requires that the lessee, at the expiration of the lease term, either buy the goods or renew the lease for as long as the goods have economic life. The rationale behind this factor seems to be the same as that for the previous factor; the lessee will have contracted for the use and possession of the goods for their entire economic life. Note that there is no reason to inquire into the consideration the lessee must give to perform its contractual duty to renew or buy. The value of the consideration is not germane.

The third and fourth factors involve option provisions that give the lessee the right to renew the lease or become the owner of the goods. The third factor is the lessee has the option to renew the lease for no additional consideration or nominal consideration. The fourth factor is the lessee has the option to become the owner of the goods for no additional consideration or nominal consideration. Inclusion of a nominal or no-consideration option is an indication that the initial lease term equals the entire economic life of the leased goods, leaving no residual value for return to the lessor. The next three paragraphs discuss nominal consideration.

Section 1-203(d) provides guidance on when consideration is nominal and when it is not. Under subsection (d), the option consideration *is not nominal* if it is the fair market rent for use of the goods (in an option to renew) or the fair market value of the goods (in an option to purchase), determined at the time the option is to be performed. Preventing the option consideration from being nominal simply requires that the parties agree that the consideration the lessee will pay to exercise the option is fixed by the fair market value of the goods or the fair market rent determined as of the time the lessee chooses to exercise the option. This is easily accomplished by a term in the lease agreement. For example, consideration is not nominal in a lease agreement that fixes the consideration to become owner of the goods as "the fair market value of the goods at the time the lessee exercises the option to purchase the goods."

The option consideration *is nominal* under subsection (d) "if it is less than the lessee's reasonably predictable cost of performing under the lease agreement if the option is not exercised." Pursuant to section 1-203(e), reasonably predictable cost of performing is "determined with reference to the facts and circumstances at the time the transaction is entered into." This requires that *nominal* is determined by judging the values the parties predicted at the beginning of the transaction, not by comparing the value at the time of exercise of the option with the value the parties fixed when they created the lease and judging how accurate their predictions were. Current market rent or value is apparently not relevant to the determination. This seems fair because whether the transaction is a lease or a security interest should be fixed by the economic facts in existence and foreseeable by the parties when they enter the transaction, not by subsequent events that may be uncontrollable, such as market valuations.

Determining whether the option consideration is nominal requires comparing that consideration with the cost of performing under the lease and not exercising the option. The cost of performing under the lease and not exercising the option is the cost of the obligations the lessee agreed to undertake at the expiration of the lease term. Such cost could be simply the cost of get-

ting the leased goods to the lessor, or could entail extensive repairing, reha-
bilitating, or processing the goods or any other obligation the parties have set.
Because nominal consideration means simply that the consideration is less
than the cost of performing under the lease, the option consideration could be
a substantial sum and still be nominal. The relevant factor is the comparison
of the option consideration with the reasonably predictable cost of performing under the lease, not the dollar amount of the consideration.

Section 1-203(c) lists six factors that do not create a security interest. The
section declares that "[a] transaction in the form of a lease does not create a
security interest merely because" it includes one of the listed factors. Use of
"merely" indicates that the inclusion of one of the enumerated factors does
not itself create a security interest. Nevertheless, under the basic rule of section 1-203(a), the facts of the case must be examined in order to determine if
the transaction is a security interest and a court could consider any of the six
factors in determining whether the transaction is a security interest. The following paragraphs discuss these factors.

A security interest is not created simply because the lease requires the lessee
to pay total rent that has a present value equal to or greater than the fair market value of the goods at the inception of the transaction. *Present value* is defined
in section 1-201(b)(28). The concept of present value is that money to be received
in the future is less valuable than money received today because the person who
receives money today can use it to make more money. For our purposes, it
means that the total rent under the lease is discounted to the value it has today.
A lease wherein the present value of the rent equals the purchase price of the
goods leased exemplifies this factor. Although including such a provision in a lease
seems to indicate a security interest because the lessee is "paying" the price of
the goods, section 1-203(c)(1) precludes it from being *the* factor that creates a
security interest. Remember that section 1-203 focuses partly on whether the
goods returned to the lessor at the end of the lease have economic value. A lease
fixing the rent as equal to the purchase price of the goods does not indicate
whether any economic value remains at the expiration of the lease.

A lessee's assumption of risk of loss to the goods, or its obligation to pay taxes,
insurance, filing fees, and maintenance costs pertaining to the leased goods, does
not alone create a security interest. A person might argue that these owner-
ship-like obligations compel a finding that the transaction is a sale coupled
with a security interest. However, section 1-203(c) declares that their presence
does not create a security interest.

The lessee's option to renew the lease or to become the owner of the goods
does not signify a secured transaction. Only the nominal option, discussed
previously, indicates a security interest.

The lessee's option to renew the lease or become the owner of the goods does not create a security interest when the option consideration equals or exceeds the *reasonably predictable* fair market value or fair market rent which the goods will have at the time the option is to be performed. Section 1-203(e) provides that *reasonably predictable* "must be determined with reference to the facts and circumstances at the time the transaction is entered into." This means the option price is compared to the value of the goods that is based on facts and circumstances existing when the parties enter the lease. To protect the transaction from being a security interest, the lease should fix the option price at an amount that is equal to or greater than the predicted value or rental value. For example, suppose lessor and lessee agree that the lessee has the option to purchase the goods at the expiration of the lease term. When the parties enter the lease, they predict, based on the facts and circumstances then known, that the goods will have a value of $10,000 at the expiration of the lease term. They fix the option consideration at $10,000. The option satisfies the conditions of section 1-203(c)(6) and does not signify that the transaction is a security interest.

In working with the factors that create a security interest and those that do not, remember that a court is to review all facts of the transaction to determine whether it creates a security interest regardless that the factors listed in section 1-203 do not create a security interest. *Duke Energy Royal, LLC v. Pillowtex Corporation*, 349 F.3d 711 (3rd Cir. 2003), exemplifies that approach. There the court examined the facts of the transaction to determine if it was a lease or a security interest notwithstanding its finding that the transaction did not satisfy the requirements for a security interest under section 1-203(b).

b. Filing a Financing Statement for a Lease — Section 9-505

Grave consequences can result from a court determining that a transaction in the form of a lease is nevertheless a security interest if the lessor, who is now a secured party, did not perfect the security interest. In a conflict over priority in the goods, the unperfected security interest of the lessor/secured party is most likely subordinate to other persons who also claim an interest in the goods. Given these consequences, a lessor in a lease of goods transaction should file a financing statement covering the goods as a precautionary measure regardless of whether the lessor thinks the transaction is a lease and not a security interest. Section 9-505(a) authorizes a lessor of goods to file a financing statement. If the transaction is determined to be a security interest, the filing perfects it, assuming that the lessor/secured party satisfies all other requirements of perfection. The requirements of an effective financing statement are discussed in Chapter 3.

Section 9-505(b) provides a safe harbor for the person who wisely chooses to file a financing statement. The safe harbor protects the lessor from a court which might think the filing of a financing statement is a factor that indicates the transaction is a security interest. Section 9-505(b) provides the "filing ... is not of itself a factor in determining whether the collateral secures an obligation." Arguably, the phrase *is not of itself a factor*, allows a court to consider the filing along with other factors. Official Comment 2 to section 9-505 rejects that argument by stating that section 9-505(b) authorizes filing "without affecting the substantive question of classification of the transaction." Of course, the Official Comments are not law. However, the last sentence of section 9-505(b) supports the comment: "If it is determined for another reason that the collateral secures an obligation, a security interest ... is perfected by the filing." *Another reason* indicates the filing of a financing statement is not a determining factor.

C. Exclusions — Sections 9-109(c), (d)

After studying the vast scope of Article 9, it might surprise you to find that Article 9 excludes some transactions which otherwise it would govern. Sections 9-109(c) and (d) exclude certain transactions from Article 9's governance, regardless of whether the transactions fit the definition of security interest. The exclusions are of two types. *First*, under section 9-109(d), Article 9 is inapplicable to certain types of transactions that ostensibly create an interest in property to secure an obligation or otherwise satisfy the definition of security interest. *Second*, under section 9-109(c), Article 9 is inapplicable to the extent that federal law preempts Article 9, or to the extent that law of a state or foreign country expressly governs one or more aspects of a security interest created by a state, foreign country, or governmental unit of the state or country. "To the extent" means that Article 9 could be partly inapplicable; it could govern some, but not all, aspects of a security interest.

However, a person is not precluded from creating an interest in its property to secure an obligation simply because Article 9 does not govern the interest. For example, section 9-109(d)(13) declares that Article 9 does not apply to a consumer debtor's assignment of her personal checking account to secure her consumer debt. That exclusion does not stop a creditor from demanding such an assignment. But any such assignment is not governed by Article 9, consequently leaving the so-called "secured party" without the protection of Article 9's scheme of creation and priority of security interests.

1. Section 9-109(d) Exclusions

Section 9-109(d) provides a list of transactions excluded completely from Article 9's governance, except where the section indicates otherwise. Many of the express exclusions of section 9-109(d) need no comment because they are types of secured transactions you will never study in law school or rarely see in law practice. Section B.4.b. of this Chapter examined the inapplicability of Article 9 to certain sales and assignments of accounts, chattel paper, payment intangibles, and promissory notes. A few others warrant review.

a. Insurance

Under section 9-109(d)(8), Article 9 is inapplicable to a transfer of an interest in or an assignment of a claim under a policy of insurance, except when the interest in insurance represents proceeds of collateral or is an assignment of a health-care-insurance receivable. For example, Article 9 does not govern a transaction where a beneficiary of an insurance policy assigns her right to payment under a life insurance policy to secure a debt she owes. Likewise, Article 9 does not govern a transaction where an insured assigns her claim for payment under a casualty insurance policy.

The proceeds exception of section 9-109(d)(8) (and the meaning of *exception* is that the Article 9 *governs* the transaction) is an important addition to the rights of a secured party. Suppose the debtor grants the secured party a security interest in her automobile. The automobile is damaged in an accident. Article 9 makes the insurance payable under the debtor's insurance policy a proceed of the automobile collateral and the secured party has a security interest in it. Article 9 governs the security interest and the insurance exclusion does not apply. Chapter 2 examines the proceeds security interest.

The other exception of section 9-109(d)(8) pertains to a *health-care-insurance receivable*, defined in section 9-102(a)(46) as "an interest in or claim under a policy of insurance which is a right to payment of a monetary obligation for health-care goods or services provided." The assignment *by* or *to* a health-care provider of a health-care-insurance receivable and any subsequent assignment of the right to payment are covered by Article 9. An example of an assignment governed by Article 9 is when a person who receives health care goods or services, the patient, from a provider of such goods or services, the doctor, assigns her right to payment under an insurance policy to the provider. Many recipients assign their right to payment without knowing they have created a security interest by simply signing the consent to treatment form that includes an assignment. This assignment hardly seems to warrant inclusion in Article 9 because it is unlike a financing transaction. Article 9's drafters recognized this and, in section 9-309(e), granted automatic perfection of such a security interest upon attachment.

A provider of health care goods and services can obtain many such rights to payment, and may want to assign such rights to its creditor as collateral for a debt. That assignment, whether a sale or a true security interest, is more like a financing transaction, and is covered by Article 9 (assignment *by* a health-care provider), and the assignee/creditor must perfect the security interest to obtain the protection of Article 9.

Article 9 governs a security interest in an insurance policy "account." Section 9-102(a)(2) defines *account* as including the right to payment of a monetary obligation for a policy of insurance issued or to be issued. Typically, the *monetary obligation* for a policy of insurance is the premium that the policyholder must pay to the insurance company as a condition to obtaining insurance. For example, an insurer who sells or creates a security interest in its right to receive payment of an insurance policy premium creates a security interest that is covered by Article 9 pursuant to sections 9-109(a)(1) and (a)(3). This type of security interest does not involve a transfer of an interest in or an assignment of a claim under a policy of insurance.

b. Tort Claims

Under section 9-109(d)(12), Article 9 does not apply to an assignment of a claim arising in tort, except when the claim is a commercial tort claim or the tort claim is a proceed of collateral. Consequently, Article 9 does not govern an assignment of a tort claim by a person injured in an accident who has a negligence claim and who assigns the claim as collateral for a debt.

The proceeds exception for tort claims is similar to the proceeds exception for an assignment of an interest in an insurance policy. For example, if the negligent destruction of collateral creates a tort claim, the tort claim is a proceed of the collateral and Article 9 governs the security interest in the proceed.

The other exception is for an assignment of a *commercial* tort claim. Article 9 governs an assignment of a commercial tort claim. Under the definition in section 9-102(a)(13), a *commercial tort claim* exists if the claimant is an organization, or the claimant is an individual and the claim arose in the individual's business or profession and does not include damages for personal injury or death. The following examples illustrate the difference between the two types of tort claims. Suppose a person's negligent act causes the destruction of an individual's household goods. If the individual assigns the resulting tort claim to a creditor as collateral for an obligation, Article 9 does not apply to the assignment. Suppose, however, a person's negligent act causes the destruction of an individual's business property. (For example, an irate client damages your office.) If the individual assigns the resulting tort claim, Article 9 applies to the assignment.

c. Consumer Transaction Deposit Account

Assignments of deposit accounts in consumer transactions are excluded from Article 9's coverage under section 9-109(d)(13). A deposit account is typically a checking or savings account maintained with a bank or other organization engaged in the business of banking, such as a credit union. A consumer transaction requires that an individual incur an obligation for personal, family, or household purposes and secure the obligation with collateral held primarily for personal, family, or household purposes. For example, if a law student borrows money to take a vacation and grants the lender an interest in his personal checking account at his bank, Article 9 does not govern the transaction, regardless of whether the parties label the transaction a "security interest." If that same law student has a business selling law books on eBay and maintains a separate checking account for his business, and grants an interest in that account to secure his vacation loan, Article 9 governs that transaction because the collateral is not primarily used for personal, family, or household purposes.

d. Statutory Liens

Statutory liens, liens arising by rule of law — statutory or case law — are excluded from Article 9. These liens arise by rule of law and are not consensual. They attach to personal property, in favor of a person who supplies services or materials to the property. All states have enacted statutes that grant liens to persons who perform services or provide materials but are not paid by the recipient of the service or materials. For example, if you hire a mechanic to repair your vehicle and you never pay for the repairs, state law typically awards the mechanic a lien on your vehicle. (This is not a mechanic's lien; a mechanic's lien pertains to real property.) The lien secures an obligation, but Article 9 does not govern the lien, other than to determine priority between the lienholder and a secured party. (Priority is discussed in Chapter 6.) Remember, however, that Article 9 expressly governs agricultural liens.

2. Section 9-109(c) Exclusions

Unlike the exclusions in section 9-109(d), where Article 9 is totally inapplicable, the exclusions of section 9-109(c) make Article 9 inapplicable to security interests only to the extent that law other than Article 9 preempts Article 9. To the extent that Article 9 is not preempted, it applies to the security interest. Section 9-109(c)(1) provides that Article 9 does not apply to a transaction to the extent that federal law—a statute, regulation, or treaty—preempts Article 9. The inapplicability of Article 9 depends on whether and to what extent federal law preempts it, not whether federal law also covers transactions covered by Article 9. Consequently, a federal law might preempt Article 9's perfection provisions, but not its priority provisions. For example, the Federal Copyright Act preempts Article 9 with respect to perfection of a security interest in a registered copyright, but not with respect to a security interest in an unregistered copyright. (*See* In re World Auxiliary Power Co., 303 F.3d 1120, 1128 (9th Cir. 2002).) Other federal acts preempting provisions of Article 9 include the Ship Mortgage Act, the Federal Aviation Act, and the Food Security Act.

Section 9-109(c) also excludes from Article 9 governance certain security interests *created by* governmental debtors, whether the debtor is a state, a foreign country, or a governmental unit of either, to the extent the government has enacted laws that preempt Article 9. These types of security interests otherwise are covered by Article 9. However, under sections 9-109(c)(2) and (c)(3), Article 9 does not apply to the extent that a state or foreign country has law other than Article 9 that governs the issue in question. Similar to federal preemption, this is not necessarily total preemption. Article 9 is preempted only to the extent that the law governs the issue. For example, suppose the Illinois State Department of Highways borrows money from a Kentucky bank and creates a security interest in favor of the bank. The security agreement provides that Kentucky's Article 9 governs the security interest. Illinois law includes statutes that apply to creation of a security interest by state governmental units. Consequently, Illinois law governs creation of the security interest and Kentucky law governs other aspects of the security interest.

The remaining exclusion of section 9-109(c) involves a letter of credit. However, the exclusion is not absolute; Article 9 applies to some security interests involving letters of credit. A letter of credit is a three-party undertaking where the applicant of the letter requests the issuer of the letter, typically a bank, to promise to pay the beneficiary of the letter an obligation that the applicant owes the beneficiary, regardless of the applicant's ability or willingness to pay. For example, suppose a foreign seller of goods to a New York buyer wants assurance that the buyer will pay the purchase price of the goods. To provide that assurance, the buyer requests its bank to issue a letter of credit to the seller whereby the bank promises to pay the seller the purchase price upon the seller's demand. The buyer is the applicant, the bank is the issuer, and the seller is the beneficiary.

Article 9 governs a security interest in a letter-of-credit right. A beneficiary of a letter of credit can *assign* its right to receive payment or performance under the letter of credit, without transferring its other rights created in the transaction. Pursuant to section 9-102(a)(51), this right to receive payment or performance constitutes a *letter-of-credit right*. A letter-of-credit right includes only the beneficiary's right to payment or performance, not the beneficiary's right to demand payment from the issuer. A beneficiary's *assignment* of its letter-of-credit right as security for an obligation creates a security interest. The assignee of the letter-of-credit right is the secured party and the beneficiary/assignor is the debtor.

In addition to creating a security interest by assigning its right to receive payment, a beneficiary of a letter of credit can *transfer* all its rights in the letter of credit and such transferee becomes a *transferee beneficiary*. In that situation, section 5-114(e) makes the rights of a transferee beneficiary independent of and superior to the assignee's letter-of-credit rights. Section 9-109(c)(4) excludes from Article 9 the rights of a transferee beneficiary under a letter of credit to the extent such person's rights are independent and superior under section 5-114(e).

The issuer of a letter of credit can designate a person to perform the letter of credit. Under section 5-102(a)(11), *nominated person* "means a person who the issuer (i) designates or authorizes to pay, accept, negotiate, or otherwise give value under a letter of credit and (ii) undertakes by agreement or custom and practice to reimburse." In that situation, section 5-114(e) makes the rights of a nominated person independent of and superior to the assignee's letter-of-credit rights. Section 9-109(c)(4) excludes from Article 9 the rights of a nominated person under a letter of credit to the extent such person's rights are independent and superior under section 5-114(e).

Checkpoints

- Article 9 governs any transaction, regardless of form, that creates a security interest in personal property.

- A security interest exists when a creditor has an interest in the personal property or fixtures of the debtor as collateral to secure the payment or performance of an obligation owed to the creditor.

- Article 9 does not govern a security interest in real property except for a security interest in fixtures and a security interest in a right to payment that is secured by an interest in real property.

- Article 9 governs agricultural liens and consignment transactions.

- Article 9 governs a sale of an account, chattel paper, promissory note, and payment intangible, as well as a security interest in that property.

- Article 9 governs a transaction structured as a lease of goods that includes the factors of section 1-203(b) that make it a security interest in the goods.

- Article 9 excludes from its governance the secured transactions listed in section 9-109(d).

- Article 9 does not apply to security interests to the extent federal law preempts Article 9.

- Article 9 does not apply to security interests created by state or foreign governmental debtors to the extent that the state or foreign country has laws that preempt Article 9.

Chapter 2

Creating a Security Interest — Attachment and Enforceability

Roadmap

- The Article 9 requirements to creating an enforceable security interest
- The debtor's authentication of a security agreement
- Describing the collateral in the security agreement
- The secured party's possession of the collateral
- Establishing control of the collateral
- Security interests that attach automatically
- Attachment of a security interest in sale of a receivable
- Attachment of a security interest of a new debtor
- After-acquired property security interests
- Future advance security interests
- Request by debtor for list of collateral or statement of obligation

---

A. Introduction

Although the parties to a secured transaction may intend and desire to create a security interest, a security interest is not valid under Article 9 until there is fulfillment of Article 9's minimal, formal requirements. Unfortunately, the drafters of Article 9 did not compose a section of Article 9 labeled "Requirements for Creating a Security Interest." Instead, they use the terms "attach" and "enforceable" to describe the requirements for creating an effective security interest. The use of two terms naturally leads one to think that there are two sets of requirements—requirements to *attach*, and requirements to be *enforceable*. That is not the case. Section 9-203(a) provides that a security interest *attaches* to the collateral when it becomes *enforceable* against the debtor. Section 9-203(b) establishes the requirements for enforceability. Article 9 adds no additional requirements for attachment. The parties can agree "expressly" to postpone attachment, but the cases where postponement occurs are rare and there is rarely any advantage to the secured party in postponing attachment.

Prior to the 1972 Official Text of Article 9, the requirements for creating a security interest were split between requirements for attachment and requirements for enforceability. With the 1972 text, those requirements were united into the requirements for *enforceability*, and Revised Article 9 continues that scheme.

Most attorneys and judges use the terms *attach* and *attachment* when discussing whether a secured party has created an effective security interest. For example, an attorney might question, "Whether the security interest has attached." I too will use that terminology. However, I remind you again that Article 9 establishes requirements for the enforceability of a security interest, and attachment is automatic upon satisfaction of those prerequisites, unless expressly postponed.

Section 9-203(b) establishes three prerequisites to the existence of a valid security interest: 1) the secured party gives value; 2) the debtor has rights in the collateral or the power to transfer rights in the collateral to a secured party; and 3) either the debtor authenticates a security agreement describing the collateral, the secured party has possession of the collateral, or, for certain types of collateral, the secured party achieves control. (Sections 9-313 and 9-203(b)(3)(D), respectively, specify the property a secured party can possess and control.) Satisfying these requirements makes the security interest enforceable against the debtor and other persons claiming an interest in the collateral. However, for most secured transactions the secured party must take additional steps to *perfect* the security interest to protect it against other claimants. Perfection of a security interest is discussed in Chapters 3, 4, and 5.

B. Value and Rights in the Collateral — Sections 9-203(b)(1), (2)

1. Secured Party Gives Value — Sections 9-203(b)(1), 1-204

Section 9-203(b)(1) provides that the secured party gives value as a requirement of attachment. Literally, section 9-203(b)(1) requires "value has been given," without designating which party must give value. Logically and practically, the secured party must give the value, and the courts unanimously agree. Although contract consideration is not a requirement for attachment, you can think of the secured party's giving value as the consideration it gives to obtain the security interest. However, the UCC definition of value establishes clearly that value is more expansive than consideration. Section 1-204 provides:

> [A] person gives 'value' for rights if he acquires them: (1) in return for a binding commitment to extend credit or for the extension of immediately available credit, whether or not drawn upon and whether or not a charge-back is provided for in the event of difficulties in collection; (2) as security for, or in total or partial satisfaction of, a preexisting claim; (3) by accepting delivery under a preexisting contract for purchase; or (4) in return for any consideration sufficient to support a simple contract.

Typically, a secured creditor gives value through a loan of money, providing a line of credit, or making a credit sale of collateral. For example, a secured creditor gives value when it loans the debtor money. A binding promise to make a loan at some future date is also value. Because value includes taking rights as security for a pre-existing claim, a secured party can obtain a valid security interest when the debtor grants a security interest to secure a debt the debtor previously incurred to the secured party. That is an important tool for creditors. For example, suppose Lender loans Debtor $10,000 with repayment due in six months. Three months later, Lender learns that Debtor, although not in default, is having financial difficulties. Lender asks Debtor to grant it a security interest to secure repayment of the $10,000. If Debtor agrees and grants Lender a security interest, the pre-existing debt satisfies the value requirement.

2. Debtor's Rights in the Collateral— Section 9-203(b)(2)

Section 9-203(b)(2) requires that the debtor have rights in the property given as collateral or the power to transfer rights in the collateral to a secured party. *Rights* is not a defined term in Article 9. Rights in the collateral typically exist if the debtor has full ownership of the collateral. In that situation, the debtor has the right to grant a security interest in the collateral. A debtor who has less than full ownership in the collateral nevertheless may have sufficient rights for a security interest to attach. However, in such case the security interest attaches only to the rights the debtor has. For example, a joint owner of property could create a security interest in the jointly owned property that would attach to the extent of the debtor's rights in the property.

A commonly occurring security interest is created when the debtor acquires rights in property and creates a security interest in the property in the same transaction. For example, suppose a debtor purchases property in an installment sale and grants the seller a security interest in the property it purchases. The debtor has sufficient rights in the collateral to enable a security interest to attach as of the time the debtor and the seller enter the sale agreement, although the debtor has not paid the entire purchase price. This transaction creates a special type of security interest known as a purchase-money security interest.

If the debtor does not have rights in the collateral at the time the secured party fulfills other attachment requirements, attachment and enforceability of the security interest are postponed until the debtor acquires the necessary rights. For example, suppose the debtor authenticates a security agreement and the secured party loans the debtor money to purchase equipment from the seller. The debtor acquires rights in the collateral when it purchases the equipment from the seller one month later. The security interest attaches at that time. However, a debtor could have rights in the collateral as early as the time the seller identifies specific equipment as the subject of the debtor-seller contract because section 2-501 awards a purchaser of goods a special property and an insurable interest in the goods at the time of their identification.

Courts have ruled that a debtor has sufficient rights to enable a security interest to attach to goods a debtor possesses under a contract with the owner of the goods to process them into a finished product, regardless that the debtor has no authority from the owner to create a security interest in them. *See* Litwiller Mach. & Mfg., Inc. v. NBD Alpena Bank, 184 Mich. App. 369, 457 N.W.2d 163 (1990). The facts in such cases follow a similar pattern. Owner delivers goods to Manufacturer for the purpose of manufacturing the goods into finished products, either with or without the addition of other materials owned by Manufacturer. Owner expressly reserves title to the goods it delivers. Secured Creditor has a perfected security interest in Manufacturer's inventory, including work in process. Manufacturer defaults on the secured debt and Secured Creditor repossesses Owner's goods in the possession of Manufacturer. Owner argues that Secured Creditor's security interest cannot attach to Owner's goods because Manufacturer does not have sufficient *rights in the collateral* for attachment. Courts have disagreed and held that sufficient rights exist to enable the security interest to attach because Manufacturer has the right to use, possess, and transform the goods. Owner can be protected from that security interest because the Owner-Manufacturer transaction creates a purchase-money security interest for Owner and a purchase-money security interest in inventory can have priority over other security interests under section 9-324(b). (Purchase-money security interests are discussed in Chapter 8.)

The attachment requirement of section 9-203(b)(2) also is met when a debtor has the "power to transfer rights in the collateral to a secured party," regardless of whether the debtor has rights in the collateral. That provision accommodates sections 9-318 and 9-319, discussed in Chapter 1, which empower a debtor with the right to grant a security interest in its previously sold accounts and chattel paper, and in goods consigned to it by an owner of the goods.

C. The Debtor's Agreement to Give a Security Interest — Section 9-203(b)(3)

The third requirement for attachment and enforceability is the debtor's agreement to create a security interest. Section 9-203(b)(3) provides four methods by which the parties can indicate the debtor's agreement: 1) the debtor authenticates a security agreement that provides a description of the collateral; 2) the secured party takes possession of the collateral; 3) collateral that is a certificated security is delivered to the secured party; or 4) for deposit accounts, electronic chattel paper, letter-of-credit rights, investment property, or electronic documents collateral, the secured party establishes *control* of the collateral. A secured party is not restricted in its choice of method except that some methods of attachment are restricted for use with specific types of collateral. For example, a secured party who takes a security interest in a debtor's deposit account could evidence the debtor's agreement to create a security interest in a deposit account by establishing control or by having the debtor authenticate a security agreement that contains a description of the collateral.

1. Satisfying the Debtor's-Agreement Requirement with an Authenticated Security Agreement — Sections 9-203(b)(3)(A), 9-108

For most security interests, the parties comply with the debtor's-agreement requirement of section 9-203(b)(3) by using the section 9-203(b)(3)(A) option of having the debtor authenticate a writing, typically labeled "Security Agreement," that embodies the debtor's giving of a security interest in the collateral and describes the collateral. Although the parties to the security agreement undoubtedly will include many other provisions, especially provisions relating to the debtor's obligation and default, a security agreement requires no other terms.

Section 9-102(a)(73) defines *security agreement* as "an agreement that creates or provides for a security interest." To satisfy that definition, a written security agreement need only include words that indicate the debtor is creating a security interest in the collateral. Article 9 mandates no particular words or phrase as indispensable to creating an effective security interest. For example, a security agreement that provides, "Debtor grants Creditor a security interest in all its equipment," satisfies the security agreement requirement. A security agreement has many attributes of a contract, and contract law governs interpretation of the security agreement unless a section of the UCC displaces it.

The debtor must *authenticate* the security agreement to satisfy section 9-203(b)(3)(A). Section 9-102(a)(7) defines *authenticate* as: "(A) to sign; or (B) to execute or otherwise adopt a symbol, or encrypt or similarly process a record in whole or in part with the present intent of the authenticating person to identify the person and adopt or accept a record." This definition, by authorizing signing or encrypting, allows for both written and electronic security agreements. A mark, symbol, or printed signature is a sufficient authentication if the person makes it with the intent to adopt or accept the record. Official Comment 37 to section 1-201 includes the example of a "letterhead" signature as a type of printed signature that could satisfy the *sign* requirement if the person intends it as an adoption or acceptance of the record. Also supporting an electronic security agreement is the section 9-102(a)(69) definition of *record* as "information that is inscribed on a tangible medium or which is stored in an electronic or other medium...."

It is possible that the debtor and the obligor are not the same person. Section 9-102(a)(28) defines *debtor* as a person having an interest in the collateral regardless of whether the person is also the obligor of a debt. For example, if a borrower secures his loan to the secured creditor by granting a security interest in his mother's automobile (with his mother's authorization), his mother is the debtor and she is the person who must authenticate the security agreement. A secured party would also want the obligor to authenticate the security agreement, but a security interest can attach regardless of whether the obligor authenticates the security agreement.

There is no requirement that the secured party authenticate the security agreement. The purpose of the security agreement is to create the security interest. A debtor creates a security interest in its collateral. Consequently, only the debtor need authenticate the security agreement. Frequently, however, the secured party will authenticate the security agreement. The security agreement could establish obligations of the secured party, and in that situation the debtor would want the secured party to authenticate the security agreement.

a. Description of Collateral — Sections 9-203(b)(3)(A), 9-108

To comply with section 9-203(b)(3)(A), the security agreement must provide a description of the collateral and, if the security interest covers timber to be cut, a description of the land concerned. Neither section 9-203 nor its comments provide any elaboration of "description of the collateral." Section 9-108, however, establishes a general rule for a sufficient description and also supplies examples of sufficient and insufficient descriptions. Although section 9-108 does not declare expressly that it applies to security agreement descriptions, Official Comment 1 to section 9-108 indicates clearly that it does. The rules of section 9-108 also establish sufficiency for a description of collateral in a financing statement. A financing statement is a record filed to perfect a security interest, and is discussed in Chapter 3.

Section 9-108(a) states that a description of collateral "is sufficient, whether or not it is specific, if it reasonably identifies what is described." Official Comment 2 to section 9-108 notes that:

> The test of sufficiency of a description under this section ... is that the description do the job assigned to it: make possible the identification of the collateral described. This section rejects any requirement that a description is insufficient unless it is exact and detailed (the so-called "serial number" test).

Although section 9-108(a) establishes a broad, general rule for the sufficiency of a description, section 9-108(b) provides a list of ways to describe the collateral that satisfy the description requirement — a "safe harbor" for describing the collateral.

Section 9-108(b) declares that a description of collateral using one of the methods listed in section 9-108(b) "reasonably identifies the collateral." *Reasonably identifies* is the standard for sufficiency of a description under section 9-108(a). Consequently, a description is sufficient if it identifies the collateral by using a section 9-108(b) method. Section 9-108(b) authorizes descriptions by "specific listing," "category," "a type of collateral defined in [the Uniform Commercial Code]," "quantity," "computational or allocational formula or procedure," or "any other method, if the identity of the collateral is objectively determinable." For example, a description "all cattle owned by the debtor" is a sufficient description of a security interest in cattle because *cattle* identifies the collateral by *category*, which is specifically authorized by section 9-108(b)(2). Also sufficient would be the description "100 head Angus cattle owned by the debtor" because it is a *specific listing* of the collateral. "All farm products" is a sufficient description of collateral under section 9-108(b)(3) as a listing by *type of collateral defined in the Uniform Commercial Code.* (Section 9-102(a)(34) defines *farm products.*)

Using the adjective "all" preceding a description of collateral by category or type of collateral should be sufficient whenever the security interest is in *all* of a type of debtor's property. Generic descriptions of collateral, such as description by *category* and *type of collateral defined in the UCC*, are authorized in sections 9-108(b)(2) and (b)(3), respectively, and *all* simply indicates the quantity of the collateral.

Section 9-108(c) expressly makes one type of generic description (or, as section 9-108(c) labels it, *supergeneric*) insufficient. A security agreement description of collateral as "all of the debtor's assets" or "all of the debtor's personal property" or "words of similar import" is not a sufficient description under section 9-108(c). However, section 9-504 validates that type of description for a financing statement. (Financing statements are discussed in Chapter 3.)

Sections 9-108(d) and (e) establish specific rules pertaining to the safe harbor description of section 9-108(b)(3): a description by type of collateral defined in the UCC. Description of collateral by type is sufficient to describe certain types of investment property collateral but is not sufficient for a consumer-transaction security interest in investment property. *Investment property*, defined in section 9-102(a)(49), includes securities, a security entitlement, a securities account, a commodity contract, or a commodity account. Section 9-108(d)(1) validates a description of collateral that uses the terms "securities entitlement," "securities account," "commodity account," or "investment property." Section 9-108(d)(2) validates a description of the underlying financial asset or commodity contract in the securities or commodity account. Additionally, section 9-108(d)(1) provides that the description "all of the debtor's existing and after-acquired investment property" is sufficient for a security interest in all of the debtor's investment property.

Section 9-108(e) declares that a description of collateral by type is insufficient for commercial tort claim collateral. An example of a commercial tort claim is a corporation's tort claim. (Commercial tort claims are discussed in Chapter 1.) Sufficiency of a description of a commercial tort claim is judged by the standard of 9-108(a): does it reasonably identify what is described? For example, the description "debtor's tort claim against ABC Corporation for destruction of equipment" should be sufficient. It reasonably identifies the tort claim described by the description. The description "debtor's tort claim against ABC Corporation" should be sufficient because it *makes possible the identification of the collateral described*, assuming debtor has only one tort claim against ABC Corporation. Official Comment 5 to section 9-108 goes so far as to validate the description "debtor's tort claim for destruction of equipment," if the tort-feasor's identity is unknown when the security interest attaches.

Section 9-108(e) also provides that a description by type of collateral is insufficient in a consumer transaction security interest when the collateral is consumer goods, a security entitlement, a securities account, or a commodity account. Consequently, the description "all consumer goods of the debtor" is not sufficient under section 9-108(e). The description "all kitchen appliances of the debtor" should be sufficient because it *reasonably identifies what is described*, kitchen appliances, thus satisfying the section 9-108(a) standard. The description "all of the debtor's securities accounts" is insufficient under section 9-108(e) in a consumer transaction security interest. A sufficient description of investment property requires greater specificity and is judged under section 9-108(a). For example, "all securities accounts of the debtor with XYZ Broker" should be sufficient because it makes possible the identification of what is described.

A *consumer transaction*, defined in section 9-102(a)(26), exists when an individual incurs an obligation "primarily" for personal, family, or household purposes and secures the obligation with a security interest in collateral "primarily" held or acquired for personal, family, or household purposes. An example is a debtor borrowing money to purchase home furnishings (an obligation incurred for personal purposes) and granting a security interest in the furnishings purchased (collateral held for personal use).

The Federal Trade Commission has adopted a further restriction on a security interest in consumer goods. FTC Consumer Lending Regulation 16 C.F.R. 444 makes it an unfair act for a lender or retail installment seller to take a security interest in household goods of a consumer, unless the security interest is a purchase-money security interest or a possessory security interest. The regulation defines household goods.

1. Description of Timber to Be Cut — Section 9-203(b)(3)(A)

If the collateral is timber to be cut, section 9-203(b)(3)(A) requires that the description of the collateral include "a description of the land concerned." The standard for sufficiency of a land description under section 9-108(a) is the same as for any description: "a description ... is sufficient, whether or not it is specific, if it reasonably identifies what is described." Although the comments to sections 9-108 and 9-203 do not amplify the requirements of a sufficient land description, there is no indication in either code or comment that a description of *land concerned* requires a metes and bounds description. Official Comment 5 to section 9-502 concurs with that statement, although section 9-502 pertains literally to the sufficiency of a land description in a financing statement. Nevertheless, that comment cites to section 9-108 and its standard that a "description ... must be sufficient to reasonably identify it." The comment states: "This formulation rejects the view that the real property description must be by metes and bounds, or otherwise conforming to traditional real-property practice in conveyancing." Land can be identified without a metes and bounds description, although such a description is certainly sufficient. What is necessary is that the description allows the land to be located readily. A security agreement description of land that gives an address and directions to the land described should be sufficient. Timber to be cut is the only type of collateral for which the security agreement must include a description of the land concerned.

b. Description Deficiencies

A secured creditor who specifically identifies collateral in the security agreement rather than using a general description can cause problems for itself. An exemplary case is *Shelby County State Bank v. Van Diest Supply Co.*, 303 F.3d 832 (7th Cir. 2002). Van Diest sold agricultural chemicals, fertilizers, and fertilizer materials to the debtor on credit and took a security interest to secure the debt. Van Diest drafted the security agreement, describing the collateral as "[a]ll inventory, including but not limited to agricultural chemicals, fertilizers, and fertilizer materials sold to Debtor by Van Diest Supply Co. whether now owned or hereafter acquired including all replacements, substitutions and additions thereto ..."

In a priority dispute after the debtor filed bankruptcy, the bankruptcy court found the description language to be ambiguous and susceptible to two interpretations: 1) Van Diest's security interest extends to all of the debtor's inventory; or 2) Van Diest's security interest is limited to inventory Van Diest sold to the debtor. Applying Iowa law on contract interpretation, the court limited the security interest to inventory Van Diest sold to the debtor. The Seventh Circuit labeled the security agreement description "a textbook example of ambiguous language" and, using principles of Iowa contract law and the parties' course of dealing, resolved the ambiguity against Van Diest, limiting the security interest to inventory Van Diest sold to the debtor. Although the opposite result seems reasonable, the lesson is clear: ambiguity in a description allows the court to determine the extent of the security interest.

Because Article 9 explicitly allows descriptions by a type of category defined in Article 9, such as inventory, secured creditors should use that type of description. The description "all inventory of the debtor" would have been sufficient under section 9-108(b)(2) to describe a security interest in all inventory and would have avoided the interpretation question. Of course, if the debtor and Van

Diest intended to limit the security interest to inventory sold to the debtor by Van Diest, they accomplished their goal.

In addition to the requirement of sufficiency, a secured creditor should be aware that when it describes the collateral in the security agreement differently from the description in the financing statement, the security agreement determines the collateral the security interest attaches. For example, suppose the security agreement describes the collateral as "dairy cattle," but the financing statement describes the collateral as "all farm products, inventory, accounts receivable and livestock." In that situation a court likely will limit the security interest to dairy cattle. The security agreement is the agreement of the parties. It should control over the financing statement, a document whose purpose is to give notice of a possible security interest, not to indicate the debtor's agreement.

c. Using Other Writings as the Security Agreement

Creating an effective security agreement is not difficult, costly, or time-consuming. Nevertheless, in many cases the secured party fails to do so. Instead, the secured party contends that a filed financing statement, along with other documents, supplies the debtor's agreement to create a security interest. The issue in those cases is whether the aggregate documentation creates or provides for a security interest; specifically whether a "grant" of a security interest is a requirement for a valid security interest. The judicially named *composite document rule* permits other documents to evidence the debtor's agreement to give a security interest in the absence of an authenticated security agreement.

Courts rarely hold that attachment of a security interest requires a clause expressly granting or conveying a security interest. Article 9 does not require such provisions. Section 9-203(b)(3)(A) requires only an authenticated security agreement that provides a description of the collateral. Section 9-102(a)(73), the *security agreement* definition, requires only an agreement creating or providing for a security interest. No Article 9 section requires a "granting" clause in the security agreement; nor should one be required. Any writing or writings that can be interpreted as evidencing the parties' intent and agreement to create or provide for a security interest meets the definition and should be sufficient.

Courts have held that a security interest attaches in situations where the documentation consists of a financing statement and a promissory note. In the typical fact scenario, the promissory note includes a term stating that it is "secured by UCC financing statement," while the financing statement indicates it, "covers collateral securing note for advanced money." In one case, attachment occurred where the financing statement was accompanied by the debtor's corporate resolution directing its clerk to prepare a financing statement with the corporation as debtor and the creditor as secured party to cover the creditor's security interest in the corporate property. Also satisfying the security agreement requirement was the combination of a signed financing statement and a signed letter providing that the debt "shall be evidenced by an installment note secured by a lien … which shall be perfected by a UCC-1 Statement to be filed upon the signing of this letter," although the debtor never signed the security agreement submitted by the secured party. What is necessary for a written security agreement is that the writing or writings objectively indicate that the debtor intended to create or provide for a security interest. The lack of a granting clause or of a document headed *Security Agreement* should not preclude an agreement from creating or providing for a security interest. A security agreement evidenced by an electronic record should be judged by the same standard.

However, even the composite document rule has its limitations. None of the illustrative cases noted above involved a situation where a financing statement was the only documentation evidencing a security agreement. The great majority of courts have held that a security interest does not attach when the financing statement is the only documentation of a security interest. An effective financing statement must include only the parties' names, addresses, and a description of the collateral, so it does not show the debtor's agreement to create or provide for a security interest and by itself does not signify the existence of a security interest. (The requirements for a financing statement are discussed in Chapter 3.) Additionally, section 9-502(d) allows a secured party to file a financing statement before a security agreement is made or the security interest attaches. Consequently, the presence of a filed statement does not indicate the debtor's agreement to create a security interest.

Courts created the composite document rule when Article 9 required the debtor's signature on the financing statement. That signature gave the secured party a basis for asserting that the financing statement indicates the debtor's agreement to give a security interest. Article 9 no longer requires the debtor's signature. That deletion presents an additional ground for contending that a financing statement alone cannot function as the security agreement: without the debtor's signature on the financing statement, there is nothing to indicate agreement.

2. Satisfying the Debtor's-Agreement Requirement Through Possession of Collateral — Sections 9-203, 9-313

a. Possession by Secured Party — Section 9-313

Section 9-203(b)(3)(B) authorizes a secured party to satisfy the section 9-203(b)(3) debtor's-agreement requirement for attachment and enforceability by possessing the collateral pursuant to the debtor's security agreement, regardless of whether the debtor also authenticates a security agreement. The meaning of *debtor's security agreement* in section 9-203(b)(3)(B) is different from the meaning of the security agreement that a debtor *authenticates* in section 9-203(b)(3)(A). Recall that Article 9 defines a security agreement as an agreement that creates or provides for a security interest. There is no requirement that a security agreement be a written or electronic document. A debtor's oral agreement giving a secured party a security interest is a security agreement. Consequently, the secured party can possess collateral pursuant to a security agreement even without a written or electronic security agreement. However, an oral agreement to give a security interest is not sufficient as an authenticated security agreement because authentication requires a signature or other act of adopting the record as one's own. Most secured parties want a written or electronic security agreement to document the agreement of the parties and to help resolve disputes, regardless of whether they use it to satisfy the attachment requirements.

Section 9-313(a) specifies the types of collateral a secured party can possess. Although section 9-313(a) expressly pertains to perfection of a security interest by possession of collateral, section 9-203(b)(3)(B) provides that possession of collateral under section 9-313 satisfies the attachment requirement. A secured party can possess tangible negotiable documents, goods, instruments, money, or tangible chattel paper. A secured party possessing other types of collateral does not satisfy the attachment requirement regardless of whether the collateral seemingly is tangible personal property, except when the secured party possesses a registered form certificated security, discussed later in this chapter. For example, a debtor who grants a security interest in an account might deliver the contract or other document evidencing the account to the secured party. Because an account is not listed in section 9-313(a) as property which a secured party can possess, the secured party's possession of such document is not *possession* of collateral under 9-203(b)(3)(B). Section 9-207 bestows rights and imposes duties on the secured party for the custody and preservation of the collateral it possesses.

A secured party in possession of collateral satisfies the attachment requirement only while it maintains possession. The secured party does not relinquish possession by delivering the collateral to another person, except for delivery to the debtor or a lessee of debtor, if the secured party complies with the requirements of section 9-313(h). However, delivery of the collateral to the debtor or to a lessee in the ordinary course of debtor's business terminates the secured party's possession.

Section 9-313(h) states that the secured party does not relinquish possession of collateral by delivery of it to a person *if* the secured party instructs the person, at or before delivery, to hold the collateral for the secured party's benefit or to redeliver the collateral to the secured party at the conclusion of the purpose for delivery. Additionally, section 9-313(i) states that the secured party does not relinquish possession even if delivery to the person violates the rights of debtor. However, depending on the agreement between secured party and debtor, such delivery might be a breach of contract, subjecting the secured party to liability for damages. The person who receives delivery of the collateral owes no duty to the secured party unless applicable law otherwise provides or the person so agrees. Typically, however a secured party would want an agreement from the transferee covering, at a minimum, return of and care of the collateral.

b. Possession by Agent of Secured Party — Section 9-313

A secured party can possess the collateral through its agent. Agency law determines whether a person is considered an agent of the secured party. Typically, an agent is a representative of the secured party and is authorized to act on behalf of the secured party. Courts have properly rejected arguments by secured parties that a secured party can achieve possession of the collateral by having the debtor possess the collateral in trust for the secured party, as the agent of the secured party, or constructively for the secured party. However, Official Comment 3 to section 9-313 provides that a person could be an agent for both the secured party and the debtor so that the agent's possession qualifies as the secured party's possession. When a person is the agent of both the debtor and the secured party, it is possible that the agent is so controlled by or connected to the debtor that the debtor effectively has retained possession of the collateral notwithstanding the agent's agreement to possess the collateral on behalf of the secured party. In that situation the secured party would not have possession of the collateral and the security interest would not attach unless the debtor authenticates a security agreement. To avoid that problem, a secured party should maintain sole control of an agent.

c. Possession by a Third Person — Section 9-313(c)

Section 9-313(c) establishes standards for how a secured party can possess collateral, other than certificated securities or goods covered by a document of title, that is in the possession of a third person who is not the agent of the secured party or the debtor, nor a lessee of the collateral from the debtor. This differs from possession by an agent in which the secured party is deemed to possess the collateral because the agent acts for the secured party. A secured party possesses collateral in the possession of a third person when that person authenticates a record acknowledging that it holds the collateral for the secured party's benefit or takes possession of the collateral after authenticating a record acknowledging that it will hold the collateral for the secured party's benefit. This rule allows the third person to authenticate the record of acknowledgement either before or after it takes possession of the goods. Section 9-313(g) states that either type of acknowledgement is effective to give the secured party possession of the collateral, even if the acknowledgement violates the rights of the debtor. The definitions of *authenticate* and *record*, sections 9-102(a)(7) and (a)(69), respectively, allow for either a written or an electronic acknowledgement.

The secured party does not control the third person and consequently cannot force the person to acknowledge that it holds or will hold the collateral for the secured party's benefit. Section 9-313(f) expressly provides that a third person is not required to acknowledge it holds property for the secured party's benefit. Consequently, a secured party who plans to perfect through possession of the collateral by a third person should be prepared to perfect the security interest using another method of perfection. A third person who acknowledges the secured party's interest owes no duty to the secured party from the act of acknowledging.

3. Satisfying the Debtor's-Agreement Requirement Through Delivery of a Registered Form Certificated Security — Section 9-203(b)(3)(C)

Section 9-203(b)(3)(C) provides a possession option for satisfying the debtor's-agreement requirement when the collateral is a registered form certificated security. Delivery of a registered form certificated security to the secured party pursuant to the debtor's security agreement and in a manner conforming to the section 8-301(a) delivery requirements satisfies section 9-203(b)(3). Recall that a debtor's oral agreement creating a security interest is effective as a security agreement. Section 8-102(a)(13) defines a *registered form certificated security* as a security represented by a certificate that specifies a person entitled to the security and the transfer of which can be registered on books maintained by the issuer. The most common example of a registered form certificated security is a stock certificate that specifies the owner of the stock the certificate represents.

Section 8-301(a) establishes three ways that delivery of the certificate to the secured party can occur: 1) the secured party has actual possession; 2) another person has possession of the certificate on behalf of the secured party; or 3) a securities intermediary (a stock broker is a typical securities intermediary) acting on behalf of the secured party has possession. Literally, section 8-301(a) uses the term "purchaser" to describe the person to whom the certificated security is delivered. However, a secured party is a purchaser because the definitions of *purchase* and *purchaser* (sections 1-201(b)(29) and (30)) include acquiring rights through a security interest.

Under section 8-301(a)(1), delivery occurs when the secured party acquires possession of the certificate. Under section 8-301(a)(2), delivery to a secured party occurs when a person, other than a securities intermediary, either acquires possession of the certificate on behalf of the secured party or, having previously acquired possession, acknowledges that it holds the certificate for the secured party. The person must acknowledge that its possession is on behalf of the secured party only if the person already possesses the certificate when it agrees to act on behalf of the secured party. Because Article 8 establishes no requirements for an acknowledgement, a sufficient acknowledgement could be written, electronic, or oral. Moreover, section 8-301 does not compel such person to acknowledge that it holds the certificate for the secured party. If the person is noncompliant, the secured party must have the debtor authenticate a security agreement or give possession of the certificate to a person who will hold it on behalf of the secured party.

Under section 8-301(a)(3), delivery to a secured party occurs when a securities intermediary, acting on behalf of secured party, acquires possession of the registered form certificated security and the certificate is either registered in the name of the secured party, payable to the order of the secured party, or specially indorsed to the secured party by an effective indorsement and has not been indorsed either to the securities intermediary or in blank. The typical securities intermediary is a brokerage company or investment bank. Registration refers to issuer's registration of transfer of the certificate.

4. Satisfying the Debtor's-Agreement Requirement Through Control—Section 9-203(b)(3)(D)

Section 9-203(b)(3)(D) provides an optional method for satisfying the debtor's-agreement requirement for a security interest in a deposit account, electronic chattel paper, investment property, letter-of-credit right, and an electronic document. A secured party can satisfy that requirement if it establishes "control" of such property under the requirements of the applicable UCC section and pursuant to the debtor's agreement to give a security interest. The UCC drafters designed the control requirements in such a manner that a secured party who establishes control has power over the collateral without obtaining further consent of the debtor. A debtor's oral agreement creating a security interest suffices as the security agreement. Although control obviates the necessity of a written or electronic security agreement, the parties likely will want such an agreement to document their rights and duties and help resolve disputes.

Control is also a method of perfecting a security interest in those types of collateral. Since the control requirements are essentially the same for attachment and perfection, if you studied control in Chapter 4, this should be a review.

a. Deposit Account — Section 9-104

Article 9 governs a security interest in a deposit account, whether the security interest arises directly in the deposit account or as proceeds of collateral. However, under section 9-109(d)(13), Article 9 does not govern a security interest in a deposit account created by a debtor in a consumer transaction except when the security interest arises as *proceeds* of collateral in a consumer transaction. The deposit account exclusion is discussed in Chapter 1.

Section 9-102(a)(29) defines a *deposit account* as a "demand, time, savings, passbook, or similar account maintained with a bank." The definition of *bank* includes savings banks, savings and loan associations, credit unions, and trust companies. Section 9-102(a)(9) includes a deposit account in the definition of *cash proceeds*.

A *certificate of deposit* can be a deposit account or an instrument. A certificate of deposit is a transaction in which the depositor deposits money with a bank to be repaid by the bank with interest at the expiration of a stated period. A certificate of deposit is like a "time" or "similar account maintained with a bank" and fits the deposit account definition. However, the definition of deposit account excludes accounts evidenced by an instrument. Such accounts are classified as instruments, not as deposit accounts. Consequently, it is possible, though unlikely, that a certificate of deposit is an instrument rather than a deposit account. Official Comment 12 to section 9-102 declares that if no certificate or other writing evidences the certificate of deposit, it remains a deposit account. Frequently, however, some type of writing evidences a certificate of deposit. In that situation, one must review the transaction to determine if it satisfies the definition of instrument, and if it does, the certificate of deposit is classified as an instrument, not a deposit account.

Instrument is defined in section 9-102(a)(47) as a "negotiable instrument or any other writing that evidences a right to the payment of a monetary obligation, is not itself a security agreement or lease, and is of a type that in ordinary course of business is transferred by delivery with any necessary indorsement or assignment." While it is unlikely that the writing embodying a certificate of deposit is a negotiable instrument because typically it lacks the necessary order or bearer language, it nevertheless evidences a depositor's right to the payment of a money obligation from a bank. However, the certificate is not an instrument unless it is transferred in the ordinary course of business by delivery and indorsement or assignment. Typically, a certificate of deposit evidenced by a writing is not transferred in that manner. Consequently, most certificates of deposit are deposit accounts.

Section 9-104 provides three separate methods by which a secured party can establish control of a deposit account. *First*, control is established automatically if the secured party is the bank with which the deposit account is maintained. For example, a bank has control when it takes a security interest in its depositor's account to secure an obligation the depositor owes the bank.

Second, control is established when the debtor, the secured party, and the bank with which the deposit account is maintained all agree in an authenticated record that the bank will comply with the secured party's instructions directing disposition of the account's funds without further consent of the debtor. The *authenticated record* can be written or electronic. This agreement establishes control even if the debtor retains a right to direct disposition of the account's funds or the agreement is subject to conditions, such as that the secured party's power exists only in the event of the debtor's default. Section 9-342 authorizes a bank to refuse to enter a control agreement even if its customer requests it to do so. Consequently, if the secured party and the debtor agree to attach a security interest in a deposit account by control but the bank refuses to enter a control agreement, the secured party must require the debtor to move its account to a bank that will enter a control agreement, establish control by another method, or have the debtor authenticate a security agreement.

Third, the secured party establishes control if it becomes the bank's customer as to the deposit account. A person becomes the bank's *customer*, pursuant to UCC Article 4, by having an account with a bank. The deposit account that will be the collateral is the debtor's deposit account. Consequently, the secured party cannot become the bank's customer as to the debtor's deposit account unless the debtor agrees to allow the secured party to become a party to the account, either solely or jointly with the other account owners. A secured party with control of a deposit account is subject to the duties imposed by sections 9-207(c) and 9-208(b)(1) and (2).

b. Electronic Chattel Paper—Section 9-105

Electronic chattel paper, defined in section 9-102 (a)(31), is chattel paper evidenced by a record consisting of information stored in an electronic medium. *Chattel paper*, defined in section 9-102(a)(11), basically is a record that evidences a monetary obligation and a security interest. (Chattel paper is discussed in Chapter 1.) Section 9-105 provides six requirements to establish control of electronic chattel paper. The significance of the requirements is that control requires creation of a system that establishes an "authoritative copy" of the chattel paper and makes the unauthorized assignment or revision of the electronic chattel paper practically impossible. The control requirements are flexible to allow the secured party and debtor to create a system that achieves control. Section 9-105 requires: 1) a single unique, identifiable, and authoritative copy of the electronic chattel paper; 2) identifying the secured party as the assignee of the chattel paper; 3) the authoritative copy is communicated to and maintained by the secured party or its designated custodian; 4) revisions that add or change an identified assignee can be made only with the participation of the secured party; 5) any copy of the authoritative copy is readily identifiable as a copy; and 6) any revision of the authoritative copy is readily identifiable as an authorized or unauthorized revision. A secured party, other than a buyer, with control of electronic chattel paper is subject to the duties imposed by sections 9-207(c) and 9-208(b)(3).

c. Letter-of-Credit Right—Sections 9-107, 5-114

Section 9-107 states that a secured party establishes control of a letter-of-credit right if the issuer or nominated person has consented to the assignment of the letter-of-credit proceeds under section 5-114 or under other applicable law or practice. *Letter-of-credit right*, defined in section 9-102(a)(51), means a right to payment or performance under a letter of credit. A letter of credit is an undertaking by the issuer of the letter at the request of the obligor that the issuer will honor a demand for payment made by the beneficiary of the letter of an obligation incurred by the obligor in a separate transaction. Letter-of-credit right is the beneficiary's right to payment or performance under a letter of credit. The beneficiary (the debtor of the security interest) can grant a security interest in its letter-of-credit right as collateral for its obligation owed to the secured party. A security interest in a letter-of-credit right refers to the assignment to the secured party by the beneficiary of the letter of credit of its right to the proceeds of a letter of credit.

Under section 5-114(d), neither the issuer nor the nominated person is obligated to consent to the assignment. Consent is not to be withheld unreasonably, however, if the secured party/assignee possesses and exhibits the letter of credit and presentation of the letter is a condition to the issuer or nominated person's duty to honor the letter. If the secured party cannot obtain the necessary consent, the secured party can satisfy the attachment requirement by having the debtor authenticate a security agreement. Sections 9-208(a) and (b)(5) obligate a secured party with control of a letter-of-credit right to send an authenticated release of control after receiving payment of the secured obligation.

In a letter of credit transaction, the issuer of a letter of credit may designate a person — labeled a *nominated person* — to pay under a letter of credit. Consequently, both the issuer and the nominated person of a letter of credit may be obligated to pay the beneficiary. A secured party can establish control against both the issuer and the nominated person or against one such person, depending on whether both persons have consented to the beneficiary's security interest assignment.

d. Investment Property

A secured party achieves control of investment property under various provisions of Article 8 or Article 9, depending on the type of investment property. *Investment property*, defined in section 9-102(a)(49), includes securities, a security entitlement, a securities account, a commodity contract, or a commodity account. Section 8-106 governs control of a security — certificated or uncertificated — and a security entitlement. Section 9-106 governs control of a commodity contract, a commodity account, and a securities account.

1. Certificated Security in Bearer or Registered Form — Section 8-106

A *certificated security* is a security, such as a share of stock, represented by a certificate. For example, a certificate representing ownership of 100 shares of stock in ABC Corporation is a certificated security. Control of a certificated security is dependent on whether the security is in bearer form or registered form. Section 8-102 defines both terms. A *bearer form* certificated security exists when the terms of the certificate make the security payable to the bearer of the certificate. A *registered form* certificated security exists when the terms of the certificate specify a person entitled to it (somewhat like the payee of a check) and its transfer can be registered on the books of the issuer of the security.

Under section 8-106(a), a secured party has control of a bearer form certificated security if the security is delivered to it. Literally, the control provisions of section 8-106(a) refer to a *purchaser* of a certificated security. However, a secured party is a purchaser because the definitions of *purchase* and *purchaser*, sections 1-201(b)(29) and (b)(30), include acquiring rights through a security interest. Section 8-301 establishes requirements for delivery. Under section 8-301(a)(1), delivery occurs when the secured party acquires possession of the certificate. Under section 8-301(a)(2), delivery to a secured party occurs when a third person, other than a securities intermediary (such as a brokerage company), either acquires possession of the certificate on behalf of the secured party or, having previously acquired possession, acknowledges that it holds the certificate for the secured party. Because section 8-301 does not compel such person to acknowledge that it holds the certificate for the secured party, the secured party must satisfy the attachment requirement through an alternative method if the person is noncompliant.

Under section 8-106(b), a secured party has control of a registered form certificated security when it satisfies two requirements. First, the certificate must be delivered to the secured party. Delivery of a registered form certificated security occurs in the same manner as delivery of a bearer form certificated security (discussed in the previous paragraph), and also when a securities intermediary acquires possession of the certificate. Under section 8-301(a)(3), delivery to a secured party occurs when a securities intermediary, acting on behalf of secured party, acquires possession of the registered form certificated security, provided the certificate is registered in the name of the secured party, payable to the order of the secured party, or specially indorsed to the secured party by an effective indorsement and has not been indorsed either to the securities intermediary or in blank. The typical securities intermediary is a brokerage company or investment bank. Registration refers to issuer's registration of transfer of the certificate.

The second requirement for control of a registered form certificated security involves indorsement or registration of the certificate under section 8-106. Control requires that the certificate be indorsed to the secured party, indorsed in blank with an *effective indorsement*, or registered in the secured party's name by the issuer of the certificate. Section 8-107(b) provides that an *effective indorsement* of a security certificate occurs when the person specified by the certificate or by a special indorsement of the certificate indorses it, an authorized agent of such person indorses it, or the person entitled to the security ratifies the indorsement or is estopped from asserting its ineffectiveness.

Combining the two requirements results in establishing control of a registered form certificated security in various ways. Control is established when: 1) a secured party has possession of a properly indorsed certificate; 2) a secured party has possession of a certificate registered in the secured party's name; 3) another person has possession of a properly indorsed certificate; 4) another person has possession of a certificate registered in the secured party's name; 5) a securities intermediary acting on behalf of the secured party has possession of a properly indorsed certificate; 6) a securities intermediary acting on behalf of the secured party has possession of a certificate payable to the order of the secured party; or 7) a securities intermediary acting on behalf of the secured party has possession of a certificate registered in the secured party's name.

Note that when the collateral is a registered form certificated security a secured party can also satisfy the section 9-203(b)(3) attachment requirement by taking delivery of the certificate under the rule of section 9-203(b)(3)(C), discussed previously in this chapter. That is a much simpler method of achieving attachment. However, satisfying the control process for attachment also perfects a security interest in investment property, and a secured party who perfects a security interest in investment property by control has a higher priority than a secured party who perfects by other methods. Priority of a security interest perfected by control is discussed in Chapter 9.

2. Uncertificated Security — Section 8-106

An *uncertificated security*, defined in section 8-102(a)(18), is simply a security for which there is no certificate. Section 8-106(c) provides two ways a secured party can establish control of an uncertificated security. *First*, a secured party has control of an uncertificated security if it is delivered to the secured party. Although it seems incongruous to speak of delivery of a security for which no certificate exists, delivery of an uncertificated security nevertheless occurs pursuant to section 8-301(b) if: 1) the issuer registers the secured party as registered owner; 2) another person becomes registered owner on behalf of the secured party; or 3) the current registered owner acknowledges that it holds the uncertificated security for the secured party. Obviously, there is no physical delivery of an uncertificated security.

Second, a secured party establishes control if the issuer of the security agrees that it will comply with instructions originated by the secured party without further consent by the entitlement holder (the owner of the rights and property of the security, generally the debtor). For example, Brown, the registered owner of 100 uncertificated shares of XYZ Corporation, grants a security interest in the shares as collateral for a loan from Bank. To achieve control, Brown and XYZ Corporation must agree that XYZ Corporation will comply with instructions originated by Bank. *Instructions* means a notification communicated to the issuer of an uncertificated security directing redemption of the security or registration of transfer of the security. Section 8-106(g) directs that an issuer cannot enter a control agreement with a secured party without obtaining the registered owner's or entitlement holder's consent. However, an issuer is not required to enter such an agreement even if the registered owner or entitlement holder so directs.

3. Security Entitlement—Section 8-106

An example will help describe a security entitlement. Suppose Brown, who has a securities account with Barrelhouse, a broker, directs Barrelhouse to purchase 100 shares of ABC Corporation for Brown's securities account. When Barrelhouse credits Brown's account with the shares, Brown has a security entitlement and is the entitlement holder with respect to 100 ABC shares, although Brown is not typically the registered owner on the shareholder records of ABC Corporation. Section 8-102(a)(17) defines *security entitlement* as the rights and property interest of an entitlement holder with respect to a financial asset. The financial asset is the 100 shares of ABC Corporation. Brown is the entitlement holder of a security that was credited to his securities account, although he is not the registered owner or the holder of the security. Brown's rights as entitlement holder in the 100 shares consist of property interests and obligations in the shares, which the securities intermediary, typically a broker, owes to the entitlement holder. Those rights constitute the security entitlement. Barrelhouse is a securities intermediary under the definition of section 8-102(a)(14). Barrelhouse, or another securities intermediary, is generally the registered owner of the shares. The entitlement holder can create a security interest in the security entitlement.

Under section 8-106(d), a secured party establishes control of a security entitlement if: 1) the secured party becomes the entitlement holder; 2) the securities intermediary has agreed to comply with entitlement orders originated by the secured party without further consent by the entitlement holder; or 3) another person has control of the security entitlement on behalf of the secured party. If the debtor and the secured party agree that the secured party will establish control of the debtor's security entitlement by becoming the entitlement holder, the debtor— the current entitlement holder—will originate an entitlement order to its securities intermediary directing the securities intermediary to transfer the debtor's security entitlement in the financial asset to the secured party. The secured party becomes the entitlement holder with respect to the financial asset and has control when the financial asset is credited to the secured party's securities account.

The secured party can also establish control of the debtor's security entitlement if the debtor's securities intermediary agrees it will comply with entitlement orders originated by the secured party alone. A securities intermediary may not make this agreement without obtaining the consent of the entitlement holder. However, a securities intermediary is not required to enter such an agreement although the entitlement holder so directs. The secured party can establish control in this manner although it does not have the exclusive right to issue entitlement orders. For example, the secured party, the debtor, and the securities intermediary might agree that both the secured party and the debtor have the right to give entitlement orders. In that situation, the secured party must be aware that the debtor retains power to sell the underlying financial asset. Consequently, exclusive control in the secured party is preferable.

The secured party also establishes control of the debtor's security entitlement if another person has control of the entitlement on behalf of the secured party. For example, Brown grants Bank a security interest in her security entitlement to 100 shares of ABC Corporation in Brown's securities account with Barrelhouse Brokers. Roundhouse Brokers agrees to act as Bank's agent with respect to Brown's security entitlement. Brown, Barrelhouse, and Roundhouse all agree that Roundhouse has the right to direct entitlement orders for Brown's security entitlement in the ABC Corporation shares. Roundhouse has control of the entitlement because Barrelhouse has agreed to comply with Roundhouse's entitlement orders without further consent of Brown. Bank has control because Roundhouse has control. Bank's control is not affected by permitting Brown to direct entitlement orders to Barrelhouse.

An entitlement holder might grant a security interest in its security entitlement to its securities intermediary. In that situation, section 8-106(e) provides that the securities intermediary establishes control simply from the entitlement holder's granting the security interest to the intermediary. This is automatic control; no action by the secured party is necessary.

4. Commodity Contract—Section 9-106

Commodity contracts, defined in section 9-102(a)(15), are different from securities or other financial assets although they are traded on an exchange similar to securities trading. The typical commodity contract is a commodity futures contract pertaining to a raw material or agricultural product. In a commodity contract, a person contracts to buy or sell a commodity (the raw material or agricultural product) at a set price for delivery at a future time. Consequently, the contract may become advantageous or disadvantageous depending on whether the price of the commodity increases or decreases in the future.

A secured party who takes a security interest in a commodity contract can satisfy the section 9-203(b)(3) attachment requirement by establishing control of the commodity contract. Section 9-106(b) supplies the control provisions for a security interest in a commodity contract. It provides two methods to achieve control of a commodity contract. *First*, a secured party has control of a commodity contract if the commodity customer (typically the debtor), the secured party, and the commodity intermediary (typically a futures commission merchant; much like a stock broker) agree to apply any value distributed on account of the commodity contract as directed by the secured party without any further consent of the commodity customer. The agreement need not give the secured party the exclusive right to direct distributions. *Second*, a secured party who is also a commodity intermediary has control of its customer's commodity contract when its customer grants it a security interest in the customer's commodity contract. Such secured party has automatic control; no additional action is required.

5. Commodity or Securities Account—Section 9-106(c)

A securities account or commodity account is the account maintained by a securities or commodity intermediary in which the intermediary carries the securities entitlements or commodity contracts for the benefit of its customer. Section 9-106(c) provides that a secured party establishes control of a debtor's securities account or commodity account if the secured party has control over *all* security entitlements or commodity contracts carried in the respective accounts. Control of securities entitlements or commodity accounts requires satisfaction of the control conditions discussed in the preceding paragraphs with respect to the type of collateral involved in the secured transaction. It is logical that a secured party who has control of all security entitlements or commodity accounts in the debtor's securities or commodity account also has control over the account. Additionally, Official Comment 4 to section 9-106 declares that control of a securities or commodity account should be established if the secured party, debtor, and securities or commodity intermediary (whichever is applicable) agree that the intermediary will honor instructions from the secured party concerning the account without further consent of the debtor. Such an agreement implies that the intermediary will honor the secured party's instructions as to the particular entitlements or accounts. Although control obviates the necessity of a security agreement, the secured party nevertheless might want a written or electronic security agreement that evidences the parties' rights and duties and helps resolves disputes regarding such matters.

e. Control of Electronic Document—Section 7-106

Under section 9-102(a)(30), a *document* means a document of title. *Document of title* is defined in section 1-201(b)(16). A document of title represents goods in possession of a person who is not generally the owner of the goods, and the person in possession or control of the document has the right to receive, control, hold, and dispose of the document and the goods it covers. Typically, a person issues a document of title covering the goods when the owner of the goods delivers them to that person for storage or transportation of the goods. An *electronic document of title* is a document of title evidenced by a record consisting of information stored in an electronic medium. A document of title is either negotiable or nonnegotiable. A negotiable document of title authorizes delivery of the goods either to the bearer of the document or to the order of a person named in the document. Any other document is nonnegotiable.

Section 7-106 supplies two methods for establishing control of an electronic document. (Article 7 of the UCC governs documents of title.) *First*, under section 7-106(a), a person has control of an electronic document when it establishes a system for evidencing the transfer of the document, with the key being that the system reliably establishes the identity of the person entitled to the document. *Second*, section 7-106(b) provides a safe harbor for establishing control by providing that a person is deemed to have control if the system established by the parties satisfies six requirements. The significance of the requirements is that they create a system under which a person should be able to identify the single authoritative copy of the document. The control requirements are flexible to allow the secured party and debtor to create a system that achieves control. Section 7-106(b) requires: 1) a single unique, identifiable, and authoritative copy of the document; 2) the authoritative copy identifies the secured party as the person to whom the document was issued or most recently transferred; 3) the authoritative copy is communicated to and maintained by the secured party or its designated custodian; 4) copies or amendments that add or change an identified assignee of the secured party can be made only with the consent of the secured party; 5) any copy of the authoritative copy is readily identifiable as a copy; and 6) any amendment of the authoritative copy is readily identifiable as authorized or unauthorized. A secured party with control of an electronic document is subject to the duties imposed by sections 9-207(c) and 9-208(b)(6).

D. Automatic Attachment for Security Interests in Specific Types of Collateral — Sections 9-203(c), (f), (g), (h), (i)

1. Security Interest in Proceeds and Supporting Obligation — Sections 9-203(f), 9-315

Under section 9-203(f) a security interest automatically attaches to a supporting obligation for the collateral and gives a secured party the right to proceeds of collateral as provided by section 9-315. A security interest in a supporting obligation and in proceeds of the collateral give the secured party additional collateral it can use to obtain payment of the debt if the obligor defaults. Additionally, a security interest in proceeds is important to the secured party if the collateral is damaged or destroyed.

a. Supporting Obligation Security Interest

Under section 9-203(f), when a security interest attaches to the collateral it automatically attaches to the supporting obligation for the collateral. *Supporting obligation* is defined in section 9-102(a)(77) as a letter-of-credit right or secondary obligation that supports the payment or performance of an account, chattel paper, a general intangible, an instrument, or investment property. For example, suppose the collateral is an account — a person (the *account debtor*) owes a creditor money. If another person guarantees that it will pay the creditor if the account debtor does not, that guaranty is a supporting obligation. The creditor can grant a security interest in the account as collateral for an obligation it owes. When the security interest attaches to the account as collateral, it also attaches to the supporting obligation and the secured party has a security interest in the guaranty. Attachment occurs even if the security agreement is silent regarding a security interest in a supporting obligation.

b. Proceeds Security Interest

Section 9-315(a)(2) states that a security interest attaches to any identifiable proceeds of collateral unless the parties agree otherwise. The combination of sections 9-315(a)(2) and 9-203(f) results in the secured party having an automatic, attached security interest in identifiable proceeds of collateral. Attachment occurs even if the security agreement is silent regarding a security interest in proceeds. Additionally, there is no requirement that the security agreement include a description of the property that constitutes proceeds. For example, a security agreement that describes the collateral as *inventory* is sufficient to attach a security interest in *cash proceeds* produced by the sale of the inventory. In the unlikely situation that the debtor and secured party do not want the security interest to include proceeds of collateral, the security agreement must provide that the security interest does not attach to proceeds of the collateral.

Article 9 adopts an expansive definition of proceeds of collateral. Generally, proceeds are any property interest or right that derives from the collateral for a security interest. A common example of proceeds is when the debtor sells the collateral for cash; the cash is proceeds of the collateral. But proceeds are not limited to situations involving a disposition of the collateral. Proceeds are defined in section 9-102(a)(64) to include: 1) whatever is acquired upon the disposition of the collateral—such as cash acquired from the sale of collateral; 2) whatever is collected on or distributed on account of the collateral—such as cash collected from the account debtor of account collateral; 3) rights arising out of collateral—such as stock options granted to the owner of investment property collateral; 4) claims arising out of the loss, nonconformity, or interference with the use of collateral, defects or infringement of rights in the collateral, or damage to the collateral, up to its value—such as a copyright infringement cause of action arising from an infringement of copyright collateral; and 5) insurance payable for such claims, to the extent payable to the debtor or secured party, up to the value of the collateral—such as insurance proceeds received from damage to the collateral.

Proceeds are not restricted to property received by the debtor. Official Comment 13 to section 9-102 declares that it is necessary only that the proceeds be traceable to the original collateral, not that they be received by the debtor. For example, suppose the debtor sells collateral to a buyer in a transaction where the security interest continues in the collateral. What the debtor receives from the buyer is proceeds. The buyer then resells the collateral. What the buyer receives is proceeds, and the security interest will attach them if the secured party can identify them as proceeds of its collateral.

Proceeds also include proceeds of proceeds collateral (sometimes called *second generation proceeds*). The definition of collateral accomplishes that feat. Section 9-102(a)(12) defines *collateral* as including "proceeds to which a security interest attaches...." Consequently, proceeds are collateral. When *proceeds collateral* is sold, leased, etc., the resulting property is proceeds. Thus, proceeds of proceeds are collateral for the security interest.

Section 9-315(a)(2) provides that a security interest attaches to proceeds to the extent they are identifiable as proceeds of collateral. In many cases identification is possible simply by tracing the proceeds to the collateral. However, in cases where proceeds are commingled with other property (as in cash proceeds commingled with other cash), a secured party may have difficulty identifying its proceeds from the other property. Section 9-315(b) provides two rules to aid the secured party in identifying proceeds. Section 9-315(b)(1) adopts the commingled goods rule of section 9-336 when the proceeds are goods commingled with other goods in such a manner that the identity of the proceeds is lost. The typical situation of commingled goods involves fungible goods, such as grain. Under section 9-336, the security interest does not exist in the particular goods commingled, but a security interest attaches to the product or mass that results when the goods become commingled. Consequently, when the proceeds of the collateral are fungible goods mixed with similar fungible goods, the security interest automatically attaches to the commingled mass of goods. (Commingled goods are discussed in Chapter 9.)

For non-goods proceeds, section 9-315(b)(2) authorizes a secured party to identify proceeds by using tracing principles permitted under non-UCC law with respect to the type of property involved. Section 9-315(b)(2) applies primarily to cash proceeds. The official comment to section 9-315 adopts a very workable rule for a situation that looks hopeless: how to identify the cash proceeds of the collateral that the debtor has commingled with other cash. Official Comment 3 to section 9-315 expressly permits use of the *lowest intermediate balance rule*, a rule originating in trust law, for identifying commingled cash proceeds. (*See* Restatement (Second) of Trusts § 202 cmt. J for elaboration on this rule.)

The *lowest intermediate balance rule* simplifies the process of identifying cash proceeds that the debtor commingles with other cash, whether in a bank account or otherwise. The first step in identifying commingled proceeds is that the secured party must prove that its cash proceeds were commingled with the other cash in which the secured party is asserting its security interest. If the secured party accomplishes that, the lowest intermediate balance rule directs that the debtor's subsequent withdrawals and deposits of cash to the commingled cash do not affect the amount of the proceeds security interest, provided the total amount of cash never is less than the amount of proceeds commingled with the cash. If the total amount becomes less than the amount of proceeds commingled, the security interest is limited to that value regardless of later infusions of non-proceeds cash. The security interest is lost only if the debtor dissipates all the cash.

For example, suppose Lender has a security interest in Debtor's equipment. Debtor sells an item of equipment for $7,000 and deposits the money in its bank account that has a balance of $17,000 after the deposit. If Lender can prove that Debtor deposited the proceeds from the collateral sale in Debtor's bank account, then Lender has identified $7,000 of the account as its proceeds security interest. Subsequent deposits or withdrawals by Debtor of non-proceeds cash do not affect Lender's security interest. However, if the account balance falls below $7,000, the proceeds are identifiable only to the amount of the remaining balance. Lender's security interest in the proceeds commingled in the bank account ends if Debtor withdraws all funds in the account. Debtor's subsequent deposits of non-proceeds cash do not revive the security interest.

Official Comment 9 to section 9-315 declares that Article 9 does not determine whether an agricultural lien continues in the proceeds of collateral. Section 9-315(a)(2) provides that a *security interest* attaches to proceeds of collateral. An agricultural lien, although governed by Article 9, is not a security interest. Consequently, the law creating the agricultural lien governs whether the lien continues in proceeds of the collateral.

2. Security Interest Arising under Articles 2, 2A, 4, or 5 — Section 9-203(c)

Section 9-203(c) provides that the attachment rules of section 9-203(b) are subject to UCC provisions governing the security interest of a collecting bank (section 4-210), of an issuer or nominated person of a letter of credit (section 5-118), or arising under Article 2 or 2A (section 9-110). Each of those sections allows the respective security interest to attach and be enforceable regardless of whether the section 9-203(b)(3) debtor's-agreement requirement is satisfied. In essence, those sections allow the security interest to attach without the debtor authenticating a security agreement, the secured party possessing the collateral, or the secured party establishing control. These types of security interests are discussed in Chapter 1. Also noteworthy is that each of the security interests listed in section 9-203(c) is perfected upon attachment without additional action under the rules of section 9-309(6), (7), and (8).

3. Security Interest in a Financial Asset — Section 9-203(c)

Section 9-203(c) provides that the attachment requirements of section 9-203(b) are subject to section 9-206, the section that governs security interests arising in a transaction involving purchase or delivery of a financial asset. The complete definition of *financial asset* is in section 8-102(a)(9), but essentially a financial asset is securities and securities entitlements. A person who buys a financial asset through a securities intermediary (such as a stock broker) typically is obligated to pay for the asset at the time of the purchase. However, it is common for the intermediary to credit the financial asset to the buyer's securities account before the buyer pays the intermediary. In such cases, section 9-206(a) automatically creates a security interest in the financial asset that secures its purchase price regardless of whether the securities intermediary, the secured party, fulfills the section 9-203(b) attachment requirements. The conditions to the creation of this security interest are: 1) purchase of a financial asset through a securities intermediary; 2) in a transaction in which the buyer is obligated to pay the purchase price at the time of purchase, meaning that the parties did not contemplate a credit transaction; and 3) the securities intermediary credits the financial asset to the buyer's securities account before the buyer pays the securities intermediary. Section 9-203(c) establishes automatic attachment of this security interest by declaring that section 9-203(b) is subject to it.

For example, suppose Black directs Barrelhouse, her broker (a securities intermediary), to purchase 1000 shares of ABC Corporation (a financial asset) for her securities account with Barrelhouse. Black is to pay Barrelhouse for the shares within three days of execution of the trade. Black pays with a check on the third day. On that day, Barrelhouse credits the shares to Black's securities account, although at that time Black's bank has not paid the check. Black acquires a security entitlement to the financial asset when Barrelhouse credits it to Black's securities account. Section 9-206 gives Barrelhouse a security interest in Black's security entitlement securing Black's duty to pay. Official Comment 2 to section 9-206 labels this a "broker's lien."

In some financial markets, trading of certificated securities and other financial assets represented by writings is still settled by physical delivery of the certificate or the writing representing the financial asset. It is possible that delivery of the asset by the seller or the seller's securities custodian will precede payment, notwithstanding the parties' agreement that delivery of the property is conditioned upon payment. In that situation, sections 9-206(c) and (d) create a security interest in favor of the person delivering the certificate to secure that person's right to receive payment. This security interest is created when a certificated security or other financial asset represented by a writing and ordinarily transferred by delivery with indorsement, is delivered pursuant to an agreement between persons in the business of dealing with such securities or financial assets and the agreement conditions delivery upon payment. The effect of section 9-203(c) is that a person obtains an enforceable security interest without complying with the section 9-203(b) attachment requirements. Notice that this security interest arises only if the agreement is between persons in the business of dealing with securities or financial assets.

4. Security Interest in a Mortgage, Security Interest, or Other Lien — Section 9-203(g)

Section 9-203(g) provides that attachment of a security interest in a right to payment or performance that is secured by a security interest or other lien on personal or real property is also attachment of a security interest in the security interest or other lien. For example, suppose Lender has a right to payment from its debtor — an account — and a security interest in the debtor's equipment secures the obligation of the account. Lender borrows money from Bank and grants Bank a security interest in the account to secure payment of its debt. Under 9-203(g), Bank's attachment of its security interest in Lender's account is also attachment of a security interest in Lender's security interest in the equipment. Attachment to the supporting security interest or other lien is automatic; it does not depend on the debtor's agreement.

If the right to payment is secured by a real property mortgage, attachment of a security interest in the right to payment results in attachment of a security interest in the mortgage. This is one of the few instances when Article 9 applies to an interest in real property. However, the secured party does not have a mortgage, it has only a security interest in the mortgage.

5. Security Interest in Securities and Commodity Accounts — Sections 9-203(h), (i)

Sections 9-203(h) and (i) provide that attachment of a security interest in a securities account or commodity account is attachment of all securities entitlements and commodity contracts in the respective accounts. (Securities and commodities accounts are discussed previously in this chapter.) Debtor's grant of a security interest in its securities or commodity account is more efficient than granting a security interest in each of its securities entitlements or commodity contracts because it is simpler for a secured party to comply with the attachment requirements of section 9-203(b) for the securities or commodity account than to comply with those requirements for each entitlement or contract in the account. Attachment to the entitlements or contracts is automatic upon attachment to the account; it does not depend on the debtor's agreement.

E. Attachment of a Security Interest Created by a Sale of Accounts, Chattel Paper, Payment Intangibles, and Promissory Notes — Section 9-203

Because Article 9 covers sales of accounts, chattel paper, payment intangibles, and promissory notes (commonly known as *receivables*), the buyer of such property must comply with the attachment provisions of Article 9. (Official Comment 5 to section 9-102 discusses the various types of receivables.) The usual attachment provisions of section 9-203(b) apply — secured party gives value, debtor has rights in the collateral, and debtor authenticates a security agreement that provides a description of the collateral or the secured party complies with one of the other debtor's-agreement requirements. When Article 9's definitions of *secured party*, *debtor*, and *collateral*, sections 9-102(a)(72), (28), and (12), respectively, are applied to sales of receivables, the buyer of such property is a secured party, the seller is a debtor, and the property sold is the collateral.

A buyer of those receivables normally satisfies the attachment requirements regardless of its possible lack of knowledge that the sale is a transaction governed by Article 9. A buyer typically gives value by purchasing the receivable with cash or some other valuable property. Section 1-204 defines value, and it includes any consideration sufficient to support a simple contract. A seller of receivables usually has either (or both) the right or the power to sell the property because it is generally the owner of the property. Section 9-318(b) (discussed in Chapter 1) supplies the seller's rights in accounts or chattel paper collateral if the seller has previously sold the accounts or chattel paper. The seller of the receivable satisfies the debtor's-agreement requirement when it authenticates an agreement for sale of the receivable, regardless of whether the parties understand that the sale creates a security interest or whether the agreement is labeled *security agreement*. Section 9-102(a)(73) defines *security agreement* as "an agreement that creates or provides for a security interest." Section 1-102(b)(35) defines *security interest* as including the interest of a buyer of accounts, chattel paper, a payment intangible, or a promissory note in a transaction subject to Article 9. An agreement for sale of such receivables is, by definition, an agreement that creates a security interest and consequently is a security agreement. If the seller authenticates the agreement, the debtor's-agreement requirement is fulfilled.

Section 9-203(b)(3) adopts optional methods of satisfying the debtor's-agreement requirement for chattel paper and promissory notes. An authenticated security agreement is not required when the collateral is *electronic* chattel paper if the secured party has *control* under section 9-105, or when the secured party takes possession of *tangible* chattel paper or a promissory note under section 9-313, as discussed previously in this chapter.

F. Attachment and New Debtors — Sections 9-203(d), (e)

A *new debtor*, defined in section 9-102(a)(56), is a person that becomes bound as the debtor under section 9-203(d) by a security agreement previously entered into by another person, the *original debtor*, defined in section 9-102(a)(60). The typical situation of a new debtor is not as complicated as the definition makes it sound. Suppose Green Corporation is a debtor in a secured transaction and authenticates a security agreement granting a security interest to Lender. Green Corporation merges with Brown Corporation in a transaction where Brown Corporation is the surviving entity and it agrees to be liable for all obligations of Green Corporation. Brown Corporation is a *new debtor*. An issue that might concern Lender is whether its security interest attaches and is enforceable against Brown Corporation to the extent of the collateral described in the security agreement, especially since Brown Corporation has not authenticated a security agreement in favor of Lender. Section 9-203(e) declares that it does.

Essentially, section 9-203(e) creates an exception to the debtor's-agreement requirement of section 9-203(b)(3). The exception allows a security agreement entered into by the *original debtor* to be effective against property of the *new debtor* even though the *new debtor* has not authenticated a security agreement, nor has the secured party complied with any of the statutory alternatives to the authenticated security agreement established by sections 9-203(b)(3)(B)–(D). Section 9-203(e) operates when a "new debtor becomes bound as debtor" by a security agreement entered into by the *original debtor*. *Original debtor* "means a person that, as debtor, entered into a security agreement to which a new debtor has become bound under section 9-203(d)." If a new debtor becomes bound, then section 9-203(e)(1) makes the security interest created by the original debtor enforceable against the new debtor and the security interest attaches the new debtor's existing and after-acquired property to the extent such property is described in the security agreement. Consequently, the property of the new debtor becomes part of the collateral described in the security agreement and it secures the obligation incurred by the original debtor. This result does not depend on the presence of a security agreement authenticated by the new debtor. Section 9-203(e)(2) expressly provides that a new security agreement is not required.

For example, suppose New Corporation becomes bound as debtor under a security agreement entered into between Bank and Old Corporation that described the collateral as Old Corporation's existing and after-acquired equipment. Because New Corporation becomes bound as debtor, the security interest created by Old Corporation attaches to New Corporation's existing and after-acquired equipment.

Section 9-203(e) applies to collateral other than any collateral previously owned by the original debtor and subsequently sold to the new debtor. A security interest continues in that collateral under the rule of section 9-315(a), discussed in Chapter 7.

Section 9-203(d) establishes when a person becomes bound as debtor—a new debtor—under the security agreement of the original debtor. *First*, a person becomes bound as debtor under the original debtor's security agreement if the original debtor's security agreement becomes effective to create a security interest in the person's property under applicable law, other than the UCC. The *applicable law* typically is corporation law. For example, if the corporate law of the governing jurisdiction provides that New Corporation becomes the debtor under Old Corporation's security agreement when Old Corporation merges into New Corporation, then Old Corporation's security interest is effective against New Corporation's property and New Corporation becomes bound as debtor and is a new debtor.

Second, a person becomes bound as debtor under the original debtor's security agreement if the original debtor's security agreement becomes effective to create a security interest in the person's property under a contract entered into by the parties. For example, if a merger agreement between New Corporation and Old Corporation provides that New Corporation becomes the debtor under Old Corporation's security agreements when Old Corporation merges into New Corporation, then Old Corporation's security interest is effective against New Corporation's property and New Corporation becomes bound as debtor and is a new debtor.

Third, a person becomes bound as debtor under the original debtor's security agreement if, under contract or non-UCC law, the person becomes generally obligated for the obligations of the original debtor, including the secured obligation, and acquires or succeeds to all or substantially all of the assets of the original debtor. For example, suppose Old Corporation merges into New Corporation in a transaction in which New Corporation acquires all of Old Corporation's property and agrees to become obligated for all of Old Corporation's obligations. New Corporation becomes bound as debtor under Old Corporation's security agreement and is a new debtor.

Secured parties need to be cognizant of the effect of sections 9-203(d) and (e). The property of the new debtor is now collateral, to the extent described in the original debtor's security agreement, for the original debtor's debt without the new debtor having authenticated a security agreement. However, the new debtor is not automatically personally obligated for original debtor's debt. The personal liability of the new debtor depends on the parties' contract or applicable law. Regardless of personal liability, the secured creditor of the original debtor now has additional collateral securing the obligation. This creates interesting priority questions when a secured party of the new debtor already has a security interest in that same property or takes a security interest in such property. (Priority is discussed in Chapter 7.)

G. Attachment of After-Acquired Property and Future Advance Security Interests — Section 9-204

In many secured transactions the parties agree to secure the obligation with collateral that the debtor will sell (such as inventory collateral) or collect (such as accounts collateral) and replace with new collateral (such as subsequent purchases of inventory). When a security interest includes collateral that the debtor will acquire after the security interest has attached to the original collateral, the secured party has a security interest in the debtor's *after-acquired property*. A common example is a secured party who secures the obligation owed by the debtor with a security interest in the debtor's existing and after-acquired inventory.

The parties to a security interest may also agree that the collateral will secure the initial value the secured party gives the debtor (such as the loan to the debtor) and any subsequent value the secured party gives the debtor (such as loans to the debtor made in the future). When the collateral secures the initial value and any subsequent value, the secured party has a security interest that secures *future advances*.

Section 9-204 validates a security agreement that includes the parties' agreement that the collateral for the security interest includes after-acquired property and that the collateral secures future advances or other value. When the security agreement includes those agreements, a single security agreement will cover a series of secured transactions between the debtor and the secured party involving multiple advances of credit by the secured party to the debtor and collateral the debtor acquires after the security interest initially attaches.

1. After-Acquired Property Security Interest — Sections 9-204(a), (b)

a. Creation of After-Acquired Property Security Interest — Section 9-204(a)

Section 9-204(a) validates a security agreement that creates or provides for a security interest in property the debtor acquires after the security interest initially attaches — an after-acquired property security interest. The effect of such a provision is that property the debtor acquires after the security interest initially attaches secures all obligations covered by the security agreement. The secured party has a security interest in the collateral that existed when the security interest attached and any collateral the debtor acquires subsequently. Section 9-204(a) does not require that the security agreement include any particular words to create a security interest in after-acquired collateral. Words such as "now owned or hereafter acquired" are sufficient to indicate the debtor's agreement to create a security interest in its after-acquired property. For example, a security agreement that states the debtor grants a security interest in "the debtor's existing and after-acquired equipment" creates a security interest in the debtor's existing equipment and all equipment the debtor acquires subsequently.

One of the important advantages of including an after-acquired property clause in the security agreement is that when the debtor acquires additional property of the type described in the security agreement, the security interest automatically attaches to the property without further action by the secured party — no additional security agreement is necessary. Recall that the attachment requirements are that the secured party gives value, the debtor has rights in the collateral, and the secured party complies with the debtor's-agreement requirement, typically by having the debtor authenticate a security agreement that describes the collateral. The *value* for the after-acquired property security interest is the same value given for the attachment of the initial security interest. The debtor has *rights in the collateral* when the debtor acquires its interest in the after-acquired property. The *security agreement* for the after-acquired collateral is the original security agreement that includes the after-acquired property clause. The after-acquired property clause in the security agreement creates a security interest in the after-acquired property. Consequently, all attachment requirements are satisfied.

A secured party who wants an after-acquired property security interest must be careful that its description of collateral in the security agreement is not too narrow. The generic description "all," followed by a type of collateral and an after-acquired property clause — for example "all existing and after-acquired equipment" — establishes a security interest in the debtors existing and after-acquired equipment of any type. However, a category-specific description, such as "all computer equipment and after-acquired equipment" creates an ambiguity that could result in the after-acquired property security interest being limited to computer equipment only. An item-specific description is even more troublesome. For example, if the security agreement describes inventory collateral as "20 claw hammers, 15 vise grips, 30 screwdrivers, and after-acquired inventory," the security interest might not cover the debtor's subsequent acquisition of 20 handsaws (inventory), despite the inclusion of the after-acquired inventory clause. If the security agreement had described the collateral as "existing and after-acquired inventory," or even "existing and after-acquired hand tool inventory," the security interest would attach to the after-acquired handsaws.

In the absence of an after-acquired property clause in the security agreement, the only way a secured party can obtain a security interest in after-acquired property is if the debtor agrees to create another security interest and authenticates another security agreement covering such property or authenticates an amendment to the existing security agreement. Because the secured party will have already given value to the debtor in the initial transaction, the debtor might not agree to create a new security interest.

Some courts, however, have interpreted a security interest in inventory or receivables (such as accounts and chattel paper) as attaching after-acquired property of that type even if the security agreement does not include an after-acquired property clause. A representative case is Paulman v. Gateway Venture Partners III, L.P. (*In re* Filtercorp), 163 F3d 570 (9th Cir. 1998), where the court considered whether the words "accounts receivable and inventory of [debtor] (see UCC-1 filing and attached inventory listing)," created a security interest in after-acquired accounts and inventory. The court adopted the majority view that a security interest in inventory or receivables presumptively includes after-acquired property because both parties to a security interest understand that those types of property are repeatedly depleted and replenished. According to the court, the presumption does not stem from the parties' use of certain language in the security agreement, such as "all inventory," but from the cyclical nature of that type of collateral. The court was undoubtedly correct in assessing the parties' understanding of the nature of inventory and receivables collateral. Parties to a security interest in inventory or receivables understand that such collateral will be depleted and replenished, and normally intend that after-acquired property secures the obligation. Regardless of the case law, a secured party should include an after-acquired property clause to prevent disagreements over the inclusion of after-acquired property. Courts have not created this presumption for collateral other than inventory or receivables.

As the *Filtercorp* court noted, courts have adopted a presumption that a security interest attaches after-acquired inventory and receivables. A presumption can be rebutted, and in *Filtercorp* it was. Because the security agreement provided for an "attached inventory listing," the court found the parties intended that the security interest attach only the inventory existing at attachment rather than inventory as a floating mass, despite the fact that no list was ever attached. The reference to the list in the security agreement, coupled with the lack of a list, created an ambiguity the court interpreted against the secured party who drafted the security agreement. The *Filtercorp* decision reinforces the wisdom of including an after-acquired property clause regardless of the nature of the collateral and describing the collateral using, when possible, an Article 9 category, rather than a listing of the collateral.

b. Exceptions — Section 9-204(b)

Article 9 limits the effectiveness of an after-acquired property clause for security interests in consumer goods and commercial tort claims. Section 9-204(b)(1) states that a security interest does not attach to after-acquired property when the collateral is consumer goods, other than accessions, unless the debtor acquires rights in the consumer goods within ten days after the secured party gives value to the debtor. Consequently, an after-acquired property security interest in consumer goods collateral is effective for ten days after the secured party gives value, unless the consumer goods are accessions. An accession is a good that is physically attached to another good, for example the tires on motor vehicle. *Accession* is defined in section 9-102(a)(1), and discussed in Chapter 9.

For example, suppose Bank makes a loan to a consumer and secures it with a security interest in the debtor's "existing and after-acquired jewelry" to secure a loan. The jewelry is *consumer goods*, under the section 9-102(a)(23) definition, to the extent it is used or bought for use primarily for personal, family, or household purposes. The debtor acquires additional jewelry one month after the security interest attaches. The security interest does not attach the new jewelry. The Bank can obtain a security interest in the new jewelry by having the debtor grant it a new security interest in the jewelry, which would require the debtor's authentication of another security agreement. Had the debtor acquired the new jewelry within ten days of when the Bank gave value, the security interest would have attached to it.

The other exception to the validity of an after-acquired property security interest is for commercial tort claim collateral. Section 9-204(b)(2) states that an after-acquired property clause is not effective to attach a security interest in an after-acquired commercial tort claim. The secured party can obtain a security interest in an after-acquired commercial tort claim by having the debtor grant a new security interest in the tort claim, which would require the debtor's authentication of another security agreement that describes the claim as collateral.

c. Perfection and Priority of After-Acquired Property Security Interest — Sections 9-502(d), 9-322(a)

A security interest in after-acquired property is perfected if that property is described in a properly filed financing statement. (Perfection of a security interest by filing a financing statement is discussed in Chapter 3.) Although the financing statement is filed before the debtor acquires the after-acquired property (assuming the secured party perfected its security interest in the original collateral by filing a financing statement), section 9-502(d) validates a financing statement that is filed before the security interest attaches. A broad description of the collateral in the financing statement is sufficient to describe after-acquired property. For example, if the financing statement describes the collateral as "all inventory," and the security agreement creates a security interest in "all of the debtor's inventory, now owned or hereafter acquired," then the security interest in additional inventory is perfected when debtor acquires it.

Section 9-204 does not make the validity of an after-acquired property clause depend on placing the clause in the financing statement. The official comments to sections 9-204 and 9-502 note that there is no requirement or need to include an after-acquired property clause in the financing statement. In fact, if the secured party places an after-acquired property clause in the financing statement but not in the security agreement, it is unlikely that a security interest in after-acquired property exists. The debtor must agree to create a security interest in after-acquired property. The security agreement is the record that evidences the debtor's agreement, and section 9-204 validates an after-acquired property security interest created in the security agreement. Because the debtor does not sign or otherwise authenticate a financing statement, it does not evidence the debtor's agreement. Consequently, an after-acquired property clause contained only in the financing statement does not create a security interest in after-acquired property.

The security interest in after-acquired property has the same priority as the security interest in the initial collateral. Priority of a security interest, under the rule of section 9-322(a), dates from the earlier of the time the financing statement is filed or the time the security interest is perfected. In the typical after-acquired property situation, the same financing statement covers the initial collateral and the after-acquired property. Since the same financing statement covers all collateral, all collateral has the same priority date. This does not mean that a security interest in after-acquired property automatically defeats all other interests in the collateral; the priority rules resolve conflicts over collateral. Priority of a security interest is discussed in Chapters 6–9.

2. Future Advance Security Interest — Section 9-204(c)

The parties to a security agreement may contemplate that the debtor will seek additional loans or other value from the secured party after the secured party gives the initial value for the security interest. A secured party that makes an additional loan likely wants the loan secured by collateral. To accomplish that, the security agreement of the parties could include an agreement that the collateral described in the security agreement secures all obligations the debtor owes to the secured party now or in the future. Section 9-204(c) validates such an agreement. It states that a security agreement "may provide that collateral secures ... future advances or other value, whether or not the advances or value are given pursuant to commitment." Such a provision in a security agreement commonly is called a *future advance clause* and is a boilerplate provision of the typical security agreement. Article 9 does not require particular words to create an agreement securing future advances. Words in the security agreement such as "the collateral described secures the indebtedness created in this transaction and any future indebtedness" create a security interest in later advances of credit from the secured party to the debtor. When the security agreement includes a future advance clause, the collateral described in the security agreement secures the original value and all subsequent value given by the secured party. Typically, the future advance is a further loan or additional credit sale, although "other value" in section 9-204(c) authorizes value that is not a loan or credit sale. Recall that the UCC broadly defines *value* in section 1-204.

If the security agreement for a security interest does not include a future advance clause, a secured party who wants to make a subsequent loan and secure it with a security interest must satisfy Article 9's attachment requirements, specifically the requirement that the debtor authenticate a security agreement or satisfy one of the alternatives to an authenticated security agreement. The main benefit of including a future advance clause in a security agreement is that a future advance made pursuant to a future advance clause does not need a new security agreement; the original security agreement functions as the security agreement for all obligations. However, if a secured party wants to secure the future advance with collateral not described in the original security agreement, it must satisfy the attachment requirements for the additional collateral, typically by having the debtor authenticate a security agreement that includes a description of that collateral.

There is no requirement that a future advance clause be placed in the financing statement. Official Comment 7 to section 9-204 declares that the financing statement need not include a future advance clause nor refer to future obligations. That is consistent with the rule of section 9-204(c) that declares a *security agreement* may provide for future advances or other obligation.

A future advance made pursuant to a future advance clause in the security agreement is covered by the security interest regardless of whether the secured party has committed to make the advance or makes the advance at its discretion. An advance made *pursuant to commitment* is defined in section 9-102(a)(68) as generally meaning an advance or other value the secured party promises to make. For example, a debtor that needs regular loans to purchase raw materials could seek a promise from a secured party that the secured party would make loans as needed by the debtor. If the secured party agrees, the loans made are *pursuant to commitment*. Article 9 treats an advance made pursuant to commitment the same as a discretionary advance with one exception: the priority of an advance pursuant to commitment can differ from the priority of a discretionary advance. The priority of a future advance security interest is determined by sections 9-322 and 9-323, discussed in Chapter 8.

Courts have questioned whether a future advance clause is effective to secure loans or obligations not of the *same class* as the original obligation. For example, suppose a security agreement that secures a loan made to enable the debtor to buy equipment includes a future advance clause securing "all indebtedness owed by debtor to secured party of whatever nature, now in existence or hereafter created, whether created directly or arising by assignment." (Professor Grant Gilmore's colorful label for such a clause is "a dragnet clause." Professor Gilmore was the principal drafter of the original Article 9 and in 1965 wrote the definitive treatise on security interests, *Security Interests in Personal Property*.) The breadth of this clause allows the secured party to argue that the security interest covers any type of obligation the debtor owes it. For example, a secured party that is the debtor's bank could assert that an overdraft on the debtor's checking account with the secured party is secured, that all obligations arising from the debtor's use of an unsecured credit card issued by the secured party are secured, or that a previously unsecured loan from the secured party to the debtor is now secured. A common situation involves a consumer debtor who grants a security interest to secure a purchase-money obligation and later borrows money for general purposes from the same secured party and the secured party asserts that the later loan is secured under the future advance clause.

In deciding whether such obligations are secured, courts have asked whether they are of the *same class* as the original secured obligation. That inquiry seeks to determine whether the future advance clause conforms to the intent of the parties. The court would ascertain whether the parties intended for the security interest to cover the advance or other value. However, some courts shortcut the process of determining the parties' intent. They simply compare the types of advances. If the type of the later (or earlier) advance is different from the type of the initial value under the security agreement, the obligations are not of the same class, and presumably the debtor did not intend for the later (or earlier) advance to be secured under the security agreement.

The drafters of Revised Article 9 expressed their rejection of the same-class test in Official Comment 5 to section 9-204:

> Determining the obligations secured by collateral is solely a matter of construing the parties' agreement under applicable law. This Article rejects the holdings of cases decided under former Article 9 that applied other tests, such as whether a future advance or other subsequently incurred obligation was of the same or similar type or class as earlier advances and obligations secured by the collateral.

The drafters would judge the scope of a future advance clause by interpreting the parties' agreement, not by applying a same-class test. Although the drafters' comment is new, the words of section 9-204(c) essentially remain as they were in former Article 9. Consequently, one can speculate whether courts will adopt the rationale of the comment to Revised Article 9, or continue to address the issue using case law principles established under former Article 9. Where the parties to the security agreement are sophisticated commercial parties, it is likely that courts will follow the official comment. However, dragnet clauses have achieved "boilerplate" status in security agreements, and it will not be surprising if courts continue to apply the same-class rule in cases where the debtor is a consumer. The secured party typically drafts a future advance clause so broadly that any obligation, preexisting or subsequent, conceivable or inconceivable, fits under the clause. Perhaps the definition of good faith will protect debtors, but a court could guard against overreaching by the creditor by limiting the coverage of a future advance clause to obligations of the same class or obligations that the parties clearly contemplated.

H. Debtor's Request for a List of Collateral and a Statement of Account— Sections 9-210, 9-625

Section 9-210 establishes a procedure whereby a debtor can obtain information from the secured party about the amount of the secured obligation and the collateral that secures the obligation.

1. Debtor's Request—Section 9-210

Section 9-210 requires the secured party to respond to a request by the debtor for any of three types of information. *First*, the debtor can request an *accounting*: a request that the secured party provide an accounting of the unpaid obligations secured by collateral. *Second*, the debtor can request a *list of collateral*: a request that the secured party approve or correct a list of what the debtor believes to be the collateral securing the obligation. *Third*, the debtor can request a *statement of account*: a request that the secured party approve or correct a statement of what the debtor believes to be the aggregate amount of unpaid obligations secured by collateral as of a specified date.

A secured party's duty to respond arises only from a request of a debtor. The secured party is not required to respond to a request from any other person, including an obligor that is not the debtor or a current or prospective secured party. Additionally, the duty arises only after the secured party receives a request that conforms to the requirements of section 9-210. The request must be in an authenticated record, allowing a written or electronic request, and it must reasonably identify the transaction that is the subject of the request.

A debtor is entitled without charge to one response during any six-month period. The secured party can charge up to $25 for each additional response. Although the secured party can charge the debtor for each additional response, it nevertheless must respond to each proper request. A failure of the secured party to respond results in liability for any loss the failure causes and in limitation of the security interest against certain persons. However, a secured party that is a buyer of accounts, chattel paper, payment intangibles, or promissory notes, or that is a consignor, has no duty to respond.

2. Secured Party's Response—Section 9-210

The secured party complies with the request by sending an authenticated response to the debtor within fourteen days after it receives the request. The contents of the response vary depending on the type of information sought by the request, the extent of the secured party's security interest, and whether the secured party claims a security interest in the collateral. *Send*, defined in section 1-201(b)(36), means to properly address and deposit in the mail or deliver for transmission with postage or cost of transmission paid.

Section 9-210(d) requires that a person respond to a debtor's request for a list of collateral if the person previously claimed a security interest in the collateral, although it claims no interest when it receives the request. Section 9-210(e) requires the same response from a person who receives a request for an accounting or for a statement of account, but who no longer claims an interest in the obligation that the debtor owes. Such person complies with the request by sending the debtor an authenticated record, within fourteen days after it receives the request, disclaiming any interest in the collateral or the obligation and providing, if known to the person, the name and mailing address of any assignee or successor to the person's interest.

3. Result of Failure to Respond — Section 9-625

A secured party who fails to respond to a debtor's request suffers the consequences established in section 9-625. The secured party is liable in damages for any loss resulting from its failure to respond to the debtor's request. Loss includes the debtor's inability to obtain or the increased cost of obtaining alternative financing. In addition to actual damages, the debtor or a consumer obligor can recover $500 from a person that without reasonable cause fails to comply with a request. Section 9-625(f) declares that a recipient of a request "has a reasonable excuse for its failure to comply" if it never claimed an interest in the collateral or obligations that are the subject of the request.

A serious consequence of a secured party's failure to respond to the debtor's request can be the limitation of its security interest. Section 9-625(g) limits the security interest of a secured party that fails to comply with the debtor's request to the collateral or obligations included in the request as against a person "reasonably misled by the failure." Although section 9-625 provides no guidance on the meaning of "reasonably misled," an existing or prospective creditor of the debtor could be a person "reasonably misled by the failure" because a basic method of a creditor to obtain knowledge regarding the collateral or obligations is through the debtor's request. The failure of a secured party to approve or correct an account or list could cause a creditor to enter a credit transaction with the debtor when it otherwise would not if it had that information. The debtor also could be a person "reasonably misled by the failure."

Checkpoints

- An attached and enforceable security interest requires that the secured party give value to the debtor, the debtor have rights in the collateral, and the debtor indicate its agreement to give a security interest in the collateral.

- The debtor can indicate its agreement to give a security interest by authenticating a security agreement that creates a security interest and includes a description of the collateral.

- The debtor can indicate its agreement to give a security interest by allowing the secured party to take possession of tangible collateral itself or through an agent or third person on behalf of the secured party.

- The debtor can indicate its agreement to give a security interest by allowing the secured party to establish control of a deposit account, electronic chattel paper, letter-of-credit right, investment property, or an electronic document.

- Attachment of a security interest in proceeds of the collateral is automatic.

- A security agreement can include an after-acquired property clause that enables the security interest to attach to property the debtor acquires after the security interest attaches to the original collateral.

- A security agreement can include a future advance clause that enables the security interest to secure existing and future obligations the debtor owes the secured party in addition to the initial value the secured party gives the debtor.

Chapter 3

Perfection of a Security Interest or Agricultural Lien by Filing a Financing Statement, Taking Possession of the Collateral, or by Federal Law or State Certificate-of-Title Statutes

---

Roadmap

- Perfection of a security interest
- Perfection by filing a financing statement
- Requirements of a financing statement
- Place of filing a financing statement
- Duration of effectiveness of a financing statement
- Errors in a financing statement
- Events occurring after filing that affect perfection
- Amendment, termination, or assignment of a financing statement
- Perfection of a security interest by the secured party taking possession of the collateral or a document that represents the collateral
- Perfection of a security interest by complying with federal law or state certificate-of-title statutes

---

A. Introduction and General Rule of Perfection — Section 9-308

One would think that with all the definitions included in Article 9 the drafters would have defined perfection. Unfortunately, that is not the situation. Article 9 includes sections on how to perfect a security interest and when a security interest is perfected, but no substantive definition on what it means to have a perfected security interest. A functional definition of perfection is that perfection is a status which a security interest or agricultural lien can attain. For most security interests and agricultural liens, attaining perfection requires a further act of the secured party beyond attachment and enforceability. Consequently, a security interest can be perfected or unperfected.

When perfected, a security interest or agricultural lien has all the rights and protection of Article 9 it can attain. That is not to say that a perfected security interest or agricultural lien is superior to all other persons who have an interest in the same collateral. Certain purchasers, secured creditors, holders of statutory liens, and lien creditors may obtain an interest in the collateral that has priority over a perfected security interest or agricultural lien under the rules of Article 9 that determine priority of conflicting interests. (Chapters 6–10 discuss priority of a perfected security interest or agricultural lien.) Nevertheless, perfection is the most protected status that a security interest or agricultural lien can attain and a secured party should always strive to perfect the security interest or agricultural lien. Failure to perfect leaves a secured party vulnerable to practically every competing interest other than the debtor. Perfection of the security interest is not necessary for priority over the debtor.

Section 9-308(a) adopts a general rule for when a security interest is perfected. It declares that "[e]xcept as otherwise provided ... a security interest is perfected if it has attached and all of the applicable requirements for perfection in Sections 9-310 through 9-316 have been satisfied." The policy behind the action required for perfection is that it generally will give notice to interested persons that the secured party claims a security interest in the collateral. That information is relevant to a person who contemplates a secured transaction with the debtor.

Attorneys and judges speak of *perfecting* a security interest as meaning performing the action required by sections 9-310 through 9-316. Although a secured party must perform that action to perfect a security interest, section 9-308(a) declares that perfection also requires satisfaction of the attachment requirements. In most cases, the requirements for attachment are different from those for perfection. (Chapter 2 discusses attachment.) Typically, a secured party satisfies the attachment requirements before performing the additional act required for perfection. However, Article 9 does not require that a secured party perform the attachment and perfection steps in any particular order. A secured party can perform the act sections 9-310 to 9-316 require before it satisfies the attachment requirements. The important point to remember is that when the secured party satisfies all attachment and perfection requirements, in any order, the security interest is perfected. However, having noted the dual requirements, when the phrase "perfecting the security interest" is used in this chapter, it means performing the act required by sections 9-310 to 9-316.

A similar dual-requirement rule applies to perfecting an agricultural lien. Section 9-308(b) provides that "[a]n agricultural lien is perfected if it has become effective and all of the applicable requirements for perfection in Section 9-310 have been satisfied." An agricultural lien becomes effective when the lienholder satisfies the requirements of the statute that creates the lien. Because an agricultural lien is not a security interest, the attachment requirements for a security interest do not apply to an agricultural lien. (Agricultural liens are discussed in Chapter 1.)

B. Perfection by Filing a Financing Statement — Section 9-310

One of the principles behind requiring perfection of a security interest is that the act required for perfection will place other persons on notice of the secured party's claim of a security interest in the collateral. To fulfill the notice purpose, section 9-310(a) establishes a general perfection rule that a financing statement must be filed to perfect all security interests and agricultural liens unless Article 9 authorizes another method. Consequently, the great majority of security interests are perfected by filing a financing statement. A secured party can file the financing statement as soon as the debtor authorizes the filing, which could occur before the security agreement is authenticated or before the security interest otherwise attaches. This early-filing right is beneficial because Article 9 generally determines the priority of a security interest according to priority in time of filing a financing statement. Authorization to file a financing statement is discussed later in this chapter.

Section 9-102(a)(39) defines *financing statement* as "a record or records composed of an initial financing statement and any filed record relating to the initial financing statement." *Record*, defined in section 9-102(a)(69), allows a written or electronic financing statement. Article 9 does not define *initial fi-*

nancing statement, but the term seems to mean just what it says: the first financing statement the secured party files against the debtor. Records *relating to the initial financing statement* include amendments to the initial financing statement that add collateral, add debtors or secured parties, continue the effectiveness of the financing statement, or terminate the effectiveness of the financing statement. Consequently, the Article 9 definition of financing statement includes filings in addition to the initial record a secured party files to perfect the security interest. Nevertheless, courts and attorneys continue to use the term *financing statement* to refer to the document initially filed to perfect a security interest, while using terms such as *continuation statement, termination statement,* and *amendment* to refer to those specific actions. I will follow the common usage and employ the term *financing statement* when referring to perfection of the security interest by filing a financing statement.

Although filing a financing statement will perfect a security interest, there are two reasons why a filed financing statement does not necessarily mean there is a perfected security interest. *First,* a filed financing statement does not signify that the secured party has satisfied the attachment requirements. *Second,* a filed financing statement does not perfect a security interest unless the financing statement complies with Article 9's information and place of filing requirements.

1. Requirements of a Sufficient and Effective Financing Statement — Sections 9-502, 9-504, 9-509, 9-516

Perfection by filing a financing statement creates three principle questions: What is filed? Where is it filed? How long is the filing effective? This section examines what is filed.

Article 9 establishes information requirements for creating a *sufficient* financing statement. These requirements, though few in number, are the essence of a financing statement. Section 9-502(a) provides that a financing statement is "sufficient" if it provides the name of the debtor, the name of the secured party or a representative of the secured party, and indicates the collateral covered by the financing statement. A sufficient financing statement does the job it is designed to do: perfect the security interest. A financing statement that is not sufficient does not perfect the security interest, regardless of whether a secured party files it. Don't get too comfortable with those three requirements because in a later section we will see that the Article 9 drafters inexplicably adopt additional information requirements for the financing statement in a different section of Article 9.

Section 9-502(c) authorizes a mortgage record to be effective as a financing statement when filed as a fixture-filing or when covering collateral that is timber to be cut or as-extracted collateral. To be effective as a financing statement, the mortgage record must comply with the requirements of sections 9-502(a) and (b).

a. Sufficiency of Names of Parties — Section 9-503

Section 9-503 supplies detail for the name requirement. Most subsections of section 9-503 pertain only to the name of the debtor; the section provides scant detail regarding the name of the secured party. That is logical because financing statements are indexed in the name of the debtor, not the secured party. A person searching the UCC index is more concerned with the name of the debtor than that of the secured party.

Failing to indicate correctly the debtor's name is probably the most common error found on financing statements. That failure will likely make the financing statement ineffective, and consequently the security interest will be unperfected and vulnerable to other claimants to the collateral.

A financing statement sufficiently provides the name of the debtor if it complies with section 9-503(a). The rules of the section are divided by the type of debtor. For registered organization debtors (primarily corporations, limited partnerships, and limited liability companies), a financing statement is sufficient if it provides the name of the debtor indicated on the public record of the debtor's jurisdiction of organization. *Registered organization* and *jurisdiction of organization* are defined at sections 9-102(a)(70) and (50), respectively. To insure sufficiency, a secured party should obtain the name of the registered organization from the public agency in the jurisdiction of organization that maintains the record of organization, which is typically the state's secretary of state office. That insures the financing statement contains the debtor's correct name. Notice that section 9-503(c) declares that a financing statement that provides only the debtor's trade name does not sufficiently show the debtor's name.

Less common types of debtors are decedents' estates and trusts. A financing statement sufficiently indicates the name of a decedent's estate debtor if it provides the name of the decedent and indicates that the debtor is an estate. For a trust debtor or a trustee acting on behalf of a trust, a financing statement is sufficient if provides the name of the trust as specified in the trust agreement and indicates that the debtor is a trust or trustee acting with respect to a trust. If the trust has no name, sufficiency is achieved by using the name of the settlor (or settlors) of the trust, plus information sufficient to distinguish the debtor from other trusts having one of more of the same settlors.

For all other types of debtors, the financing statement sufficiently indicates the debtor's name if it provides the name of the debtor or, if the debtor has no name (for example, a partnership without a name), if it provides the names of the partners, members, associates, or other persons comprising the debtor. This rule pertains to individual debtors and to organizations that are not registered organizations. *Organization* is defined broadly by section 1-201(b)(25) to include all legal, governmental, and commercial entities. Remember that section 9-503(a)(1) adopts a specific rule for the name of a registered organization.

Although Official Comment 4h to section 9-101 notes that one purpose of section 9-503 is to "clarify when a debtor's name is correct," section 9-503 provides no definitive answer to the question perplexing secured creditors and courts of what is the name of an individual debtor. Section 9-503(a)(4)(A) advises simply that a financing statement "sufficiently provides the name of the debtor ... only if it provides the individual ... name of the debtor." The issue typically arises when the secured party uses the debtor's nickname on the financing statement, rather than the debtor's legal name.

Does a filed financing statement sufficiently provide the name of the debtor when it indicates the debtor as *Terry J. Kinderknecht* but the debtor's legal name is *Terrance J. Kinderknecht?* In Clark v. Deere & Co. (*In re* Kinderknecht), 308 B.R. 71, 72 (B.A.P. 10th Cir. 2004), the Tenth Circuit Bankruptcy Appellate Panel (BAP) held that a financing statement is sufficient under Kansas law only if the secured creditor lists an individual debtor by his or her legal name, not a nickname. Recognizing that section 9-503 provides no specific answer to the question, the court based its holding on the purpose of section 9-503, a reading of the section as a whole, and practical considerations. Requiring the debtor's legal name on a financing statement supports the drafters' intent to "clarify" when a name is sufficient, the BAP stated, because it presents an easy test for courts to apply. Reviewing the entire section 9-503, the BAP noted that the sufficient name for a registered organization debtor is the name indicated on the public record; a trade name alone is not sufficient. The BAP did not believe a different standard should apply for individual debtors. Lastly, the BAP listed four "practical considerations" supporting its decision: 1) requiring the debtor's legal name sets a clear test to simplify the drafting of financing statements; 2) requiring the legal name simplifies the parameters of UCC searches; 3) the legal name requirement avoids litigation over the appropriateness of a nickname; and 4) obtaining the debtor's legal name is not a difficult task for a secured creditor.

The opposite holding is found in Nazar v. Bucklin Nat'l Bank (*In re* Erwin), 50 UCC Rep. Serv. 2d 933 (Bankr. Kan. 2003), where a Kansas bankruptcy court held a financing statement sufficient even though it contained the debtor's nickname rather than the debtor's legal name. (*Nazar* preceded *Kinderknecht* by approximately ten months and was cited, but disagreed with, by the *Kinderknecht* BAP.) The financing statement indicated the debtor as *Mike Erwin.* The debtor's legal name was *Michael A. Erwin.* The court concluded that the full legal name of the debtor is not required in order for a financing statement to be sufficient because section 9-503(a)(4)(A) does not specify that "individual name" means legal name, nor does it expressly prohibit nicknames or common derivatives.

Article 9 hints that the name of an individual is the legal name, not a nickname. Official Comment 2 to section 9-503 notes that the section "reflects the view prevailing under former Article 9 that the actual individual ... name of the debtor on a financing statement is both necessary and sufficient...." *Actual* ostensibly means the legal name. Another indication is found in section 9-521(a), the uniform form for a financing statement (known as "Form UCC1" or simply "UCC 1"). Above the box for the debtor's name appears the instruction: "[D]EBTOR'S EXACT FULL LEGAL NAME." A nickname would not be sufficient as the *full legal name*. Requiring the debtor's legal name provides a clear test that will help avoid litigation. However, ascertaining a debtor's legal name seems to be dependent upon seeing the debtor's birth certificate, and a debtor might have difficulty locating the birth certificate. It is likely that the UCC drafters will resolve the issue with an amendment to section 9-503 or its comment, or by issuing a Permanent Editorial Board Commentary.

Section 9-503 (b)(1) states that a financing statement complying with the name requirement of section 9-503(a) it "is not rendered ineffective" because it omits a trade name or other name of the debtor or the names of the partners, members, etc. Consequently, a debtor's trade name, other name, or names of its partners are not required for sufficiency. For example, if the debtor is an individual, Jackie Brown, who does business under a trade name, Desserts by Jackie, the financing statement sufficiently indicates the debtor's name by providing *Jackie Brown*. Likewise, if the debtor is G,B & B Inc., a corporation doing business under the name, Just Solutions, the financing statement sufficiently shows the name of the debtor by providing *G,B & B Inc.* However, a financing statement that indicates the required name and also includes the trade name or members' names should be sufficient because such a financing statement complies with section 9-503(a) by including the individual or partnership name. Remember the rule of section 9-503(c) that a financing statement does not sufficiently show the debtor's name if it provides only the debtor's trade name. For example, a financing statement indicating the debtor's name as "Desserts by Jackie" is not sufficient if the debtor is Jackie Brown.

Subsections 9-503(d) and (e) adopt two additional rules pertaining to sufficiency of names. *First*, a financing statement may provide the name of more than one debtor or more than one secured party. This permits a single financing statement to be effective against several debtors and in favor of several secured parties. *Second*, a financing statement is sufficient whether or not it indicates the representative capacity of the secured party. For example, when the secured party is a representative, such as when a bank acts as the agent for the actual secured party, a financing statement is sufficient if it names the bank as the secured party regardless of whether it indicates the representative capacity. Subsections 9-503(d) and (e) are the only provisions of section 9-503 that pertain to the name of the secured party.

All is not lost if the secured party fails to provide correctly the names of the debtor and secured party. Section 9-506(a), discussed in detail later in this chapter, makes a financing statement effective even though it contains "minor errors," that are "not seriously misleading." Incorrectly indicating the debtor's name is an error. Section 9-506(b) declares that a financing statement that fails sufficiently to provide the name of the debtor is seriously misleading. However, section 9-506(c) saves a financing statement from being seriously misleading if a search under the "debtor's correct name, using the filing office's standard search logic" would disclose the financing statement. Consequently, the financing statement is effective regardless of the error if a search of the financing statement index using the correct name of the debtor and the search logic of the filing office would disclose the financing statement.

b. Indication/Description of Collateral — Section 9-504

Section 9-502(a)(3) requires that to be sufficient a financing statement must indicate the collateral it covers. This is the description requirement for a financing statement. Requiring that the financing statement indicate the collateral helps fulfill the notice function of a financing statement because a person searching the financing statement index has notice that a security interest might exist in the collateral indicated in the financing statement. Any indication of collateral is sufficient if it satisfies that purpose. However, section 9-504 adopts two safe harbors for describing collateral. Under section 9-504, a financing statement sufficiently indicates the collateral it covers if the financing statement provides a description of the collateral in accordance with the rules established in section 9-108 or if it indicates that it covers all assets or all personal property of the debtor.

A description in a financing statement is sufficient under section 9-504(2) if it indicates the collateral by using the words "all assets" or "all personal property." A secured party can use the "all personal property" description when the debtor grants a security interest in all its personal property. This type of description simplifies the burden of the secured party to indicate sufficiently the collateral because it is not necessary to list the collateral by type, category, or item. Recall however, that section 9-108(c) declares that *all assets* or *all personal property* is not a sufficient description of the collateral for the *security agreement* even if debtor has granted a security interest in all its assets or personal property. The section 9-504(2) safe harbor is only for the description in a financing statement.

The other safe harbor of section 9-504 validates a description that complies with the rules of section 9-108. Only a summary discussion of those rules is given here because Chapter 2 provides a detailed discussion. Section 9-108 adopts a general rule for a sufficient description and also supplies examples of sufficient descriptions that operate as a safe harbor. The general rule of section 9-108(a) is that a description "is sufficient, whether or not it is specific, if it reasonably identifies what is described." Official Comment 2 to section 9-108 states that the "test of sufficiency of a description under this section … is that the description … make possible the identification of the collateral described. This section rejects any requirement that a description is insufficient unless it is exact and detailed (the so-called 'serial number' test)." To achieve sufficiency a secured party must describe the collateral in a manner that enables identification of the collateral.

Section 9-108(b) adopts examples of descriptions that satisfy the section 9-108(a) standard and consequently are sufficient — the safe harbors. A description is sufficient, unless section 9-108 provides otherwise, if it identifies the collateral by *specific listing, category, a type of collateral defined in the UCC, quantity, computational or allocational formula or procedure,* or *any other method if the identity of the collateral is objectively determinable.* However, section 9-108(e) expressly invalidates collateral-type descriptions for a security interest in a commercial tort claim or, in a consumer transaction, for consumer goods, a security entitlement, a securities account, or a commodity account. A *consumer transaction,* defined in section 9-102(a)(26), exists when an individual incurs an obligation "primarily" for personal, family, or household purposes and secures the obligation with a security interest in collateral "primarily" held or acquired for personal, family, or household purposes.

A secured party who takes a security interest in every item of a type of property and uses a safe harbor description can describe the collateral as "all" of the collateral. For example, a financing statement description of "all of the debtor's inventory" is sufficient because it identifies the collateral by *a type of collateral defined in Article 9 of the UCC.*

Additionally, sections 9-108(d) and (e) expressly validate collateral-type descriptions for security interests in investment property, except for a security interest in a consumer debtor's investment property. A description is sufficient if it uses the terms *securities entitlement, securities account, commodity account,* or *investment property.* For example, a description *all debtor's investment property* is sufficient.

c. Financing Statement Information Required by Section 9-516(b)

1. Address of the Debtor and the Secured Party— Sections 9-516(b), 9-520

A sufficient financing statement under all previous versions of Article 9 required not only the parties' names and an indication of collateral, but also the parties' addresses. The parties' addresses are no longer required for a *sufficient* financing statement under section 9-502(a). However, for reasons unexplained by the drafters of Revised Article 9 (and thus somewhat baffling), sections 9-516(b)(4) and (5) and 9-520(a) combine to compel a filing office to refuse to accept for filing a financing statement that does not include the debtor's and secured party's mailing addresses. Does this mean mailing addresses are required for a sufficient financing statement? The answer is pragmatically—yes, statutorily—yes and no.

Section 9-520(a) declares that a filing office must refuse to accept a financing statement for filing if it does not comply with the requirements of section 9-516(b). Sections 9-516(b)(4) and (b)(5)(A) specify that filing does not occur if the filing office refuses a financing statement that fails to provide mailing addresses of the secured party and the debtor. The result is that a financing statement must include the addresses of the parties or the filing office should refuse to accept it for filing. Consequently, the secured party should always include the addresses of the parties in the financing statement.

However, section 9-520(c) declares that a "filed financing statement is effective" if it satisfies the requirements of section 9-502(a) (and section 9-502(b) if the financing statement relates to real property), although the filing office was required to refuse to accept it. The Article 9 drafters must think it is possible that a filing office might accept a financing statement it was required to refuse. Consequently, a financing statement that includes the section 9-502(a) information is effective if the filing office accepts it for filing although it does not contain the debtor's or secured party's address and the filing office should have refused it. Although section 9-520(c) does not define *effective*, the unmistakable implication is that *effective* means the financing statement will do what it is supposed to do—perfect a security interest. Official Comment 3 to section 9-520 declares that such a financing statement is "fully effective."

This problem should arise infrequently because the official form financing statement adopted by Article 9 in section 9-521(a) (UCC 1) provides blank spaces for including the parties' mailing addresses. Most filers will complete all relevant blank spaces on the official form and thus include the addresses.

2. Organizational Information — Sections 9-516(b)(5)(B), (C)

Section 9-516(b)(5) compels the same result for information about the status of the debtor. Section 9-516(b)(5)(B) declares that filing does not occur if a filing office refuses to accept a financing statement that fails to indicate whether the debtor is an individual or an organization. Additionally, if the debtor is an organization, section 9-516(b)(5)(C) adopts the same rule when the financing statement fails to include the type of organization, the jurisdiction where the organization is organized, and an organizational identification number or an indication that the debtor has none. Section 9-520(a) requires the filing office to refuse to accept a financing statement that does not contain such information. However, section 9-520(c) declares that the financing statement is effective if the filing office nevertheless accepts for filing a financing statement that omits the section 9-516(b)(5) information. Because the official form financing statement (UCC 1) provides spaces for including this information, a secured party using the form will likely include the required information.

3. Other Reasons for Refusal — Section 9-516(b)

Section 9-516(b) specifies other grounds that justify a filing office's refusal to accept a financing statement for filing with the consequence being that filing does not occur. For example, filing does not occur if the filing office refuses a financing statement because the filer does not tender the filing fee. Although these grounds arise less frequently than the requirements discussed in the previous paragraphs, they are no less troublesome. A secured party must comprehend and comply with the requirements adopted by section 9-516(b) to prevent the filing office's rightful refusal to accept the financing statement for filing. Remember that a financing statement that the filing office properly refuses to accept for filing does not perfect the security interest. An unperfected security interest likely is subordinate to other claimants to the collateral other than the debtor. A secured party whose financing statement is not accepted for filing can supply the information it omitted and resubmit the financing statement for filing.

d. Authorization — Sections 9-509 and 9-510

The debtor's signature on the financing statement is not a requirement of a sufficient financing statement. In lieu of the signature, section 9-510(a) states that a filed record — a written or electronic financing statement — is "effective" only if section 9-509 authorizes the person to file it. A financing statement that is not effective does not perfect a security interest. Additionally, a person who files a financing statement without authorization is liable for statutory damages of $500 under section 9-625(e) as well as actual loss caused. Article 9 does not answer the question of whether an unauthorized financing statement becomes effective by subsequent authorization. Subsequent authorization arguably ratifies the unauthorized filing.

Section 9-509 establishes three ways a person is authorized to file a financing statement. *First*, section 9-509(a)(1) provides that a debtor can authorize the filing of a financing statement in an "authenticated record." The definitions of *authenticate* and *record*, sections 9-102(a)(7) and (a)(69), respectively, allow fulfillment of this requirement with a written or electronic document. Consequently, a debtor can authorize a secured party to file a financing statement by signing a statement authorizing the filing.

Section 9-509(a)(2) authorizes the holder of an agricultural lien to file a financing statement covering the collateral that the lien attaches if the lien is effective at the time of filing. The agricultural lien's effectiveness depends on the lienholder's compliance with the statute creating the lien. (Agricultural liens are discussed in Chapter 1.)

Second, section 9-509(b) provides that a debtor authorizes the filing of a financing statement when it authenticates a security agreement. Official Comment 4 to section 9-509 labels this authorization "*ipso facto* authorization." This authorization is automatic upon the debtor's authentication of the security agreement. Most secured parties will obtain authorization to file a financing statement by this method, because a secured party usually satisfies the debtor's-agreement attachment requirement by having the debtor authenticate a security agreement.

The section 9-509(b) authorization permits the filing of a financing statement covering the collateral described in the security agreement and property that becomes collateral as proceeds of collateral. For example, suppose the debtor authenticates a security agreement that describes its inventory as the collateral. The secured party is authorized to file a financing statement covering inventory. The debtor sells the inventory for cash and purchases equipment with the cash. The equipment is proceeds of collateral and proceeds are, by definition, collateral. Section 9-509(b)(2) provides that the secured party is authorized to amend the financing statement or file a new financing statement to cover the equipment collateral because the security interest automatically covers proceeds under the rule of section 9-315(a)(2). (Proceeds are discussed in Chapter 2.)

Section 9-509(b) also provides that a "new debtor" who becomes bound as debtor under an "original debtor's" security agreement authorizes a secured party to file a financing statement against the new debtor for the collateral covered in the security agreement and its proceeds. This authorization is automatic; a secured party needs no additional authorization from a new debtor. (*New debtor* and *original debtor* are discussed in Chapter 2.)

Third, under section 9-509(c) a person who acquires collateral in which a security interest continues under section 9-315(a)(1) authorizes the filing of a financing statement covering the collateral and any proceeds of it. A person who acquires collateral is a debtor because section 9-102(a)(28) defines *debtor* as including a person who acquires collateral that is subject to a security interest, regardless of the person's lack of personal liability for the secured obligation. The most common example of this situation is when the debtor in a security interest sells the collateral to a buyer and that buyer becomes the debtor. For many such security interests, section 9-507, discussed later in this chapter, continues perfection of the security interest without requiring the filing of a financing statement in the name of the debtor who acquired the collateral. If a filing is required, the debtor's acquisition of the collateral automatically authorizes the filing of a financing statement in the name of the debtor.

e. Financing Statement for Security Interest Related to Real Property—Section 9-502(b)

Financing statements for security interests in collateral related to real property require additional information for sufficiency. A financing statement that covers as-extracted collateral or timber to be cut, or that is filed as fixture filing must include the information specified in section 9-502(b) in addition to all the requirements of sections 9-502(a) and 9-516(b). A sufficient financing statement must: 1) indicate it covers that type of collateral; 2) indicate it is to be filed in the real property records; 3) provide a description of the real property to which the collateral is related; and 4) if the debtor does not have an interest of record in the real property, provide the name of a record owner. The official form financing statement adopted in section 9-521(a) (UCC 1) provides spaces for including the required information in the financing statement. Accordingly, the additional information should not cause any problems for secured parties that use the form.

The only requirement that needs elaboration is the description of real property. The most frequently asked question relating to the description is whether a legal description is required for sufficiency. Although such a description is sufficient, it is not always required. Official Comment 5 to section 9-502 reiterates the section 9-108 standard for sufficiency of a description: "a description of real property must be sufficient to reasonably identify it." The comment, citing section 9-108, declares that: "This formulation rejects the view that the real property description must be by metes and bounds, or otherwise conforming to traditional real-property practice in conveyancing." More helpful is the comment's statement that the proper test for sufficiency of a financing statement description of real property is whether the description allows the financing statement to "fit into the real-property search system and be found by a real-property searcher." Because these financing statements are filed in the real property records, it is appropriate to judge the sufficiency of the real property description by whether the description allows the financing statement to fit into the recording system. Consequently, in a jurisdiction that has adopted a grantor-grantee index for real property records, a description of the real property by address should be sufficient when coupled with the name of the debtor (assuming the debtor is the record owner) because the financing statement is indexed in the name of the grantor. If the jurisdiction has adopted a tract index for real property records, a metes and bounds description is probably necessary for sufficiency because the financing statement is indexed according to the legal description of the property.

2. Place of Filing a Financing Statement — Section 9-501

Where does a secured party file the financing statement? The section 9-501 of each jurisdiction establishes an office in that jurisdiction as the place of filing to perfect a security interest or agricultural lien. Consequently, the first step in determining where to file a financing statement is to ascertain the jurisdiction that governs perfection of the security interest in accordance with sections 9-301 to 9-307, discussed in Chapter 10. After determining the governing jurisdiction, a secured party must file in the office designated by that jurisdiction. The following discussion will examine the rules of the uniform section 9-501, although many jurisdictions have enacted a variation of the uniform section.

For a financing statement covering *as-extracted collateral* or *timber to be cut*, or that is filed as a *fixture filing* for goods that are or are to become fixtures, section 9-501(a)(1) designates the office in which a mortgage on the related real property would be filed or recorded as the place of filing. This type of filing is commonly known as local filing, because typically it is a filing in the office of the county clerk or county recorder where the real property is located. This section complements section 9-502(b)(2) which requires that these types of financing statements indicate they are to be filed in the real property records.

A security interest in timber to be cut creates an interesting filing issue. Once the timber is cut, it is no longer timber *to be cut*; it is timber, an ordinary good. The filing office for a financing statement covering ordinary goods is not the office where a mortgage on the related real property would be filed. Consequently, the filing in the real estate office ceases to be effective. To maintain perfection after the timber is cut, a secured party must file a financing statement in the office for filing an ordinary goods financing statement, typically the secretary of state's office. For example, suppose Debtor grants Bank a security interest in his standing timber growing in Kentucky. Kentucky law governs perfection of the security interest, and the proper place to file a financing statement to perfect the security interest is in the real estate records for the real property on which the timber is growing. However, to maintain perfection after the timber is cut, Bank must file a financing statement in the office for filing a financing statement for goods.

The uniform section 9-501 adopts a separate filing rule to perfect a security interest in collateral of a transmitting utility. A *transmitting utility*, defined in section 9-102(a)(79), includes debtors that operate a public transportation business, such as railroads, a traditional utilities business, such as electricity and gas utility companies, a communications business, or a pipeline business. Section 9-501(b) allows each jurisdiction to designate the office for filing a financing statement that relates to a transmitting utility debtor.

For security interests in all other types of collateral, section 9-501(a)(2) authorizes each jurisdiction to designate the office where a financing statement is filed. Most jurisdictions establish the secretary of state's office as the office in which to file a financing statement. Filing in the secretary of state's office is commonly known as central filing. Section 9-501(a)(2) covers most financing statements.

3. What Constitutes Filing of a Financing Statement — Sections 9-516, 9-520

The rules of sections 9-516 and 9-520 determine whether a financing statement is filed or not filed. The sections produce four different outcomes. *First*, section 9-516(a) states that a financing statement is filed, unless otherwise provided in section 9-516(b), when it is communicated to the filing office accompanied by the proper fee, or communicated to the filing office and accepted by the office. *Communicate*, defined in section 9-102(a)(18), allows for electronic transmission of a "record." Many jurisdictions authorize a secured party to file a financing statement electronically.

Second, a filing office might erroneously accept a financing statement for filing it is required to refuse — a wrongful acceptance. Because the financing statement was communicated and accepted for filing, the rule of section 9-516(a) declares it filed. Section 9-520(c) also establishes this result. It declares that a filed financing statement complying with the requirements of section 9-502(a) and (b) is effective to perfect the security interest even if the filing officer was required to refuse it for noncompliance with section 9-516(b). For example, the filing office is required to reject a financing statement that omits a mailing address for the debtor. However, the financing statement is sufficient under section 9-502, although it does not contain the debtor's address. Consequently, the financing statement perfects the security interest if the filing office accepts it for filing. However, a financing statement wrongfully accepted for filing is not effective to perfect the security interest if it does not satisfy the requirements of section 9-502. The presence of a filed financing statement does not determine conclusively whether the accompanying security interest is perfected. An interested person should examine a filed financing statement carefully to determine if the financing statement complies with section 9-502.

Third is the situation of a wrongful rejection of a financing statement. Section 9-516(d) provides that a financing statement communicated to the filing office, containing all required information, and accompanied by the proper fee but wrongfully rejected for filing, is nevertheless effective as a filed record. Consequently, it will perfect the security interest.

However, that financing statement is not effective against a purchaser of the collateral who gives value in reasonable reliance on the absence of the record from the files. (Remember that the definitions of purchase and purchaser include acquiring rights by taking a security interest.) According to Official Comment 3 to section 9-516, reasonable reliance exists when a person searches the filing records and acts upon the apparent absence of the financing statement from the files. The purchaser must give value *after* reasonably relying on the record. The life of a wrongful rejection should be short-lived because the filing office is required to communicate the refusal and the reason for the refusal. The secured party can correct the filing office as to its error.

Fourth, section 9-516(b) states that filing does not occur if the filing office refuses to accept the filing for any of the reasons listed in section 9-516(b). A secured party must comply with the section 9-516(b) requirements to avoid the filing office's rightful rejection of the financing statement. Generally, those requirements involve the parties' names, addresses, and organization information. Some of the section 9-516(b) requirements are also required for a sufficient financing statement under section 9-502.

Section 9-520(a) declares, somewhat cryptically, that a filing office is required to refuse to accept a financing statement that fails to comply with section 9-516(b), and may refuse to accept a financing statement only for the section 9-516(b) grounds. The section contains two principles. One principle is that the filing office should review a financing statement to determine whether it complies with the requirements of section 9-516(b), and if it does not, the filing office should refuse to accept it. The other principle is that the only reason a filing office can refuse to accept a financing statement for filing is that it fails to satisfy the section 9-516(b) requirements. Section 9-516(c) adds that a financing statement does not provide the information required by section 9-516(b) if the filing office is unable to read or decipher the information included in it. Consequently, the filing office's review of the financing statement prior to accepting it for filing is simply to determine whether the financing statement legibly includes all the information section 9-516(b) requires. It does not review the accuracy of the information. Official Comment 3 to section 9-516 notes that the filing officer is not required or authorized to determine or even consider the accuracy of information provided in the financing statement. Section 9-520(b) compels a filing office that refuses to accept a financing statement for filing to communicate to the filer the refusal and the reason for the refusal.

4. Duration of Effectiveness of a Financing Statement — Sections 9-515, 9-510(c), 9-516(b)(7)

a. Length of Effectiveness — Section 9-515(a)

How long is a filed financing statement effective? Section 9-515(a) makes a filed financing statement effective for five years after the date of filing, except as otherwise provided by Article 9. This means that a security interest perfected by filing a financing statement is perfected for five years from the date of filing, unless the parties sooner terminate the financing statement because there is no outstanding obligation or commitment to make a loan. Termination of a financing statement is discussed later in this chapter.

The security interests for which Article 9 provides otherwise are in sections 9-515(b), (f), and (g). If the debtor is a transmitting utility, the financing statement is effective until a termination statement is filed. A mortgage record filed as a financing statement for a fixture security interest is effective until the mortgage is released or satisfied, or its effectiveness terminates. If the financing statement relates to a public-finance transaction security interest, the financing statement is effective for 30 years from the date of filing. A *public-finance transaction*, defined in section 9-102(a)(67), basically is a secured transaction where either the debtor or the secured party is a state or governmental unit of a state that issues debt securities with a maturity of at least 20 years.

If the financing statement relates to a "manufactured-home transaction," the financing statement is effective for 30 years from the date of filing. A manufactured-home transaction is a purchase-money security interest in a manufactured home, other than a manufactured home held as inventory. Section 9-102(a)(54) defines *manufactured-home transaction,* while section 9-102(a)(53) provides a very detailed definition of *manufactured home.* Succinctly, a manufactured home is a trailer home used as a dwelling. Note that in some jurisdictions a manufactured home is a good covered by a certificate of title, and the certificate-of-title statutes of the jurisdiction may require a secured party to perfect a security interest by complying with the applicable certificate of title statute (discussed later in this chapter), not by filing a financing statement.

b. Lapse of Effectiveness — Section 9-515(c)

Section 9-515(c) states that the effectiveness of a filed financing statement lapses on the expiration of the applicable period of effectiveness — five years for most security interests. This lapse can be prevented if the secured party timely files a continuation statement, as discussed in the next section. There are two serious consequences of lapse of the effectiveness of a financing statement. *First,* under section 9-515(c) a security interest or agricultural lien perfected by the financing statement becomes unperfected, unless the security interest is perfected otherwise. An unperfected security interest is vulnerable to other security interests, buyers, a bankruptcy trustee, and other lien creditors. It is possible, although not common, that a secured party would perfect by filing and also by another method. In that situation, the lapse of the financing statement would not affect perfection. A secured party whose security interest has become unperfected should reperfect as soon as it discovers the lapse. However, because the perfection lapsed, there is a gap in perfection and the security interest will have a new priority date that is later than the original priority date.

Second, if the security interest or agricultural lien becomes unperfected, section 9-515(c) declares that the security interest or agricultural lien is "deemed never to have been perfected as against a purchaser of the collateral for value." This rule is called the *retroactive unperfection rule,* an apt description of its effect. It means that a security interest that had been perfected and protected against other interests, is now treated as though it never were perfected as against a purchaser of the collateral for value and likely is subordinate to such person. The beneficiary of this rule is a purchaser for value, whether the purchaser acquires its interest before or after the effectiveness of the financing statement lapses. Sections 1-201(b)(29) and (30) define *purchase* and *purchaser* to include secured parties and buyers, but not lien creditors. *Value* is defined in section 1-204, discussed in Chapter 2.

The following example illustrates the retroactive unperfection rule. Bank perfects a security interest in Debtor's equipment by filing a financing statement. Subsequently, Lender perfects a security interest in the same equipment by filing a financing statement. Section 9-322(a) awards priority in the collateral to Bank. Bank's financing statement lapses at the expiration of five years from the date of filing. Under section 9-515(c), Bank's security interest becomes unperfected and is deemed never to have been perfected against Lender, a purchaser for value. Section 9-322(a) awards priority to Lender, assuming its security interest remains perfected. A secured party can prevent this serious consequence from occurring by filing a continuation statement.

c. Continuing Effectiveness of a Filed Financing Statement with a Continuation Statement — Sections 9-515(c), (d), (e)

If the secured party timely files a continuation statement, section 9-515(c) provides that the effectiveness of a filed financing statement does not lapse at the expiration of five years from the date of filing or the otherwise applicable effectiveness period. (The contents of a continuation statement are discussed later in this section.) Section 9-515(d) states that a secured party can file an effective continuation statement only within six months before the expiration of the applicable period — not before or after the six-month period. That rule is reinforced by section 9-510(c) — a continuation statement that is not filed within the six-month period is ineffective — and section 9-516(b)(7) — a filing officer should refuse to accept a continuation statement not filed within the six-month period.

Under the rule of section 9-515(e), a timely filed continuation statement continues the effectiveness of a filed financing statement for a period of five years, commencing on the day on which the financing statement would have lapsed. Observe that the continuation statement's five-year life commences on the date the financing statement would have lapsed, not on the day the secured party files the continuation statement. Upon the expiration of that five year period, the financing statement lapses unless another continuation statement is timely filed. Section 9-515(e) authorizes a secured party to file successive continuation statements.

A secured party who neglects to file a continuation statement in the six-month period before lapse should file a new financing statement as soon as it realizes the effectiveness of the financing statement has lapsed. Section 9-509(b) authorizes the secured party to file the financing statement. The new financing statement reperfects the security interest. However, there is a gap in perfection, and a person acquiring an interest in the collateral in the interval between lapse and reperfection is likely superior to the security interest.

Although section 9-515 speaks of a continuation statement, the section does not specify the information a continuation statement must provide. That absence results from Article 9's treatment of a continuation statement as a type of amendment a secured party can make to a financing statement. Section 9-512(a) authorizes amendment of a filed financing statement for the purpose of continuing the effectiveness of a financing statement. However, the stated requirements of section 9-512(a)(1) pertaining to amendments are minimal—a secured party continues the effectiveness of a filed financing statement by filing an amendment that identifies, by file number, the initial financing statement to which the amendment relates. The easiest and best method of continuing the perfection of a financing statement is to use the form adopted by section 9-521(b), designated "Form UCC 1Ad." (Form UCC 1Ad is usable for all types of amendments.) Notice that a continuation statement, like a financing statement, does not require the debtor's or secured party's authentication.

5. Incorrect Information and Misindexed Financing Statements—Sections 9-506, 9-517, 9-518

a. Incorrect and Omitted Information—the Minor Error Rule— Section 9-506

A filed financing statement may contain incorrect information. For example, the financing statement could have an incorrect address or a misspelling of the secured party's name. The important question in that situation is whether that financing statement nevertheless operates to perfect a security interest. The happy answer for the filer is that in some cases, it will. Section 9-506(a) provides: "A financing statement substantially satisfying the requirements of this part is effective, even if it has minor errors or omissions, unless the errors or omissions make the financing statement seriously misleading." The section creates three prerequisites to validating a filed financing statement that includes inaccurate information or omits information: 1) the financing statement must substantially satisfy the requirements for a financing statement; 2) the error or omission must be minor; and 3) the error or omission must not make the financing statement seriously misleading. Official Comment 2 to section 9-506 notes that the section comports with Article 9's policy of simplifying formal requisites and is "designed to discourage the fanatical and impossibly refined reading of the statutory requirements in which courts occasionally have indulged themselves."

Section 9-506(a), however, is not the panacea for all financing statement inaccuracies or omissions. And the consequence of a filed financing statement

that is not sufficient or effective is drastic—the security interest is not perfected. A secured party must strive to include correct information on the financing
statement. When it has failed, section 9-506 may provide relief. A secured party
who discovers that its financing statement includes incorrect information or omits
information should file an amendment that provides the correct information
as soon as possible, and also, in the case of an incorrect debtor's name, a new
financing statement.

Section 9-506 applies to errors and omissions in a *financing statement*. The
definition of *financing statement* in section 9-102(a)(39), includes the initial financing statement and any filed record relating to the initial financing statement. An amendment is a "record relating to the initial financing statement,"
and it includes continuation statements, termination statements, and addition or deletion of collateral or parties. Consequently, section 9-506 can validate an amendment that contains inaccuracies or omissions if the requirements
for effectiveness are satisfied.

Errors in the name of the debtor usually are seriously misleading. Because the filing office indexes financing statements in the name of the debtor,
an incorrect name results in the financing statement not being found by a
person searching the financing statement index under the correct name of
the debtor. Consequently, a financing statement with an incorrect name of
the debtor does not provide notice. Section 9-506(b) concurs: "Except as
otherwise provided in subsection (c), a financing statement that fails sufficiently to provide the name of the debtor in accordance with section 9-
503(a) is seriously misleading." Section 9-503, discussed previously in this
chapter, provides standards for when a financing statement sufficiently provides the debtor's name. If the financing statement fails to comply with
those standards, it is seriously misleading and does not perfect the security
interest.

However, section 9-506(c) provides an exception to the error-in-debtor's-
name-is-seriously-misleading rule of 9-506(b). A financing statement containing an insufficient debtor's name is not seriously misleading if the financing
statement would be disclosed by searching under the debtor's *correct* name,
using the filing office's standard search logic. Each jurisdiction sets its search
logic; Article 9 includes no rules or guidelines for search logic. Generally, search
logic pertains to how the filing system treats punctuation, upper and lower case
letters, organization abbreviations, first and middle names, and initials. The
section 9-506(c) exception is fairly straightforward: the financing statement
with the incorrect name of the debtor is effective to perfect the security interest if a search under the correct name of the debtor, using the jurisdiction's
search logic, would disclose the financing statement with the incorrect name.

Errors in the name of the secured party should not disqualify the effectiveness of the financing statement because such an error does not make the financing statement seriously misleading. A financing statement is indexed in the debtor's name, not the secured party's name. Interested persons search the financing statement index under the debtor's name, not the secured party's name. Inaccuracies in the secured party's name do not hinder a person from discovering whether a financing statement is filed against a debtor. Consequently, an error in the name of the secured party does not make the financing statement seriously misleading. Official Comment 2 to section 9-506 agrees with that proposition: "[A]n error in the name of the secured party … will not be seriously misleading." Thus, a financing statement with an error in the name of the secured party is effective to perfect a security interest.

Neither section 9-506 nor its comment mentions the effect of errors in the debtor's and secured party's mailing addresses. Those errors should be treated the same as errors in the secured party's name — not seriously misleading and of no effect on the perfection of the security interest. Addresses are not required for a sufficient financing statement under section 9-502. Searches are not conducted by the parties' addresses. An omission of either party's address obligates the filing officer to reject the financing statement but, as section 9-520(c) declares, the financing statement is effective if the filing office nevertheless accepts it for filing. It is possible that an incorrect debtor's address could mislead an interested person, but likely not seriously mislead. If the person is searching the financing statement index because it is considering a credit transaction with the debtor, such person likely knows the address of its prospective debtor and can inquire whether it is the debtor named in the filed financing statement. Consequently, errors or omissions of the parties' addresses in a filed financing statement should not invalidate the financing statement.

There is a potential problem for a secured party whose filed financing statement includes an incorrect mailing address for the debtor. Section 9-338 subordinates a security interest perfected by a financing statement that includes section 9-516(b)(5) information that is incorrect at the time of filing to a conflicting security interest or other purchaser who reasonably relied on the incorrect information. (Section 9-338 is discussed in Chapter 6.)

Errors in the description of collateral are governed by section 9-506. Official Comment 2 to section 9-506 declares that section 9-506(a) "provides the standard applicable to [errors and omissions in] indications of collateral." Section 9-506(a) should validate a description that misspells the name of the collateral, if it is not a seriously misleading error. Under section 9-108, the job of the description is to make possible the identification of the collateral described, not to provide an exact and detailed description. For example, if a financing statement indicates "30 Delp computers" when the security agreement grants a security interest in "30 Dell computers," section 9-506(a) ostensibly would make the financing statement effective.

Nevertheless, an inaccurate description could cause perfection problems in the situation where collateral is indicated in the security agreement but not in the financing statement. That financing statement provides no notice to a third person that a security interest might exist in the omitted collateral. For example, if the security agreement describes the collateral as "10 Sharp copy machines and 30 Apple computers" but the financing statement indicates the collateral as "30 Apple computers," section 9-506(a) should not make the financing statement effective to perfect the security interest in the copy machines. That omission seriously misleads an interested person. However, the financing statement is sufficient as to the computers.

Section 9-506 seems most likely to function in situations where a filed financing statement misspells the debtor's name, includes erroneous information required by section 9-516(b)(5), or omits that information. Answering the question of whether the error is minor and not seriously misleading involves asking whether the filed financing statement provides notice of the existence of a security interest in the collateral against the debtor. It is no surprise that a minor error not seriously misleading to a court in one jurisdiction is seriously misleading to a court in another jurisdiction and possibly even to different judges in the same jurisdiction. Correctly indicating the information on a financing statement seems like a minor task, but the failure to do so has a major effect — the security interest might be unperfected.

b. Misindexed Financing Statements — Section 9-517

A filing office could misindex a record — file it in the wrong place in the index. For example, a filing office mistakenly could file an initial financing statement naming "Day" with debtors whose name begins with "B." In that situation, section 9-517 provides that the filing office's failure to index correctly the financing statement does not affect its effectiveness. Consequently, the financing statement perfects the security interest. The secured party does not bear the risk of mistakes by the filing office. However, an interested person searching the financing statement index might not find a misindexed financing statement. Official Comment 2 to section 9-517 states that the person searching bears the burden of the mistake. No Article 9 section subordinates a misindexed financing statement against a purchaser who reasonably relies on the absence of the financing statement.

c. Correcting an Inaccurate or Wrongfully Filed Record — Section 9-518

A debtor against whom a financing statement is filed may believe that the financing statement is inaccurate or wrongfully filed. In that situation, section 9-518(a) authorizes the debtor to file a correction statement in the office where the financing statement is filed. A correction statement must identify the filed record by the file number assigned to the initial financing statement, indicate that it is a correction statement, and provide the basis for the person's belief that the record is inaccurate or wrongfully filed. Although a correction statement becomes part of the "financing statement," section 9-518(c) states that a correction statement "does not affect the effectiveness" of any filed records. Consequently, a security interest perfected by filing is not affected by the filing of a correction statement. A court would decide whether and to what extent such a security interest is perfected.

6. Effect of Post-Filing Events on Effectiveness of Financing Statement — Sections 9-507, 9-508, 9-316

The information in an effective and sufficient filed financing statement might become inaccurate after it is filed because of changes to the parties or events involving the collateral. Sections 9-507 and 9-508 determine whether the financing statement remains effective after such changes. In most situations, the financing statement remains effective, consequently, the security interest remains perfected without amendment of the financing statement by the secured party. The minor-error rule of section 9-506 does not apply because it determines the effectiveness of a filed financing statement that contains inaccuracies at the time of filing.

a. Disposition of Collateral — Section 9-507(a)

Section 9-507(a) continues the effectiveness of a filed financing statement for collateral that is sold, exchanged, leased, licensed, or otherwise disposed of in which a security interest or agricultural lien continues. The financing statement remains effective until it otherwise would lapse under section 9-515 in accordance with the period of effectiveness of a financing statement, typically the remainder of five years. The important effect of section 9-507(a) is that the filed financing statement remains effective to perfect the security interest in the collateral although the debtor named in the financing statement might no longer retain any interest in the collateral. The transferee becomes a debtor under the definition of *debtor* in section 9-102(a)(28) because debtor includes a person having an interest in the collateral regardless of whether the person is the obligor. For example, suppose Bank perfects a security interest in ABC Corporation's equipment by filing a financing statement. ABC Corporation sells the equipment collateral to DEF Corporation in a transaction in which the security interest continues. The financing statement filed against ABC Corporation remains effective to perfect Bank's security interest in the equipment sold to DEF Corporation although ABC Corporation, the named debtor in the financing statement, is not the debtor. DEF Corporation is the debtor. This rule might cause a person who contemplates taking a security interest to ascertain the debtor's source of title to the collateral and search the financing statement index for financing statements in the name of the person who transferred the collateral to the debtor.

This continued-effectiveness rule applies when the security interest or agricultural lien *continues* in the collateral notwithstanding the disposition. Section 9-315(a), discussed in Chapter 7, determines whether the security interest or agricultural lien continues in the collateral after a disposition. The general rule is that the transferee in the disposition takes the collateral subject to the security interest unless the secured party authorizes the disposition free of the security interest or an Article 9 rule provides otherwise.

Although section 9-507(a) preserves the effectiveness of the financing statement notwithstanding the disposition of the collateral, another aspect of the disposition might necessitate a new filing. If the transferee of the collateral is located in a jurisdiction different from the jurisdiction of the debtor named in the filed financing statement, Article 9's choice-of-law rule, section 9-301, causes a change in the law governing the security interest and requires a filing in the governing jurisdiction to continue the perfection of the security interest. However, section 9-316(a) allows the security interest to remain perfected temporarily in the new jurisdiction. It provides that the security interest remains perfected until the earlier of the time perfection would have ceased under the law of the old jurisdiction or one year after the date of the transfer of collateral to the transferee in the new jurisdiction. This gives the secured party time to ascertain the jurisdiction where the debtor is located and file a financing statement in that jurisdiction. (Section 9-316(a) is discussed in Chapter 10.)

b. Change in Debtor's Name — Sections 9-507(b), (c)

The general rule of section 9-507(b) is that an effective filed financing statement does not become ineffective if the information provided in it becomes seriously misleading. However, exceptions to the rule exist if a debtor changes its name or if a new debtor becomes bound as debtor. Section 9-507(c) supplies the rule for determining whether the financing statement remains effective when the debtor changes its name. A change in name of the debtor could cause a filed financing statement to become seriously misleading. For example, suppose Bank has a security interest in ABC Corporation's existing and after-acquired equipment perfected by filing a financing statement. ABC Corporation changes its name to AAA Corporation. To identify the debtor, the financing statement should indicate the debtor as AAA Corporation, not ABC Corporation. Consequently, the name change causes the financing statement to become seriously misleading under section 9-506(b) because a financing statement "that fails sufficiently to provide the name of the debtor ... is seriously misleading."

Section 9-507(c)(1) nevertheless continues the effectiveness of the financing statement to perfect a security interest in existing collateral and any collateral the debtor acquires within four months after the name change. The security interest in that collateral remains perfected by means of the seriously misleading financing statement; no action by the secured party is required. This rule might cause a person who contemplates taking a security interest to ascertain whether its potential debtor has changed its name and, if so, search the financing statement index for financing statements filed in the previous name.

Section 9-507(c)(2) adopts a different rule for collateral the debtor acquires more than four months after the seriously misleading name change. It declares that the filed financing statement is not effective to perfect a security interest in collateral the debtor acquires more than four months after the name change unless the secured party amends the financing statement to make it not seriously misleading within four months after the name change. The appropriate amendment to the financing statement changes the debtor's name to the new name.

The result of subsections 9-507(c)(1) and (c)(2) is that a secured party remains perfected in collateral the debtor acquires within four months after the name change, but is not perfected in collateral the debtor acquires more than four months after the change unless the secured party amends the financing statement to reflect the new name of the debtor. Consequently, the security interest could be subordinate to a person that acquires an interest in the collateral after the expiration of four months.

One method a secured party can use to discover the name change is to have the security agreement require the debtor to notify the secured party of any change in its name. The secured party hopes the debtor will perform that duty. If the debtor does not, whether by design or neglect, the recourse for the secured party is that the debtor has defaulted. However, default of the debtor does not change the rule of section 9-507(c)(2). A secured party should amend the financing statement as soon as it discovers the name change.

Notice that section 9-507(c) applies when the debtor changes its name, not when there is a change in debtors, such as when debtor sells the collateral to a buyer. Section 9-507(a) covers that situation. Nor does section 9-507(c) apply if the debtor changes its organizational structure, such as from partnership to corporation, or merges with another entity. Section 9-508, discussed in the next section, determines the continued effectiveness of a filed financing statement in those situations.

c. Effect of New Debtor Becoming Bound by Security Agreement of Original Debtor — Section 9-508

When a debtor changes its organizational structure or merges with another organization, the transaction raises questions regarding the effectiveness and perfection of security interests created by the *original debtor*. A *new debtor* (either the new organization or the merger survivor) can become *bound as debtor under the security agreement of the original debtor* in accordance with the attachment requirements of sections 9-203(d) and (e), discussed in Chapter 2. Section 9-508 determines whether a financing statement filed against the original debtor is effective to perfect a security interest in the new debtor's existing and after-acquired collateral. (*Original debtor* and *new debtor* are defined in sections 9-102(a)(60) and (56), respectively.)

For example, suppose Bank has a security interest perfected by filing in ABC Corporation's existing and after-acquired equipment. ABC Corporation (the original debtor) merges with DEF Corporation (the new debtor) in a transaction where DEF Corporation is the surviving corporation and DEF Corporation becomes bound as the debtor under ABC Corporation's security agreement. Because DEF Corporation becomes bound as debtor, its existing and after-acquired equipment is now collateral for Bank's security interest. Section 9-508 determines whether Bank's financing statement, naming ABC Corporation as debtor, is effective to perfect a security interest in DEF Corporation's equipment.

Becoming bound as the debtor under the original debtor's security agreement is different from being a transferee of collateral in which the security interest continues. In the latter situation, the transferee is the debtor for the transferred collateral only. In the former situation, all property of the new debtor that fits the description of collateral in the original debtor's security agreement is collateral for the security interest. Section 9-508(c) allows section 9-507(a) (discussed in the previous section) to determine whether a filed financing statement remains effective to perfect the security interest in the collateral transferred to the new debtor.

With one exception, section 9-508(a) provides that a filed financing statement indicating an original debtor as debtor continues to be effective to perfect a security interest in a new debtor's existing and after-acquired collateral to the extent that the financing statement would have been effective against the original debtor. For example, if the financing statement would be effective to perfect a security interest in the original debtor's existing and after-acquired equipment, it will be effective to perfect a security interest in the new debtor's existing and after-acquired equipment. There is no requirement that the secured party make a new filing naming the new debtor as debtor.

Official Comment 4 to section 9-508 notes that the rule of section 9-508(a) applies when both debtors are located in the same jurisdiction. If the new debtor is located in a jurisdiction different from the jurisdiction of the original debtor, a new filing is required because Article 9's choice-of-law rule, section 9-301, causes a change in the law governing the security interest and requires a filing in the governing jurisdiction to continue perfection of the security interest. However, section 9-316(a) allows the security interest to remain perfected until the earlier of the time perfection would have ceased under the law of the jurisdiction of the original debtor or the expiration of four months after the change in the location of the debtor. (Section 9-316 is discussed in Chapter 10.)

Section 9-508(b) contains the exception to the continued-effectiveness rule. It applies when the change in name from the original debtor to the new debtor causes the filed financing statement to be seriously misleading. Section 9-506(b) declares that a filed financing statement is seriously misleading if a search under the correct name of the debtor, the new debtor, would not disclose the financing statement filed in the name of the original debtor. Consequently, the financing statement will be seriously misleading unless the name of the new debtor is the same or very similar to the name of the original debtor.

Section 9-508(b) limits, but does not extinguish, the continued effectiveness of the filed financing statement. Although the financing statement is seriously misleading, section 9-508(b)(1) continues the effectiveness of the financing statement to perfect a security interest in the new debtor's existing collateral and any collateral the new debtor acquires within four months after it becomes bound under the original debtor's security agreement. This enables the security interest to be perfected in after-acquired collateral for four months, assuming the security agreement includes an after-acquired property clause.

Section 9-508(b)(2) declares that a filed financing statement is not effective to perfect a security interest in collateral the new debtor acquires more than four months after it becomes bound as debtor, unless the secured party files an initial financing statement indicating the new debtor as debtor within four months of the change. Under section 9-509(b), the new debtor authorizes the filing of the initial financing statement by becoming bound as debtor under the original debtor's security agreement.

For example, suppose Bank perfects a security interest in ABC Corporation's existing and after-acquired equipment by filing a financing statement. ABC Corporation merges with DEF Corporation in a transaction where DEF Corporation is the surviving corporation and DEF Corporation becomes bound as debtor by ABC Corporation's security agreement. DEF Corporation's existing and after-acquired equipment is now collateral for Bank's security interest. Although the filed financing statement undoubtedly is seriously misleading, it is effective nevertheless to perfect Bank's security interest in DEF Corporation's existing equipment and in equipment DEF acquires within four months after it becomes bound by ABC Corporation's security agreement. The financing statement is not effective, however, to perfect Bank's security interest in equipment DEF acquires after the four-month period. To perfect its security interest in such collateral, Bank must file an initial financing statement indicating DEF Corporation as the debtor before expiration of four months.

A secured party who does not file the initial financing statement within the four-month period should file it as soon as it learns that the new debtor has become bound under the original debtor's security agreement. Filing the initial financing statement after the four-month period expires will perfect the security interest in collateral acquired after the date of the new filing. However, a gap in perfection will exist with respect to such collateral, and priority of the security interest in that collateral dates from the time of filing the initial financing statement against DEF Corporation, not from the time of filing the initial financing statement against ABC Corporation.

d. Change in Location of Debtor — Section 9-316

A debtor that changes its location — for example, an individual debtor changes her residence from Kentucky to Tennessee — affects the perfection of the security interest. In that situation, Article 9's choice-of-law rule, section 9-301, changes the jurisdiction that governs perfection of the security interest from the jurisdiction where the debtor was located previously to the jurisdiction where the debtor is located presently. Section 9-316, discussed in Chapter 10, determines whether a perfected security interest remains perfected after the change in governing jurisdiction.

7. Amendment of a Financing Statement — Section 9-512

Every filing made after filing an initial financing statement is an amendment under the terminology of section 9-512. Amendments of financing statements include adding or deleting collateral, adding or deleting debtors or secured parties, assigning the secured party's rights, continuing the effectiveness of the security interest, terminating the effectiveness of the security interest, or otherwise amending the information provided in the financing statement. An amendment can perform more than one task. For example, a secured party can file an amendment that both continues the effectiveness of the financing statement and adds collateral. All amendments are subject to the provisions of section 9-512. Continuation statements, termination statements, and assignments are also subject to additional provisions contained in separate sections of Article 9.

The simplest method of effectively amending a financing statement is to use the amendment form—Form UCC 1Ad—adopted in section 9-521(b). It contains spaces for all required and relevant information. Article 9 does not require a debtor's signature for any type of amendment. However, an amendment is effective only if the debtor authorizes its filing. Under section 9-509 authorization for an amendment exists when: the debtor authenticates a record authorizing the filing; the debtor authenticates a security agreement (the original security agreement); the debtor becomes bound as debtor under a security agreement (the *new debtor* situation); or the debtor acquires collateral in which a security interest continues.

Section 9-512 adopts a few noteworthy rules regarding amendments. An amendment does not extend the period of effectiveness of a financing statement unless the amendment is a continuation statement effective under section 9-515. An amendment that adds collateral is effective as to the added collateral only from the date of filing the amendment. An amendment that adds a debtor is effective as to the added debtor only from the date of filing the amendment. Additionally, the financing statement is effective as to the added debtor and added collateral only for the remaining period of effectiveness of the financing statement.

8. Termination Statement—Section 9-513

A termination statement is an amendment governed by section 9-513 in addition to the general amendment provisions of section 9-512. The purpose of a termination statement is to terminate the effectiveness of a filed financing statement. Because the effectiveness of most filed financing statements lapses five years after the date of filing under section 9-515 (unless a continuation statement is filed), a secured party is not obligated, except in the case of a financing statement covering consumer goods, to file or send the debtor a termination statement unless the debtor demands it. The financing statement ceases to be effective upon the filing of an authorized termination statement. If there is more than one secured party of record, a filed termination statement applies only against the secured party or parties who authorized the filing.

Section 9-513(a) compels a secured party of record to file a termination statement for a financing statement covering consumer goods in two situations. *First*, the secured party must file a termination statement when there is no obligation secured, such as when the debtor repays the loan, and no commitment of the secured party to make an advance or otherwise give value. *Second*, a secured party must file a termination statement if the debtor did not authorize the filing of the initial financing statement. A secured party who files an initial financing statement without authorization is also subject to statutory damages under section 9-625(e). *Consumer goods*, defined in section 9-102(a)(23), are goods the debtor uses for personal, family, or household purposes. A *secured party of record* is the secured party named in a filed initial financing statement or amendment.

The duty of section 9-513(a) is compulsory and self-executing; it does not depend upon a demand from the debtor that the secured party terminate the financing statement. Additionally, the secured party of record must file the termination statement in the proper office, not merely send it to the debtor for filing.

Section 9-513(b) directs the secured party to file the termination statement by the earlier of 1) one month after there is no obligation or commitment or 2) within 20 days after the secured party receives an authenticated demand from a debtor. Requiring the secured party to timely respond to a debtor's demand does not create a condition of demand to the existence of the duty. If the debtor makes no demand, the secured party must file the termination statement within one month after there is no obligation or commitment. Section 1-202(e) adopts rules for determining when a secured party *receives* a demand.

For all other types of collateral, section 9-513(c) requires a secured party of record to either file a termination statement or send it to the debtor *only* after receiving an authenticated demand from the debtor. The secured party must perform within twenty days of receiving the demand from the debtor. This duty arises only if there is no obligation secured by the collateral and there is no commitment to make an advance or otherwise give value, or if the debtor did not authorize the filing of the initial financing statement.

Section 9-513(c)(1) is not applicable to a financing statement that relates to a transaction where accounts or chattel paper have been sold to the secured party or when the financing statement covers goods that are the subject of a consignment. Although the debtor owes no obligation to the secured party in these types of transactions, Article 9 governs them nevertheless, and consequently the secured party typically perfects its security interest by filing a financing statement. There are two exceptions to that exception. Sections 9-513(c)(2) and (c)(3) require the secured party to file or send the termination statement if the account debtor for the receivable has paid its obligation or the consigned goods are not in the debtor's possession, and the secured party receives an authenticated demand from the debtor. (Sales of receivables and consignments are discussed in Chapter 1.)

A secured party who fails to comply with the requirements of section 9-513 activates the debtor's right to file a termination statement, in addition to being liable for statutory damages established by section 9-625(e). Section 9-509(d) authorizes the debtor or a person authorized by the debtor to file a termination statement if the secured party fails to file or send a termination statement as required by section 9-513(a) or (c). That termination statement must indicate that the debtor authorized it to be filed.

9. Assignment of Security Interest by Secured Party of Record — Section 9-514

A secured party may assign its perfected security interest to another person. In that situation, section 9-310(c) provides that the assignee is not required to make any filing to continue the perfected status of the security interest or agricultural lien. However, a secured party or lienholder who assigns its rights may want to file a record of the assignment so that the Article 9 duties placed on the secured party of record become obligations of the assignee. Section 9-514 provides two methods for indicating an assignment. *First*, an initial financing statement can reflect an assignment of all a secured party's rights by indicating the name and mailing address of the assignee as the name of the secured party. A secured party assignor could elect this option if it assigned its security interest rights before it filed the initial financing statement. *Second*, an amendment to the financing statement can reflect an assignment of all or part of a secured party's rights if it identifies the initial financing statement by file number, provides the name of the assignor, and provides the name and mailing address of the assignee. The official forms adopted in section 9-521 — Forms UCC 1 and UCC 1Ad — are specifically adapted for either type of assignment.

C. Perfection by Possession — Section 9-313

1. Possession by the Secured Party

Although a security interest in most types of collateral can be perfected by filing a financing statement, Article 9 adopts optional methods of perfection for some types of collateral. Section 9-313(a) authorizes a secured party to perfect a security interest in negotiable documents, goods, instruments, money, or tangible chattel paper by taking possession of the collateral in lieu of filing a financing statement; although filing a financing statement is effective to perfect a security interest in that collateral. A secured party who takes possession of the collateral also satisfies the debtor's-agreement attachment requirement of section 9-203(b)(3), discussed in Chapter 2, without having the debtor authenticate a security agreement. However, most secured parties will want a written security agreement regardless of whether they choose to satisfy section 9-203(b)(3) by taking possession of the collateral. Additionally, section 9-313(a) authorizes a secured party to perfect a security interest in a registered form certificated security, discussed in Chapter 4, by taking delivery of it.

If the collateral is not of a type listed in section 9-313, a secured party cannot perfect a security interest in it by taking possession. For example, when the debtor grants a security interest in an account, she might deliver the contract or other document evidencing the account to the secured party. The secured party's *possession* of such document does not perfect the security interest because an account is not listed in section 9-313(a) as a type of collateral in which a security interest can be perfected by possession.

Section 9-313(d) provides that a security interest perfected by possession of the collateral is perfected when the secured party takes possession and continues only while the secured party retains possession. However, the secured party does not relinquish possession by delivering the collateral to another person, other than delivery to the debtor or a lessee of debtor, if the secured party complies with the requirements of section 9-313(h). Delivery of the collateral to the debtor or to a lessee from the debtor in the ordinary course of debtor's business terminates the secured party's possession.

Section 9-313(h) states that the secured party does not relinquish possession of collateral by delivery of it to a person *if* the secured party instructs the person, at or before delivery, to hold the collateral for the secured party's benefit or to redeliver the collateral to the secured party at the conclusion of the purpose for delivery. Additionally, section 9-313(i) states that the secured party does not relinquish possession even if delivery to the person violates the rights of the debtor. Such delivery might, however, depending on the agreement between secured party and debtor, be a breach of contract, subjecting the secured party to liability for damages. The person who receives delivery of the collateral owes no duty to the secured party unless applicable law otherwise provides or the person so agrees. Typically, a secured party would want an agreement from the transferee covering, at a minimum, return of and care of the collateral.

2. Possession Through an Agent of the Secured Party

A secured party can take possession of the collateral through its agent. The law of agency determines whether a person is an agent of the secured party. Courts properly have rejected arguments by secured parties that a secured party can achieve possession of the collateral by having the debtor possess the collateral as the agent of the secured party. However, Official Comment 3 to section 9-313 provides that a person can be an agent for both the secured party and the debtor so that the agent's possession qualifies as the secured party's possession. In that situation, the secured party must insure that the agent is not controlled by or connected to the debtor so that the debtor effectively possesses the collateral, thus precluding possession by the secured party and perfection of the security interest.

3. Possession Through a Third Person — Section 9-313(c)

Section 9-313(c) adopts standards for when a secured party can possess collateral, other than certificated securities or goods covered by a document of title, that is in the possession of a third person who is not the agent of the secured party or the debtor, nor a lessee of the collateral from the debtor. A secured party could use this perfection method when the debtor has delivered the collateral to a person for the purpose of storing the collateral. This differs from possession by an agent in which the secured party is deemed to possess the collateral because the agent acts for the secured party. A secured party possesses collateral in the possession of a third person when that person authenticates a record acknowledging that it holds the collateral for the secured party's benefit, or it takes possession of the collateral after authenticating a record acknowledging that it will hold the collateral for the secured party's benefit. This rule allows the third person to authenticate the record of acknowledgement before or after it takes possession of the goods. Section 9-313(g) states that either type of acknowledgement is effective to give the secured party possession of the collateral, even if the acknowledgement violates the rights of the debtor. The definitions of *authenticate* and *record*, sections 9-102(a)(7) and (a)(69), respectively, allow for either a written or an electronic acknowledgement. Section 9-313(c) is not applicable if the person in possession of the goods has issued a document of title covering them.

The secured party does not control the third person and thus cannot force the person to acknowledge it holds or will hold the collateral for the secured party's benefit. Section 9-313(f) expressly provides that a third person is not required to acknowledge that it holds property for the secured party's benefit. Consequently, a secured party who plans to perfect through possession of the collateral by a third person should be prepared to perfect the security interest using an alternative method of perfection. A third person who acknowledges the secured party's interest owes no duty to the secured party from the act of acknowledging.

4. Delivery of a Registered Form Certificated Security — Sections 9-313(e), 8-301

Section 9-313(e) authorizes a secured party to perfect a security interest in a registered form certificated security by delivery of the certificate to the secured party in accordance with section 8-301. Section 8-102(a)(4) defines a *certificated security* as a security represented by a certificate. *Registered form*, section 8-102(a)(13), means that the certificate specifies a person entitled to the security and transfer of the security may be registered on books maintained by the issuer for that purpose. Delivery of a certificated security under section 8-301(a) occurs in any of three situations: 1) the secured party has possession of the certificate; 2) another person has possession of the certificate on behalf of the secured party; or 3) a securities intermediary, acting on behalf of the secured party, has possession. Although section 8-301(a) uses the term *purchaser* to describe the person to whom the certificated security is delivered, a secured party is a purchaser because the definitions of *purchase* and *purchaser* in sections 1-201(b)(29) and (b)(30) include acquiring rights by taking a security interest. Section 9-313(e) states that a secured party who perfects its security interest by delivery remains perfected until the debtor obtains possession of the certificate.

Under section 8-301(a)(1), delivery occurs when the secured party acquires possession of the certificate. Under section 8-301(a)(2), delivery to a secured party occurs when a third person, other than a securities intermediary, either acquires possession of the certificate on behalf of the secured party or, having previously acquired possession, acknowledges that it holds the certificate for the secured party. Because section 8-301 does not compel such person to acknowledge that it holds the certificate for the secured party, the secured party must perfect through an alternative method of perfection if the person is noncompliant. Under section 8-301(a)(3), delivery of a registered form certificated security to a secured party occurs when a securities intermediary, such as an investment bank or brokerage company, acting on behalf of the secured party, acquires possession of the security certificate, and the certificate is registered in the name of the secured party, payable to the order of the secured party, or specially indorsed to the secured party by an effective indorsement, and has not been indorsed to the securities intermediary or in blank. "Registered" refers to the issuer's registration of transfer of the certificate.

D. Perfection of a Security Interest in Goods in Possession of a Bailee — Sections 9-312 (c), (d)

Section 9-312 establishes methods for perfecting a security interest in goods in possession of a bailee who has issued a negotiable or nonnegotiable document. *Bailee*, section 7-102(a)(1), means a person who issues a document of title acknowledging its possession of goods and its obligation to deliver the goods. Under section 9-102(a)(30), a *document* means a document of title. A document of title covers goods that are in the possession of a person who is not generally the owner of the goods. Section 1-201(b)(16) defines *document of title* as a record that gives the person in possession of it the right to control the document and the goods it covers. The typical document of title is a warehouse receipt, issued by a warehouse company when an owner of goods stores the goods in the warehouse, or a bill of lading, issued by a carrier when an owner delivers goods to the carrier for transportation of the goods. A document of title is either negotiable or nonnegotiable. A negotiable document of title authorizes delivery of the goods either to the bearer of the document or to the order of a person named in the document. A nonnegotiable document of title authorizes delivery of the goods to a person named in the document. Section 9-313(c), discussed previously in this chapter, governs perfection of a security interest in goods in possession of a person who has not issued a document of title.

Section 9-312(c) authorizes a secured party to perfect a security interest in *goods* in the possession of a bailee who issues a negotiable document of title covering the goods by perfecting a security interest in the *document*. A secured party can perfect a security interest in the document by filing a financing statement describing the document as collateral under section 9-312(a), by taking control of an electronic document under section 9-314, or by taking possession of the document under section 9-313(a).

Section 9-312(c)(2) establishes a rule for determining priority between conflicting security interests in the goods perfected during the time a bailee has issued a negotiable document and has possession of the goods. In that situation, a security interest perfected in the document has priority over a security interest perfected by any other method. For example, suppose Bank perfects a security interest in goods stored in a warehouse and covered by a negotiable warehouse receipt by filing a financing statement covering the goods. Lender perfects a security interest in the same goods by taking possession of the document. Lender has priority under the rule of section 9-312(c)(2), regardless of the fact that it was not the first secured party to perfect. The other priority rules of Article 9 determine priority if the conflicting security interests are perfected before or after the time the bailee is in possession of the goods.

Section 9-312(d) authorizes three methods by which a secured party can perfect a security interest in goods possessed by a bailee who issues a non-negotiable document of title covering the goods. *First*, a secured party can file a financing statement indicating the goods as collateral. *Second*, a security interest in the goods is perfected by the bailee's receipt of notification of the security interest. Perfection does not depend on the bailee's acknowledgement of the secured party's interest, only that the bailee receives notification of it. (Section 1-202(e) establishes rules for determining when a notification is received.) *Third*, a security interest in the goods is perfected if the bailee issues a document of title in the name of the secured party.

E. Perfection of Security Interests by Federal Law or State Certificate-of-Title Statutes — Section 9-311

Perfection of a security interest in property that is subject to federal law or state certificate-of-title statutes that adopt perfection requirements is accomplished by complying with the perfection requirements of such law or statute, not by filing a financing statement or complying with an Article 9 perfection method. With one important exception, section 9-311(a) provides that Article 9's filing provisions are *not necessary or effective* if the security interest is subject to: 1) a statute, treaty, or regulation of the United States that creates perfection requirements which enable a security interest to obtain priority over a lien creditor and that preempt Article 9's filing requirements; or 2) a jurisdiction's certificate-of-title statute which provides for indication of a security interest on the certificate of title as a condition to or result of perfection or obtaining priority over a lien creditor. When such law exists, the secured party must perfect its security interest by complying with it. A secured party who files a financing statement in an attempt to perfect the security interest does not achieve perfection. Additionally, section 9-311(c) declares that the applicable statute, treaty, or regulation also governs duration of perfection and continuation of perfection.

However, all other aspects of the security interest remain subject to the rules of Article 9. Consequently, Article 9 governs such matters as attachment, priority, and default of the security interest. Section 9-311(b) helps implement that rule by stating that compliance with the perfection requirements of the applicable law "is equivalent to the filing of a financing statement under this article." This insures that Article 9's other provisions that connect with a financing statement, such as the first-to-file-or-perfect rule of section 9-322, will apply to security interests perfected under applicable state or federal law.

The exception to the rule of section 9-311(a) pertains to inventory collateral. A certificate-of-title statute does not supplant the Article 9 perfection requirements if the collateral for the security interest is inventory held for sale or lease by a person in the business of selling such goods. In that situation, the secured party must perfect the security interest by using an authorized Article 9 method, typically by filing a financing statement; compliance with the certificate-of-title statute does not perfect the security interest. For example, suppose Bank takes a security interest in the used car inventory of Gannon Motors. A certificate-of-title statute of the jurisdiction governs perfection of a security interest in automobiles. Nevertheless, Bank must perfect its security interest by complying with Article 9, not by complying with the certificate-of-title statute. Official Comment 4 to section 9-311 reiterates that the exception applies only when the debtor is in the business of *selling* that type of collateral. If the debtor is in the business of *leasing* but not selling such collateral, the exception does not apply and the secured party must perfect according to the certificate-of-title statute.

Most certificate-of-title statutes require that perfection of a security interest in such property is achieved by indicating the security interest on the certificate of title. Jurisdictions with those statutes also establish a process for indicating the security interest on the certificate of title. Many certificate-of-title statutes cover boats and manufactured homes in addition to motor vehicles. Chapter 10 provides additional discussion of certificate-of-title statutes.

Section 9-311 is related to section 9-109(c)(1) (discussed in Chapter 1), which makes Article 9 inapplicable to a security interest to the extent that a United States statute, treaty, or regulation preempts Article 9. Section 9-109(c) allows federal law to preempt Article 9 governance over any or all aspects of a security interest. Section 9-311(a) supplants only the perfection provisions of Article 9 and only when the federal law adopts perfection requirements for a security interest.

An example of a federal law that displaces Article 9's filing provisions, but leaves other aspects of a security interest to Article 9 is the Federal Aviation Act (FAA), 49 U.S.C. §§ 44107-44111. The FAA has generated controversy over whether it is a perfection statute only or a complete preemption of Article 9. The majority of courts have held that a purpose of the FAA was to establish a national filing system for recording security interests in aircraft, not to preempt state laws governing priorities of security interests, and thus the act only preempts Article 9's perfection provisions. *See, e.g.,* Cessna Fin. Corp. v. Skyways Enter., 580 S.W. 2d 491 (Ky. 1979).

Checkpoints

- Most security interests are perfected by filing a financing statement—a written or electronic document.

- A sufficient financing statement must include the names of the debtor and the secured party and indicate the collateral in a manner conforming to the Article 9 requirements for a financing statement.

- A financing statement must include mailing addresses of the debtor and the secured party and information about the organizational status and jurisdiction of the debtor, however, a *filed* financing statement that omits that information is effective nevertheless if it sufficiently indicates the parties and the collateral.

- The financing statement must be filed in the office designated by the jurisdiction that governs perfection of the security interest.

- Most financing statements are effective for five years from the date of filing, and the effectiveness of a financing statement can be continued for five-year periods by filing a continuation statement before the financing statement lapses.

- If a financing statement lapses, the security interest becomes unperfected and is deemed never to have been perfected as against a purchaser for value.

- A financing statement that includes erroneous information is effective if the financing statement substantially complies with the Article 9 requirements and the error is minor and does not make the financing statement seriously misleading.

- Events that occur after a financing statement is filed, such as the debtor selling the collateral, changing its name, or merging with another entity, do not render the financing statement ineffective as to existing collateral, but can affect the security interest in collateral the debtor acquires more than four months after the event.

- A secured party can perfect a security interest in tangible collateral by taking possession of the collateral or by having its agent take possession or when a third person in possession of the collateral acknowledges the security interest of the secured party.

- If federal law establishes perfection requirements that preempt Article 9, a secured party must perfect the security interest under federal law.

- If a jurisdiction adopts certificate-of-title statutes that govern perfection of a security interest in goods covered by a certificate of title, a secured party must perfect the security interest in that manner, unless the collateral is inventory.

Chapter 4

Perfecting a Security Interest by Establishing Control— Sections 9-312 and 9-314

Roadmap

- Establishing control of investment property collateral
- Establishing control of deposit account collateral
- Establishing control of electronic chattel paper collateral
- Establishing control of letter-of-credit right collateral
- Establishing control of electronic document collateral

Article 9 adopts control as a method of perfection for a security interest in a deposit account, electronic chattel paper, investment property, letter-of-credit right, and electronic document of title. Control is the only method of perfection for a deposit account and letter-of-credit right, unless the security interest in that collateral arises as proceeds of collateral. For those other types of collateral, Article 9 authorizes additional methods for perfecting the security interest. The UCC drafters designed the requirements for control in such a manner that a secured party who establishes control has power over the collateral without obtaining further consent of the debtor. "Establishing control," means that the secured party has complied with the Article 9 requirements for control of the particular collateral. Section 9-314(b) states that a security interest is perfected when the secured party obtains control and remains perfected by control only while the secured party retains control. A secured party with control of collateral is subject to the duties and rights of sections 9-207(c) and 9-208.

Control is also a method of satisfying the debtor's-agreement attachment requirement of section 9-203(b)(3). Since the control requirements are essentially the same for attachment and perfection, if you studied control in Chapter 2 this should be a review.

A. Control of Investment Property —
Sections 9-106, 8-106

Sections 9-312(a) and 9-314(a) authorize a secured party to perfect a security interest in investment property by establishing control or by filing a financing statement. *Investment property*, defined in section 9-102(a)(49), includes a security, a security entitlement, a securities account, a commodity contract, or a commodity account. A secured party establishes control of investment property under the rules of Article 8 or Article 9, depending on the type of investment property. Section 8-106 governs control of a security — certificated or uncertificated — and a security entitlement. Section 9-106 governs control of a commodity contract, commodity account, and a securities account. An important reason why a secured party would choose to perfect a security interest in investment property by control rather than by filing is that a security interest perfected by control has priority over a security interest perfected by filing.

1. Certificated Security in Bearer or Registered Form —
Section 8-106

A *certificated security* is a security, such as a share of stock, represented by a certificate. For example, a certificate representing ownership of 100 shares of stock in General Electric Company is a certificated security. Control of a certificated security is dependent on whether the security is in bearer form or registered form. Section 8-102 defines both terms. A *bearer form* certificated security exists when the terms of the certificate make the security payable to the bearer of the certificate. A *registered form* certificated security exists when the terms of the certificate specify a person entitled to it (somewhat like the payee of a check) and its transfer can be registered on the books of the issuer of the security.

Under section 8-106(a), a secured party has control of a bearer form certificated security if the security is delivered to it. Literally, the control provisions of section 8-106(a) refer to a *purchaser* of a certificated security. However, a secured party is a purchaser because the UCC definitions of *purchase* and *purchaser*, (sections 1-201(b)(29) and (30), respectively) include acquiring rights by taking a security interest. Section 8-301 establishes requirements for delivery. Under section 8-301(a)(1), delivery occurs when the secured party acquires possession of the certificate. Under section 8-301(a)(2), delivery occurs when a third person, other than a securities intermediary, either acquires possession of the certificate on behalf of the secured party or, having previously acquired possession, acknowledges that it holds the certificate for the secured party. Because section 8-301 does not compel such person to acknowledge that it holds the certificate for the secured party, the secured party must perfect through an alternative method of perfection if the person is noncompliant.

Under section 8-106(b), a secured party has control of a registered form certificated security when it satisfies two requirements. First, the certificate must be delivered to the secured party. Delivery of a registered form certificated security occurs in the same manner as delivery of a bearer form certificated security (examined in the preceding paragraph), and also when a securities intermediary acquires possession of the certificate. Under section 8-301(a)(3), delivery of a registered form certificated security to a secured party occurs when a securities intermediary, such as an investment bank or brokerage company, acting on behalf of the secured party acquires possession of the security certificate, provided the certificate is registered in the name of the secured party, payable to the order of the secured party, or specially indorsed to the secured party by an effective indorsement and has not been indorsed to the securities intermediary or in blank. Registration refers to issuer's registration of transfer of the certificate.

The second requirement for control of a registered form certificated security involves indorsement or registration of the certificate under section 8-106. Control requires that the certificate be indorsed to the secured party, indorsed in blank with an *effective indorsement,* or registered in the secured party's name by the issuer. Section 8-107(b) provides that an *effective indorsement* of a security certificate occurs when the person specified by the certificate or by a special indorsement of the certificate indorses it, an authorized agent of such person indorses it, or the person entitled to the security has ratified the indorsement or is estopped from asserting its ineffectiveness.

Combining the two requirements results in establishing control of a registered form certificated security in various ways. Control is established when: 1) a secured party has possession of a properly indorsed certificate; 2) a secured party has possession of a certificate registered in the secured party's name; 3) another person has possession of a properly indorsed certificate; 4) another person has possession of a certificate registered in the secured party' name; 5) a securities intermediary acting on behalf of the secured party has possession of a properly indorsed certificate; 6) a securities intermediary acting on behalf of the secured party has possession of a certificate payable to the order of the secured party; or 7) a securities intermediary acting on behalf of the secured party has possession of a certificate registered in the secured party's name.

2. Uncertificated Security — Section 8-106(c)

An *uncertificated security*, defined in section 8-102(a)(18), is simply a security that is not represented by a certificate. Section 8-106(c) provides two ways a secured party can establish control of an uncertificated security. *First*, a secured party has control of an uncertificated security if it is delivered to the secured party. Although it seems incongruous to speak of delivery of a security for which no certificate exists, delivery of an uncertificated security nevertheless occurs pursuant to section 8-301(b) if: 1) the issuer of the security registers the secured party as registered owner; 2) another person becomes registered owner on behalf of the secured party; or 3) the current registered owner acknowledges that it holds the uncertificated security for the secured party. Obviously, there is no physical delivery of an uncertificated security.

Second, a secured party establishes control if the issuer of the security agrees that it will comply with instructions originated by the secured party without further consent by the entitlement holder (the owner of the rights and property of the security, generally the debtor). For example, Brown, the registered owner of 100 uncertificated shares of XYZ Corporation, grants a security interest in the shares as collateral for a loan from Bank. To achieve control, Brown and XYZ Corporation must agree that XYZ Corporation will comply with instructions originated by Bank. *Instructions* means a notification communicated to the issuer of an uncertificated security directing redemption of the security or registration of transfer of the security. Section 8-106(g) directs that an issuer cannot enter a control agreement with a secured party without obtaining the registered owner's or entitlement holder's consent. However, an issuer is not required to enter such an agreement even if the registered owner or entitlement holder so directs.

3. Security Entitlement — Section 8-106(d)

An example will help describe a security entitlement. Suppose Brown, who has a securities account with Barrelhouse, a broker, directs Barrelhouse to purchase 100 shares of ABC Corporation for Brown's securities account. When Barrelhouse credits Brown's account with the shares, Brown has a security entitlement and is the entitlement holder with respect to 100 ABC shares, although Brown is not typically the registered owner on the shareholder records of ABC Corporation. Section 8-102(a)(17) defines a *security entitlement* as the rights and property interest of an entitlement holder with respect to a financial asset. The financial asset is the 100 shares of ABC Corporation. Brown is the entitlement holder of a security that has been credited to his securities account, although he is not the registered owner or the holder of the security. Brown's rights as entitlement holder in the 100 shares consist of property interests and obligations in the shares, which the securities intermediary, typically a broker, owes to the entitlement holder. Those rights constitute the security entitlement. Barrelhouse is a securities intermediary under the definition of section 8-102(a)(14). Barrelhouse, or another securities intermediary, is generally the registered owner of the shares. The entitlement holder can create a security interest in the security entitlement.

Under section 8-106(d), a secured party establishes control of a security entitlement if: 1) the secured party becomes the entitlement holder; 2) the securities intermediary has agreed to comply with entitlement orders originated by the secured party without further consent by the entitlement holder; or 3) another person has control of the security entitlement on behalf of the secured party. If the debtor and the secured party agree that the secured party will establish control of the debtor's security entitlement by becoming the entitlement holder, the debtor—the current entitlement holder—will direct its securities intermediary to transfer the debtor's security entitlement in the financial asset to the secured party. The secured party becomes the entitlement holder as to the financial asset and has control when the financial asset is credited to the secured party's securities account.

The secured party can also establish control of the debtor's security entitlement if the debtor's securities intermediary agrees it will comply with entitlement orders originated by the secured party alone. A securities intermediary may not make a control agreement without obtaining the consent of the entitlement holder. However, a securities intermediary is not required to enter such an agreement although the entitlement holder so directs. The secured party can establish control although it does not have the exclusive right to issue entitlement orders. For example, the secured party, the debtor, and the securities intermediary might agree that both the secured party and the debtor have the right to give entitlement orders. In that situation, the secured party must be aware that the debtor retains power to sell the underlying financial asset. Consequently, exclusive control in the secured party is preferable.

The secured party also establishes control of the debtor's security entitlement if another person has control of the entitlement on behalf of the secured party. For example, Brown grants Bank a security interest in his security entitlement to 100 shares of ABC Corporation in Brown's securities account with Barrelhouse Brokers. Roundhouse Brokers agrees to act as Bank's agent with respect to Brown's security entitlement. Brown, Barrelhouse, and Roundhouse all agree that Roundhouse has the right to direct entitlement orders for Brown's security entitlement in the ABC Corporation shares. Roundhouse has control of the entitlement because Barrelhouse has agreed to comply with Roundhouse's entitlement orders without further consent of Brown. Bank has control because Roundhouse has control. Bank's control is not affected by permitting Brown to direct entitlement orders to Barrelhouse.

An entitlement holder might grant a security interest in its security entitlement to its securities intermediary. In that situation, section 8-106(e) provides that the securities intermediary establishes control simply from the entitlement holder's granting the security interest to the intermediary. This is automatic control; no action by the secured party is necessary.

4. Commodity Contract — Section 9-106(b)

Commodity contracts, defined in section 9-102(a)(15), are different from securities or other financial assets even though they can be traded on an exchange much like securities are traded. The typical commodity contract is a commodity futures contract pertaining to a raw material or agricultural product. In a commodity contract, a person contracts to buy or sell a commodity (the raw material or agricultural product) at a set price for delivery at a future time. Consequently, the contract may become advantageous or disadvantageous depending on the future increase or decrease in the price of the commodity.

Section 9-106(b) supplies the control provisions for a security interest in a commodity contract. It provides two methods to achieve control of a commodity contract. *First*, a secured party has control of a commodity contract if the commodity customer (typically the debtor), the secured party, and the commodity intermediary (typically a futures commission merchant; much like a stock broker) agree to apply any value distributed on account of the commodity contract as directed by the secured party without any further consent of the commodity customer. The agreement need not give the secured party the exclusive right to direct distributions. *Second*, a secured party who is also a commodity intermediary has control of its customer's commodity contract when its customer grants it a security interest in the customer's commodity contract. Such secured party has automatic control; no additional action is required.

5. Commodity or Securities Account — Section 9-106(c)

A securities account or commodity account is the account maintained by a securities or commodity intermediary in which the intermediary carries the securities entitlements or commodity contracts for the benefit of its customer. Section 9-106(c) provides that a secured party establishes control of a debtor's securities account or commodity account if the secured party has control over *all* security entitlements or commodity contracts carried in the respective accounts. Control of securities entitlements or commodity accounts requires satisfaction of the control conditions discussed in the preceding paragraphs with respect to the type of collateral involved in the secured transaction. It is logical that a secured party who has control of all security entitlements or commodity accounts in the debtor's securities or commodity account also has control over the account. Additionally, Official Comment 4 to section 9-106 declares that control of a securities or commodity account should be established if the secured party, debtor, and securities or commodity intermediary (whichever is applicable) agree that the intermediary will honor instructions from the secured party concerning the account without further consent of the debtor. Such an agreement implies that the intermediary will honor the secured party's instructions as to the particular entitlements or accounts.

B. Control of a Deposit Account— Section 9-104

Section 9-312(b)(1) states that a security interest in a deposit account can be perfected only by control, except for a security interest in a deposit account that arises as proceeds of collateral. A proceeds security interest in a deposit account is perfected automatically under section 9-315(d), discussed in Chapter 5. Deposit accounts are discussed in detail in Chapter 2, so review that material if you desire additional explanation of a deposit account.

Section 9-104 provides three separate methods by which a secured party can establish control of a deposit account. *First,* control is established automatically if the secured party is the bank with which the deposit account is maintained. For example, a bank that takes a security interest in its depositor's account to secure an obligation has control.

Second, control is established when the debtor, secured party, and the bank with which the deposit account is maintained all agree in an authenticated record that the bank will comply with the secured party's instructions directing disposition of the account's funds without further consent of the debtor. An *authenticated record* can be written or electronic. This agreement establishes control even if the debtor also retains the right to direct disposition of the account's funds or the agreement is subject to conditions, such as the secured party's power exists only in the event of the debtor's default. Section 9-342 authorizes a bank to refuse to enter a control agreement even if its customer requests it to do so. Consequently, if the secured party and the debtor agree to perfect a security interest in a deposit account by control but the bank refuses to enter a control agreement, the secured party must require the debtor to move its account to a bank that will enter a control agreement or establish control in the following manner.

Third, the secured party establishes control if it becomes the bank's customer as to the deposit account. A person becomes the bank's *customer*, in accordance with UCC Article 4, by having an account with a bank. The deposit account that will be the collateral is the debtor's deposit account. Consequently, the secured party cannot become the bank's customer as to the debtor's deposit account unless the debtor agrees to allow the secured party to become a party to the account, either solely or jointly with the other account owners. A secured party with control of a deposit account is subject to the duties imposed by sections 9-207(c) and 9-208(b)(1) and (2).

C. Control of Electronic Chattel Paper — Section 9-105

Electronic chattel paper, defined in section 9-102(a)(31), is chattel paper evidenced by a record consisting of information stored in an electronic medium. *Chattel paper*, defined in section 9-102(a)(11), basically is a record that evidences a monetary obligation secured by a security interest in specific goods. (Chattel paper is discussed in Chapter 1.) Filing a financing statement is not necessary to perfect a security interest in electronic chattel paper perfected by control. However, a security interest in electronic chattel paper can be perfected by filing a financing statement.

Section 9-105 provides six requirements to establish control of electronic chattel paper. The significance of the requirements is that control requires creation of a system that establishes an "authoritative copy" of the chattel paper and makes the unauthorized assignment or revision of the electronic chattel paper practically impossible. The control requirements are flexible to allow the secured party and debtor to create a system that achieves control. Section 9-105 requires: 1) a single unique, identifiable, and authoritative copy of the electronic chattel paper; 2) identifying the secured party as the assignee of the chattel paper; 3) the authoritative copy is communicated to and maintained by the secured party or its designated custodian; 4) revisions that add or change an identified assignee can be made only with the participation of the secured party; 5) any copy of the authoritative copy is readily identifiable as a copy; and 6) any revision of the authoritative copy is readily identifiable as an authorized or unauthorized revision. Section 9-314(b) states that a security interest is perfected when the secured party obtains control and remains perfected by control only while the secured party retains control. A secured party, other than a buyer, with control of electronic chattel paper is subject to the duties imposed by sections 9-207(c) and 9-208(b)(3).

D. Control of Letter-of-Credit Right — Sections 9-107, 5-114

Section 9-107 states that a secured party establishes control of a letter-of-credit right if the issuer or nominated person has consented to the assignment of the letter-of-credit proceeds under section 5-114 or under other applicable law or practice. *Letter-of-credit right,* as defined in section 9-102(a)(51), means a right to payment or performance under a letter of credit. A security interest in a letter-of-credit right refers to the assignment to the secured party by the beneficiary of the letter of credit of its right to the proceeds of a letter of credit. Except as a supporting obligation or as proceeds of collateral, a security interest in a letter-of-credit right can be perfected only by control.

Under section 5-114(d), neither the issuer nor the nominated person is obligated to consent to the assignment. Consent is not to be withheld unreasonably, however, if the secured party/assignee possesses and exhibits the letter of credit and presentation of the letter is a condition to the issuer or nominated person's duty to honor the letter. Sections 9-208(a) and (b)(5) obligate a secured party with control of a letter-of-credit right to send an authenticated release of control after receiving payment of the secured obligation.

In a letter of credit transaction, the issuer of the letter may designate a person — labeled a *nominated person* — to pay under a letter of credit. Consequently, both the issuer and the nominated person of a letter of credit may be obligated to pay the beneficiary. A secured party can establish control against both the issuer and the nominated person or against one such person, depending on whether both persons have consented to the beneficiary's security interest assignment.

E. Control of Electronic Document of Title — Sections 9-314, 7-106

Under section 9-102(a)(30), a *document* means a document of title. A *document of title,* defined in section 1-201(b)(16), covers goods that are in the possession of a person who is not generally the owner of the goods and the person in possession of the document has the right to receive, control, hold, and dispose of the document and the goods it covers. Typically, a person issues a document of title covering the goods when the owner of the goods delivers them to that person for storage or transportation of the goods. An electronic document of title is a document of title evidenced by a record consisting of information stored in an electronic medium. A document of title is either negotiable or nonnegotiable. A negotiable document of title authorizes delivery of the goods either to the bearer of the document or to the order of a person named in the document. Any other document is nonnegotiable.

A security interest in an electronic document of title may be perfected by control. Section 7-106 supplies two methods for establishing control. (Article 7 of the UCC governs documents of title.) *First*, under section 7-106(a), a person has control of an electronic document when it establishes a system for evidencing the transfer of the document, with the key to the system being that the identity of the person entitled to the document must be reliably established. *Second*, section 7-106(b) provides a safe harbor for establishing control by providing that a person is deemed to have control if the system established by the parties satisfies six requirements. The significance of the requirements is that they create a system under which a person should be able to identify the single authoritative copy of the document. The control requirements are flexible to allow the secured party and debtor to create a system that achieves control. Section 7-106(b) requires: 1) a single unique, identifiable, and authoritative copy of the document; 2) the authoritative copy identifies the secured party as the person to whom the document was issued or most recently transferred; 3) the authoritative copy is communicated to and maintained by the secured party or its designated custodian; 4) copies or amendments that add or change an identified assignee of the secured party can be made only with the consent of the secured party; 5) any copy of the authoritative copy is readily identifiable as a copy; and 6) any amendment of the authoritative copy is readily identifiable as authorized or unauthorized.

Checkpoints

- Control is a method of perfecting a security interest in a deposit account, electronic chattel paper, investment property, letter-of-credit right, and electronic document of title.

- Depending on the type of investment property, a secured party can establish control by delivery of the collateral to the secured party, by delivery plus indorsement or registration, or by obtaining an agreement from the appropriate person that the person will comply with orders from the secured party regarding the investment property.

- A secured party establishes control of a deposit account if the bank for the account agrees to honor instructions regarding the account originating from the secured party, the secured party becomes the bank's customer of the account, or the bank is the secured party in the account.

- A secured party establishes control of electronic chattel paper by creating a system that establishes an authoritative copy of the chattel paper and makes the unauthorized assignment or revision of the chattel paper practically impossible.

- A secured party establishes control of a letter-of-credit right if the issuer or nominated person of the letter of credit consents to the beneficiary's assignment of the letter-of-credit proceeds.

- A secured party establishes control of an electronic document of title by creating a system that establishes an authoritative copy of the document and requires the consent of the secured party to assignment of the document.

Chapter 5

Automatic Perfection, Temporary Automatic Perfection, and Perfection of Proceeds Security Interest — Sections 9-308, 9-309, 9-312, 9-315

Roadmap

- Security interests that are perfected automatically
- Security interests that are perfected upon attachment
- Security interests that are perfected automatically for twenty days
- Perfecting a security interest in proceeds of collateral

Article 9 creates exceptions to its general rule that a financing statement must be filed to perfect a security interest. Perfection of security interests in particular types of collateral occurs when the secured party satisfies the attachment requirements. A few security interests are perfected automatically. Other security interests are perfected automatically for a designated length of time — temporary automatic perfection. Finally, a security interest in proceeds of collateral is perfected automatically for a limited time or, depending on the type of proceeds, for its remaining duration. Nevertheless, a secured party who so desires can perfect most of those security interests by filing a financing statement.

A. Automatic Perfection — Sections 9-308, 9-309

1. Automatic Perfection of Secondary Collateral — Section 9-308

Section 9-308 subsections (d)–(g) establish automatic perfection of security interests in the collateral and transactions listed therein. The collateral for these security interests essentially is secondary to the principal collateral for the security interest; automatic perfection of these security interests results from perfection of the security interest in the principal collateral. There are four instances of automatic perfection: 1) a secured party who perfects a security interest in collateral automatically perfects a security interest in a supporting obligation to the collateral; 2) a secured party who perfects a security interest in a right to payment automatically perfects a security interest in a lien, mortgage, or security interest securing the right to payment; 3) a secured party who perfects a security interest in a securities account automatically perfects a security interest in the security entitlements carried in the account; and 4) a secured party who perfects a security interest in a commodity account automatically perfects a security interest in the commodity contracts carried in the account. These same security interests automatically attach under section 9-203 subsections (f)–(i), discussed in Chapter 2. Consequently, attachment and perfection of a security interest in these types of collateral is automatic if the secured party satisfies the attachment and perfection requirements for the principal collateral.

2. Automatic Perfection upon Attachment — Section 9-309

Section 9-309 lists thirteen types of security interests that are perfected when the secured party satisfies the attachment requirements. They differ from the security interests that automatically attach and are perfected under section 9-308 because a condition to perfection of these security interests is that the secured party must satisfy the attachment requirements. The following sections examine the more commonly occurring security interests that perfect automatically upon attachment.

a. Purchase-Money Security Interest in Consumer Goods — Section 9-309(1)

Section 9-309(1) provides that a purchase-money security interest in consumer goods is perfected upon attachment, unless a federal or state statute or treaty adopts a different rule. Section 9-102(a)(23) defines *consumer goods* as

goods used or bought for use primarily for personal, family, or household purposes. A purchase-money security interest is created when a seller of goods on
credit takes a security interest in the goods to secure all or part of the purchase
price or when a lender makes a loan to enable the debtor to purchase the goods
and takes a security interest in the goods to secure the loan. (Purchase-money
security interests are discussed in Chapter 8.) Automatic perfection pertains
only to purchase-money security interests in consumer goods, not to any other
purchase-money security interest.

The exception in section 9-309(1) typically applies to consumer goods governed by a certificate-of-title statute, such as motor vehicles. Certificate-of-title
statutes are enacted by states, and are not part of the UCC. Such laws supplant the automatic perfection rule of section 9-309(1). A secured party who
takes a purchase-money security interest in a consumer good motor vehicle
covered by a certificate-of-title statute must perfect the security interest by
complying with the perfection provisions of the applicable statute. Perfection
of a security interest in such property is discussed in Chapters 3 and 10.

b. Assignments of Accounts and Payment Intangibles— Section 9-309(2)

Section 9-309(2) provides that a security interest created by an assignment
of accounts or payment intangibles is perfected when it attaches, if the assignment does not alone or in conjunction with other assignments transfer a
significant part of the assignor's outstanding accounts or payment intangibles
to the assignee. Security interests in accounts and payment intangibles are discussed in Chapters 1 and 2. *Assignment* is the transfer of property or of an interest in property. It can be absolute, such as a sale of the account or payment
intangible, or for security purposes, such as the transfer of a security interest
in the account or payment intangible. For example, a security interest exists when
a debtor assigns an account or payment intangible as security for a debt and
when a debtor assigns (sells) an account or payment intangible in a sale transaction. Because both types of assignment create a security interest, the secured
party—the assignee—must satisfy Article 9's attachment and perfection requirements. However, if the assignment is of a type within section 9-309(2),
the security interest is perfected automatically when it attaches.

To be perfected upon attachment, the assignment must not transfer a significant part of the assignor's outstanding accounts or payment intangibles,
either alone or in conjunction with the assignor's other assignments to the assignee. Consequently, the assignment is examined alone and in combination
with other assignments, if any, to determine whether it transfers a significant

part of the assignor's accounts or payment intangibles. Unfortunately, section 9-309(2) gives no guidance on the meaning of *significant part*. However, Official Comment 4 to section 9-309 declares that the purpose of automatic perfection "is to save from *ex post facto* invalidation casual or isolated assignments — assignments which no one would think of filing." "*Ex post facto* invalidation" can result because an assignment creates a security interest, and if the secured party does not perfect the security interest it is subordinate (invalid) to most other claimants of an interest in the collateral. The comment further advises that "[a]ny person who regularly takes assignments of any debtor's accounts or payment intangibles should file." That is good advice. Additionally, even a casual, one-time assignment must be perfected if it transfers a significant part of the assignor's outstanding payment intangibles or accounts.

Courts have used two tests in determining whether an assignment transfers a significant part. One test follows the approach of the section 9-309 comment and permits perfection upon attachment if the assignment is casual or isolated and not part of a financing series. The second test compares the value of the accounts or payment intangibles that were assigned to the value of all such property of the debtor to determine if the transfer is a significant portion of that property. That leaves unanswered the question of how much is "significant." Courts have held that sixteen percent of a debtor's outstanding accounts is not significant, while twenty percent is significant. The lack of a bright-line test leads the careful secured party to file a financing statement to perfect any security interest created by the assignment of an account or payment intangible.

c. Health-Care-Insurance Receivables — Section 9-309(5)

Section 9-309(5) provides that a security interest created by the assignment of a health-care-insurance receivable to the provider of the health-care goods or services is perfected upon attachment. Section 9-102(a)(46) defines *health-care-insurance receivable* as "an interest in or claim under a policy of insurance which is a right to payment of a monetary obligation for health-care goods or services provided or to be provided." This receivable arises when an individual covered by medical insurance receives medical benefits (goods or services) and consequently has a claim for reimbursement (a right to payment) from her health insurance provider. The security interest arises when the individual assigns her right to the insurance payment to the provider of the health-care benefits. The assignment creates a security interest that is perfected upon attachment; the provider of health-care goods or services need not file a financing statement to perfect its security interest. The perfection-upon-attachment rule operates only for an assignment of the receivable to the provider of health care goods or services. If the provider assigns its right to the receivable to a secured party, that secured party must comply with Article 9's perfection requirements.

B. Temporary Automatic Perfection — Certificated Securities, Negotiable Documents, Instruments, or Goods Possessed by a Bailee Issuing a Nonnegotiable Document — Sections 9-312 (e)–(g)

Sections 9-312 (e)–(g) establish temporary automatic perfection of a security interest in the types of collateral listed therein. The perfection lasts for twenty days, after which the secured party must perfect the security interest by using an authorized Article 9 method. No perfection act is required during the twenty-day period.

Section 9-312(e) provides that a security interest is perfected for twenty days from the time of attachment if the secured party gives new value under an authenticated security agreement for a security interest in a certificated security, such as a stock certificate, an instrument, such as a promissory note, or a negotiable document, such as a warehouse receipt. Section 9-102(a)(57) defines *new value* as "(i) money, (ii) money's worth in property, services, or new credit, or (iii) release by a transferee of an interest in property previously transferred to the transferee." Under that definition, new value does not include taking the security interest as security for a prior debt or in payment of a prior debt. The definition of *authenticate*, section 9-102(a)(7), allows either a written or electronic security agreement.

A secured party can perfect a security interest in these types of collateral by taking possession of the collateral. Section 9-312(e)'s grant of temporary automatic perfection enables the security interest to be perfected although the secured party gives the debtor possession of the collateral. For example, suppose Bank loans money to Debtor on July 1 and takes a security interest in a promissory note (an instrument) owned by Debtor pursuant to a signed security agreement. Bank allows Debtor to retain the promissory note in order to present it for payment. Bank's security interest in the promissory note is perfected for twenty days from the time the security interest attaches without Bank taking any additional perfection action.

The perfection lapses after twenty days unless the secured party perfects the security interest using one of Article 9's authorized methods—filing a financing statement (section 9-312(a)) or taking possession of the collateral (section 9-313(a)). To maintain continuous perfection, the secured party must take the appropriate perfection action before the twenty-day period expires. A secured party who fails to perfect within that time can still perfect the security interest, but there will be a gap in perfection that allows a person who acquires an interest in the collateral during the gap to gain priority.

Section 9-312(f) maintains for twenty days the perfection of a *perfected* security interest in a negotiable document or in goods possessed by a bailee that issues a nonnegotiable document when the secured party allows the debtor to possess the goods or the document for one of the purposes specified in section 9-312(f). The purposes specified are: sale or exchange of the document or goods, and loading, unloading, storing, shipping, manufacturing, or processing the goods. This temporary perfection lapses after twenty days from the relinquishment of the goods or document unless the secured party reperfects the security interest using one of Article 9's authorized methods. Negotiable and nonnegotiable documents refer to documents of title—documents that cover the situation where the owner of goods delivers them to another person for storage or carriage.

You probably are asking why a secured party who has a perfected security interest needs the benefit of temporary automatic perfection. The answer is in the method of perfecting a security interest in this type of collateral. Section 9-312(c) authorizes a secured party to perfect a security interest in goods covered by a negotiable document by taking possession of the document. If a secured party perfects its security interest by that method and then relinquishes the document to the debtor, it does not fulfill the requirement for perfection. Consequently, the security interest would become unperfected were it not for section 9-312(f).

Section 9-312(g) maintains for twenty days the perfection of a *perfected* security interest in a certificated security or an instrument when the secured party delivers the security certificate or instrument to the debtor for the purposes listed in section 9-312(g). The purposes specified are: sale or exchange of the security certificate or the instrument, or presentation, collection, enforcement, renewal, or registration of transfer of the security certificate or the instrument. Temporary perfection benefits the secured party that perfects its security interest in an instrument or certificated security by taking possession of the collateral but agrees to allow the debtor to have possession for one of the section 9-312(g) purposes. The perfection lapses after twenty days from the relinquishment of the goods or document unless the secured party perfects the security interest using one of Article 9's authorized methods—filing or taking possession.

C. Perfecting a Security Interest in Proceeds of Collateral — Section 9-315

Section 9-315(a)(2) provides that a security interest attaches to any identifiable proceeds of collateral. Attachment of a security interest in proceeds does not depend on an agreement of the debtor to grant a security interest in proceeds. Under section 9-203(f), a security interest that attaches to collateral automatically gives the secured party the right to proceeds of collateral provided by section 9-315. Attachment of a security interests in proceeds is discussed in Chapter 2.

Section 9-315(c) provides that a security interest in proceeds is perfected if the security interest in the original collateral is perfected. Consequently, most security interests in proceeds continue perfected automatically. However, automatic perfection lasts for twenty days from the date the security interest attaches to the proceeds. On the twenty-first day after attachment, the security interest in proceeds becomes unperfected unless the security interest fits one of the situations established by section 9-315(d).

Section 9-315(d) provides a secured party with three methods to continue the perfection of a security interest in proceeds. The good news for secured parties is that two of the three methods do not require action by the secured party; if the security interest fits the rule, perfection continues automatically. The better news is that many, if not most, proceeds security interests will fit one of those two methods. However, if the security interest does not satisfy the conditions of section 9-315(d), the security interest becomes unperfected on the twenty-first day after attachment.

1. Perfecting a Security Interest in Proceeds That Are Not Cash Proceeds or Not Acquired with Cash Proceeds — Section 9-315(d)(1)

The first rule of section 9-315(d) covers all proceeds except cash proceeds and proceeds acquired with cash proceeds. *Cash proceeds* are defined in section 9-102(a)(9) as "money, checks, deposit accounts or the like." *Proceeds acquired with cash proceeds* are second generation proceeds: proceeds that the debtor acquires by using cash proceeds of the collateral. The following scenario illustrates proceeds covered and not covered by section 9-315(d)(1). Suppose Bank has a perfected security interest in Debtor's inventory. Debtor sells an item of inventory to Buyer who promises to pay in thirty days. That promise creates an account. The account is proceeds. It is not cash proceeds and Debtor did not acquire it with cash proceeds. Consequently, it is within the rule of section 9-315(d)(1). If Debtor sells an item of inventory collateral for cash, and uses the cash to buy a piece of equipment, the equipment is proceeds. However, it is not within the rule of section 9-315(d)(1)because Debtor acquired it with cash proceeds.

A security interest in proceeds continues perfected automatically under section 9-315(d)(1) if: 1) a filed financing statement covers the original collateral; 2) the secured party could perfect a security interest in the proceeds by filing a financing statement in the office where the financing statement covering the collateral was filed; and 3) the proceeds were not acquired with cash proceeds. The second condition is really two conditions: the proceeds must be a type of collateral for which Article 9 authorizes perfection by filing a financing statement, and that financing statement would be filed in the same office where the financing statement covering the original collateral was filed. Section 9-310(a) authorizes filing a financing statement to perfect a security interest for practically all types of collateral. Section 9-501, with limited exceptions, establishes the same office as the place of filing for all financing statements regardless of the type of collateral. Consequently, most proceeds security interests will fulfill the requirements of the second condition. Note that perfection of a security interest in proceeds under section 9-315(d)(1) does not require the actual filing of a financing statement, only that filing is an authorized method of perfection for the collateral and the place of filing is the same office as the financing statement already filed.

For example, suppose Lender perfects a security interest in Debtor's inventory by filing a financing statement. Debtor sells an item of inventory on open credit creating an account. The account is proceeds. Article 9 authorizes filing as a method of perfecting a security interest in an account. If Lender were to file a financing statement covering the account, it would file it in the same office where Lender filed the financing statement covering the inventory, assuming that Debtor's location has not changed. Debtor did not acquire the account with cash proceeds. Consequently, the security interest in the account remains perfected after twenty-days because all conditions of section 9-315(d)(1) are satisfied.

Section 9-315(e) provides that a security interest in proceeds perfected under section 9-315(d)(1) remains perfected until the "later of" when the filed financing statement lapses or is terminated or the twenty-first day after attachment of the security interest to the proceeds. *Later of* gives the secured party twenty-days of perfection even if the filed financing statement covering the collateral becomes ineffective during that time, such as if the five-year life of the financing statement expires during the twenty-day period.

2. Perfecting a Security Interest in Identifiable Cash Proceeds — Section 9-315(d)(2)

The second rule of section 9-315(d) applies only to proceeds that are identifiable cash proceeds. Section 9-102(a)(9) defines *cash proceeds* as money, checks, deposit accounts or the like. Section 9-315(d)(2) provides that a security interest in identifiable cash proceeds continues perfected automatically after the twenty-day period expires. There are no conditions or requirements to this automatic perfection other than that the cash proceeds are identifiable and that the security interest in the original collateral was perfected. Money deposited in a deposit account is still identifiable under the *lowest intermediate balance rule*, discussed in Chapter 2. Official Comment 7 to section 9-315 clarifies the duration-of-perfection rule of section 9-315(e). It declares that a security interest in cash proceeds remains perfected indefinitely, even if the security interest in the original collateral becomes unperfected.

3. Perfection of Other Proceeds — Section 9-315(d)(3)

The third rule of section 9-315(d) provides for continuous perfection of a security interest in proceeds *if* the secured party perfects the security interest by an applicable method of perfection no later than twenty days after attachment of the security interest to the proceeds. Compliance with this rule generally requires that the secured party fulfill Article 9's perfection requirements for the type of collateral that constitutes the proceeds — in other words, take action to perfect the security interest in the proceeds. Consequently, perfection of the proceeds security interest under section 9-315(d)(3) is not generally automatic. However, no action is necessary if the proceeds are a type of collateral in which a security interest is perfected upon attachment under section 9-309. Otherwise, the secured party must perfect the security interest within twenty days after attachment. If the secured party fails to perfect, the proceeds security interest becomes unperfected on the twenty-first day.

An example illustrates the third rule. Suppose Creditor has a perfected security interest in Debtor's inventory. Debtor sells an item of inventory for cash. As cash proceeds, the security interest is automatically perfected under section 9-315(d)(2). Debtor uses the cash to buy equipment. The equipment is proceeds. Section 9-315(d)(1) is inapplicable because the proceeds are acquired with cash proceeds. To maintain perfection after twenty days, Creditor must perfect the security interest under one of Article 9's authorized methods. Creditor can perfect this security interest by taking possession of the equipment if the debtor consents, by filing a financing statement that describes the collateral as the equipment, or by amending the filed financing statement to include the equipment. A debtor authorizes these filings under section 9-509(b).

Checkpoints

- A perfected security interest in collateral automatically perfects a security interest in a supporting obligation for the collateral.

- A perfected security interest in a right to payment automatically perfects a security interest in a lien, mortgage, or security interest securing the right to payment.

- A perfected security interest in a securities or commodity account automatically perfects a security interest in the security entitlements or commodity contracts carried in the account.

- The security interests listed in section 9-309 are perfected when the secured party satisfies the attachment requirements for the security interest.

- A security interest in a certificated security, instrument, or negotiable document is perfected automatically for twenty days if the secured party gives new value and the debtor authenticates a security agreement.

- A perfected security interest in a document, certificated security, or instrument is perfected for twenty days after the secured party relinquishes the document to the debtor for the purposes listed in section 9-312(f) and (g).

- A security interest in proceeds of collateral is perfected for twenty days after it attaches if the security interest in the collateral was perfected.

- A perfected security interest in proceeds remains perfected after twenty days if the proceeds could be perfected by filing a financing statement in the office where the financing statement covering the original collateral is filed and the proceeds were not acquired with cash proceeds.

- A perfected security interest in cash proceeds remains perfected automatically for the duration of the security interest.

- Other proceeds security interests do not remain perfected after twenty days unless the secured party perfects the proceeds security interest using a method authorized by Article 9.

Chapter 6

General Priority of a Perfected or Unperfected Security Interest and a Security Interest in Proceeds

Roadmap

- Priority of an unperfected security interest against a security interest, transferee, or lien creditor
- Priority of a perfected security interest against a perfected security interest
- Priority of a proceeds security interest
- Subordination of a security interest perfected by a financing statement containing incorrect information
- Priority of a lien arising by operation of law

A. Introduction and General Priority Rule — Section 9-201

Sections 9-317 to 9-339 establish the rules for determining priority between persons with conflicting claims to the collateral. Conflicting claims arise when the debtor creates more than one security interest in the collateral, when a creditor with a judgment obtains a lien on the collateral, or when the debtor transfers its interest in the collateral to another person, such as a sale to a buyer. If the debtor is able to satisfy all the obligations the collateral secures, no person is harmed by the presence of other interests in the collateral. However, if the debtor defaults in satisfying those obligations, then each person with an interest in the collateral will be competing for the right to have *priority* in the collateral.

Priority is the right to be first in line to use the collateral to satisfy the obligation the debtor owes. Having priority is important to the secured party because priority allows the secured party to control the disposition of the collateral if the debtor defaults. Additionally, the person with priority uses as much of the value of the collateral, even all of it, as is necessary to satisfy the obligation the collateral secures. Consequently, a person with a subordinate interest in the collateral (also known as a *junior* interest) may never be able to use the collateral to satisfy the obligation the debtor owes it and be left with only its cause of action against the debtor on the debtor's promise to pay.

For most security interests, a secured party who perfects its security interest completes all the acts Article 9 requires for achieving priority. However, a perfected security interest does not guarantee priority. Article 9's priority rules determine whether a perfected security interest has priority over the interests of other persons in the collateral. Nevertheless, a secured party should perfect its security interest because an unperfected security interest is subordinate to most other claimants to the collateral.

Section 9-201(a) functions as a general rule of priority by declaring "a security agreement is effective according to its terms between the parties, against purchasers of the collateral and against creditors" except as Article 9 otherwise provides. Under this rule, a secured party's security interest is effective against other interests in the collateral regardless of whether it is perfected. A security interest that is effective against other interests has priority over those interests. However, section 9-201(a) rarely decides priority conflicts because Article 9 adopts many rules that determine priority between competing claimants. Those rules supersede the general rule of section 9-201(a).

B. Unperfected Security Interests and Agricultural Liens — Section 9-317

Section 9-317 adopts priority rules that subordinate an unperfected security interest to buyers, lessees, licensees, lien creditors, and other secured parties. The rules operate in the same manner against an unperfected agricultural lien. Although the title of section 9-317 does not indicate that its scope is unperfected security interests, Official Comment 2 to section 9-317 remarks that the section pertains to "persons who take priority over, or take free of, an unperfected security interest." Consequently, section 9-317 is known as the section that determines the priority of an unperfected security interest.

1. Conflicting Perfected Security Interest — Section 9-317(a)(1)

It is entirely logical that an unperfected security interest is subordinate to a perfected security interest in the same collateral, and that is the effect of section 9-317(a)(1). Section 9-317(a)(1) declares that an unperfected security interest is subordinate to persons entitled to priority under section 9-322. Section 9-322 governs the priority between conflicting *perfected* security interests. If a perfected security interest is superior to another perfected security interest, it should be superior to an unperfected security interest. Section 9-322(a)(2) leaves no doubt as to that result. "A perfected security interest or agricultural lien has priority over a conflicting unperfected security interest or agricultural lien." The rule of section 9-317(a)(1) is the same as the rule of section 9-322(a)(2), although the Article 9 drafters did not use those same words in section 9-317(a)(1). Notice that the attachment times of the conflicting security interests are not relevant to priority. An unperfected security interest is subordinate to a perfected security interest although it attached first. Equally irrelevant is the secured party's knowledge of the unperfected security interest.

2. Lien Creditors — Sections 9-317(a)(2), (e)

A *lien creditor*, defined in section 9-102(a)(52), is a creditor that acquires a lien on property by "attachment, levy, or the like" or a person who is an assignee for benefit of creditors, a trustee in bankruptcy, or a receiver in equity. The latter three persons are lien creditors by Article 9 definition, not because they have taken some action against the property. Each becomes a lien creditor upon its appointment. Of these three persons, the bankruptcy trustee is the person most likely to assert rights against a secured party. A debtor seldom uses the other two mechanisms to administer property and debts.

The traditional lien creditor is a creditor that acquires a lien on the collateral by "attachment, levy, or the like." The words *attachment* and *levy* indicate the type of action a creditor takes to obtain the lien; *or the like* refers to attachment and levy so it covers other acts of law or judicial process that result in a lien. The typical lien creditor is a person who has an unsatisfied judgment against a debtor, obtains a writ of execution from the court, and instructs the sheriff to seize the debtor's property to satisfy the judgment. The lien attaches the property to the extent of the unsatisfied judgment. A lien creditor also includes a person who obtains a lien on the debtor's property by a prejudgment attachment in an action against the debtor. All jurisdictions have laws that specify the steps a creditor must take to become a lien creditor. Article 9 adopts no requirements for a lien creditor other than the definitional requirements of section 9-102(a)(52).

The other lien creditors are appointed in a federal or state proceeding. A *trustee in bankruptcy*, appointed when a debtor commences a federal bankruptcy, represents the estate created by the commencement of a bankruptcy. The estate includes all property in which the debtor has an interest. The trustee administers the debtor's property for all creditors and consequently is frequently in conflict with a secured party over the priority and validity of a security interest. An *assignee for benefit of creditors* is appointed in a state statutory proceeding that is similar to a federal bankruptcy. The assignee liquidates the debtor's property and distributes it to creditors. Like the bankruptcy trustee, the assignee seeks to control the property that serves as collateral for a security interest and may contest the validity and priority of a security interest. A *receiver in equity* is a person a state court appoints to collect and protect property of the debtor that is subject to diverse claims. The receiver might assert rights in property that conflict with the rights of a secured party.

Section 9-317(a)(2) establishes rules for determining the priority between an unperfected security interest and a lien creditor. A security interest is subordinate to a person who becomes a lien creditor before the *earlier* of perfection of the security interest or the time the secured party files a financing statement against the collateral and satisfies one of the debtor's-agreement attachment conditions of section 9-203(b)(3). The rules subordinate a security interest that the secured party delays in perfecting or fails to perfect. For example, suppose Debtor grants Bank a security interest in all its equipment. Before Bank files a financing statement or otherwise perfects its security interest, Finance Company becomes a lien creditor with respect to Debtor's equipment. Bank's unperfected security interest is subordinate to Finance Company's interest in Debtor's equipment. The result does not change if the secured party perfects its security interest after the person becomes a lien creditor—the lien creditor still has priority over the security interest. However, a security interest that is perfected before the person becomes a lien creditor has priority over the lien creditor. Section 9-317(a)(2) also subordinates an agricultural lien to a person who becomes a lien creditor before the lienholder perfects the lien.

Although unperfected, a security interest can have priority over a lien creditor under the second part of the rule, section 9-317(a)(2)(B). A security interest is subordinate to a lien creditor only if the person becomes a lien creditor before the *earlier* of perfection of the security interest or the time a financing statement is filed and the secured party has satisfied one of the debtor's-agreement attachment conditions. Consequently, an unperfected security interest is not subordinate to a lien creditor if the secured party files a financing statement and satisfies one of the debtor's-agreement conditions before the person becomes a lien creditor. Those conditions, discussed in Chapter 2, are: the debtor authenticates a security agreement; the secured party possesses the collateral; or the secured party takes delivery of a registered form certificated security collateral. This rule should motivate a secured party to file its financing statement as soon as the debtor authorizes the filing.

For example, suppose Debtor applies for a secured loan with Bank and signs all necessary documents, including a security agreement that describes the collateral as all equipment. Bank files a financing statement, although it has not decided whether to make the loan to Debtor. (Remember that the debtor authorizes the filing of a financing statement under section 9-509(b) when it authenticates the security agreement.) The security interest has not attached and is not perfected because Bank has not given value to Debtor. Before Bank decides whether to make the loan, Finance Company becomes a lien creditor with respect to Debtor's equipment. Bank then makes the loan, and that act completes the attachment and perfection of Bank's security interest. Bank's security interest is not subordinate to Finance Company because Finance Company became a lien creditor after Debtor authenticated a security agreement—one of the debtor's-agreement attachment conditions—and after Bank filed a financing statement.

Section 9-317(e) creates an exception to the priority of a lien creditor when the unperfected security interest is a purchase-money security interest. (Purchase-money security interests are discussed in Chapter 8.) If a secured party with a purchase-money security interest files a financing statement before or within twenty days after the debtor receives delivery of the collateral, the security interest is superior to a person who becomes a lien creditor between the time the security interest attaches and the time of filing the financing statement. This exception enables a purchase-money security interest to have priority over a lien creditor although the person became a lien creditor before the purchase-money security interest was perfected.

For example, on April 17 Seller finances Debtor's purchase of an item of equipment and secures the purchase price with a purchase-money security interest in the equipment. Seller delivers the equipment to Debtor on May 1. On May 15, before Seller files a financing statement or otherwise perfects its purchase-money security interest, Bank becomes a lien creditor with respect to Debtor's equipment, including the purchase-money equipment. Section 9-317(a)(2) subordinates Seller's security interest to Bank because Bank becomes a lien creditor before Seller perfects its security interest. However, Seller perfects by filing a financing statement on May 19. Seller's purchase-money security interest has priority over Bank under the rule of section 9-317(e) because Seller filed its financing statement within twenty days after Debtor received delivery of the collateral.

3. Buyers, Lessees, and Licensees — Sections 9-317(b)–(e)

A security interest generally continues in collateral under the rule of section 9-315(a) notwithstanding that the debtor sells, leases, licenses, or otherwise disposes of the collateral. (Section 9-315 is discussed in Chapter 7.) Consequently, the transferee in those dispositions takes the collateral subject to the security interest, regardless of whether it agrees to be liable for the secured debt. However, a buyer, lessee, or licensee of collateral who satisfies the section 9-317 requirements takes the collateral free of an unperfected security interest or agricultural lien.

Section 9-317(b) establishes a rule protecting a buyer who buys tangible chattel paper, tangible documents, goods, instruments, or a certificated security that is subject to a security interest. A buyer, other than a secured party, "takes free" of a security interest or agricultural lien if the buyer gives value and receives delivery of the collateral without knowledge of the security interest or agricultural lien and before it is perfected. *Takes free* means that the buyer's interest in the collateral is free of the security interest. This is not a priority rule that gives the buyer first use of the collateral to recover what it paid, leaving the secured party with whatever value remains. The secured party has no security interest in the collateral against the buyer.

The buyer must satisfy all the section 9-317(b) conditions to take the collateral free of the security interest. The buyer must: 1) buy collateral listed in section 9-317(b); 2) give value for the collateral without having knowledge of the security interest and before it is perfected; and 3) receive delivery of the collateral without having knowledge of the security interest and before it is perfected. *Value*, defined in section 1-204, includes making a loan or commitment to make a loan, having a pre-existing claim, or any consideration sufficient to support a simple contract. In the UCC, *knowledge* always means actual knowledge under the rule of section 1-202(b).

The phrase "a buyer, other than a secured party" in section 9-317(b) pertains to sales of tangible chattel paper or promissory notes (a type of instrument). Because Article 9 treats a sale of chattel paper or a promissory note as a security interest (discussed in Chapter 1), the rules governing priority between security interests determines priority between the buyer and an unperfected security interest in the chattel paper or promissory note. However, if section 9-109(d) excludes the sale from Article 9 governance, then the buyer is not a secured party and section 9-317 applies.

Section 9-317(c) adopts the same rule for lessees of goods. A lessee of goods takes free of a security interest or agricultural lien if it gives value and takes delivery of the collateral without knowledge of the security interest or agricultural lien and before it is perfected.

Section 9-317(e) creates an exception that allows a purchase-money security interest to have priority over a buyer or lessee. If a secured party with a purchase-money security interest files a financing statement before or within twenty days after the debtor receives delivery of the collateral, the security interest is superior to a person who buys or leases the collateral between the time the security interest attaches and the time of filing. For example, on April 17 Seller sells Debtor equipment and secures the purchase price with a purchase-money security interest in the equipment. Seller delivers the equipment to Debtor on May 1. On May 15, before Seller files a financing statement or otherwise perfects its security interest, Buyer buys and receives the purchase-money equipment without knowledge of the security interest. Buyer takes free of the security interest under section 9-317(b). However, Seller perfects by filing a financing statement on May 19. Consequently, Seller's purchase-money security interest has priority over Buyer under section 9-317(e) because Seller filed its financing statement within twenty days after Debtor received delivery of the collateral.

Section 9-317(d) adopts a rule enabling specific licensees and buyers to take the collateral free of an unperfected security interest. A licensee of a general intangible or a buyer, other than a secured party, of accounts, general intangibles, electronic chattel paper, electronic documents, or investment property, other than a certificated security, takes the collateral free of a security interest if the licensee or buyer gives value without knowledge of the security interest and before it is perfected. Section 9-317(d) establishes a rule similar to the rules for buyers and lessees, with the difference being that no delivery of the collateral is required because the section 9-317(d) collateral is intangible property that cannot be delivered. The phrase *buyer, other than a secured party* pertains to the sale of an account, electronic chattel paper, or a payment intangible. Because Article 9 treats a sale of such property as a security interest, the priority rules for security interests determine priority, not the rule of section 9-317(d). However, if section 9-109(d) excludes the sale from Article 9 governance, then the buyer is not a secured party and section 9-317(d) applies.

C. Priority between Perfected Security Interests or Agricultural Liens — Section 9-322

1. Priority in the Collateral — Section 9-322(a)

Frequently, two or more perfected security interests exist in the same collateral. Section 9-322 states general rules determining priority in the collateral and proceeds of the collateral between competing security interests or agricultural liens. The rules of section 9-322 are subject to Article 9's specific rules of priority that govern particular types of collateral and purchase-money security interests. Nevertheless, section 9-322 is the default rule for priority between perfected security interests; if there is no specific rule determining priority, section 9-322 applies.

Section 9-322(a)(1) states the general rule of priority for all perfected security interests and agricultural liens. It is labeled the *first-to-file-or-perfect* rule. The section determines the priority between conflicting perfected security interests based on priority in time of filing or perfection. Determining priority is a two-step process. *First*, use the rule of section 9-322(a)(1) to determine the date of priority for each security interest or agricultural lien involved in the conflict: "priority dates" from the earlier of the time a filing covering the collateral is first made or the security interest or agricultural lien is first perfected if there is no time thereafter when there is neither filing nor perfection. This simply requires determining the time when each conflicting security interest became perfected, or, if the security interest is perfected by filing, the time the financing statement was filed. The earlier of those two times is the date of priority (or *priority date*) of the security interest, provided that there is no time thereafter when there is neither filing nor perfection of the security interest. The proviso means that priority dates from the earlier time if there is no gap in the perfection of the security interest or lapse of the effectiveness of the financing statement, whichever event establishes the priority date of the security interest. *Second*, compare the priority date of each conflicting security interest. Priority goes to the security interest with the earliest priority date. A secured party's knowledge or lack of knowledge of the other security interest or agricultural lien is irrelevant to priority. In essence, the rule creates a race to file or perfect; the secured party that wins the race has priority. The rule is the same if the conflict is between agricultural liens or a security interest and an agricultural lien.

The rationale for using the first-to-file-or-perfect rule to determine priority is to protect the notice given by the filing system. When a prospective secured party checks the filing records and finds no financing statements filed against the collateral, it can rely on its financing statement as being the first financing statement filed and determinative of its priority date for its security interest. When a subsequent secured party checks the records, it will discover the financing statement of the first secured party and consequently is on notice of the potential security interest and priority of the first secured party.

The following example demonstrates the rule of section 9-322(a)(1). Bank files a financing statement on August 19 covering all equipment of Debtor after Debtor applies for a loan and authenticates a security agreement, but before Bank decides whether to make the loan. On September 1 Lender makes a loan to Debtor and perfects a security interest by filing a financing statement covering all equipment of Debtor. On September 15 Bank, with knowledge of Lender's security interest, makes a loan to Debtor which functions to complete attachment and perfection of Bank's security interest. Bank has priority; it is *the first to file or perfect*. Bank's security interest has a priority date of August 19, the earlier of the time it perfected its security interest (September 15) or filed its financing statement (August 19). Lender has a priority date of September 1, because it perfected its security interest on September 1 and filed its financing statement on September 1. Comparing the priority dates of Bank and Lender shows that Bank has the earlier priority date, and consequently it has priority.

It is possible for a secured party to change the method it uses to perfect its security interest without changing the priority date of its security interest, *provided* there is no period when there is neither filing nor perfection of the security interest. For example, on April 5 Bank acquires a temporarily perfected security interest in a negotiable document of title (twenty days of automatic perfection under section 9-312(e)). On April 15, Lender perfects a security interest in the same document by filing a financing statement. Bank files a financing statement against the document on April 22, during the twenty-day period of temporary perfection. Bank's security interest has priority because it has an earlier priority date. Although Bank changed the method of perfecting its security interest from temporary-automatic perfection to perfection by filing, there was never a period when Bank was not perfected. Consequently, its priority date remains April 5, an earlier priority date than the April 15 priority date of Lender. If Bank first files a financing statement on April 27, Lender has priority. That scenario engages the proviso of section 9-322(a)(1)—there is a period when there is neither filing nor perfection of Bank's security interest. Consequently, Bank does not retain its April 5 priority date. Its priority date is April 27, later than the April 15 priority date of Lender.

Section 9-322(a) includes two additional rules determining priority between security interests and agricultural liens. *First*, if the priority conflict is between a perfected security interest or agricultural lien and an unperfected security interest or lien, the perfected interest has priority over the unperfected interest under the rule of section 9-322(a)(2). A perfected security interest always has priority over an unperfected security interest, regardless of which security interest attached first. Knowledge of the unperfected security interest is irrelevant to priority. *Second*, if none of the conflicting security interests or agricultural liens are perfected, the first security interest to attach or, for agricultural liens, to become effective, has priority under the rule of section 9-322(a)(3).

The section 9-322(a) priority rules are subject to a special rule for the holder of an agricultural lien. Section 9-322(g) awards a perfected agricultural lien priority over a conflicting agricultural lien or security interest if the statute creating the agricultural lien so provides. Consequently, the statute that creates an agricultural lien can adopt a priority rule that supplants the rules of section 9-322(a). If it does not, section 9-322(a) determines priority.

2. Priority in Proceeds and Supporting Obligations — Section 9-322

Article 9 automatically extends a security interest in collateral to any identifiable proceeds of the collateral and to a supporting obligation of the collateral. (Proceeds and supporting obligations are discussed in Chapter 2.) Section 9-322 provides rules for determining the priority of such security interests. Unless otherwise noted, the priority rules discussed below are the same for security interests in proceeds and supporting obligations.

The first-to-file-or-perfect rule of section 9-322(a)(1) determines priority between conflicting security interests in proceeds or a supporting obligation, unless Article 9 establishes a different rule. Section 9-322(b) establishes the priority date of a security interest in proceeds or a supporting obligation for the purpose of applying the section 9-322(a)(1) priority rule. The rule states that the time of filing or perfection of the security interest in the collateral is the time of filing or perfection of the security interest in proceeds or a supporting obligation. Consequently, a security interest in proceeds or a supporting obligation has the same priority date as the security interest in the collateral that produces the proceeds or supporting obligation. Priority goes to the security interest with the earliest priority date.

For example, suppose Bank perfects a security interest in Debtor's equipment on August 17. Debtor sells an item of equipment on September 25 to a buyer who promises to pay for the equipment in thirty days. The promise to pay creates an account that is a proceed of the collateral. Bank has a perfected security interest in the account. The priority date for the account is August 17, although the account was created on September 25.

a. Priority Rules for Proceeds of "Non-filing Collateral"— Sections 9-322(c)–(e)

The proceeds and supporting obligation priority rule of section 9-322(a) is subject to the more complicated priority rules of sections 9-322(c), (d), and (e) for proceeds and supporting obligations of "non-filing collateral." These sections establish three rules that govern priority in proceeds and supporting obligations of a security interest in deposit accounts, negotiable documents, investment property, letter-of-credit rights, chattel paper, and instruments. Official Comment 8 to section 9-322 labels those types of collateral "non-filing collateral" because a secured party can, and usually does, perfect a security interest in that collateral by using a method other than filing a financing statement.

The priority rule of section 9-322(c)(1) determines priority between conflicting security interests in a *supporting obligation* when the underlying collateral is a deposit account, negotiable document, investment property, letter-of-credit right, chattel paper, or instrument. It awards priority to the security interest that would have priority in the underlying collateral under the applicable Article 9 priority rule for such collateral. (Those rules are established in sections 9-327, 9-328, 9-329, 9-330, and 9-331, discussed in Chapter 9.) For example, section 9-328 determines the priority of a security interest in investment property perfected by control. Section 9-322(c)(1) grants priority in a supporting obligation for such collateral to whichever security interest has priority in the investment property under section 9-328.

The priority rule of section 9-322(c)(2) determines priority between conflicting security interests in *proceeds* when the underlying collateral is a deposit account, negotiable document, investment property, letter-of-credit right, chattel paper, or instrument. It awards priority in proceeds to the security interest that would have priority in the underlying collateral if three conditions are satisfied: 1) the security interest in the proceeds is perfected (perfection of a proceeds security interest is discussed in Chapter 5); 2) the proceeds are cash proceeds or the same type as the underlying collateral; and 3) when the security interest is in proceeds of proceeds, all intervening proceeds are cash proceeds, the same type of proceeds as the underlying collateral, or an account created by disposition of the collateral. For example, suppose Bank perfects a security interest in all investment property of Debtor by filing a financing statement. Lender subsequently perfects a security interest in the same investment property by establishing control. Lender has priority in the investment property under the priority rule of section 9-328, regardless that it was not first to file or perfect. Debtor receives a cash dividend from the stock—*cash proceeds*.

Lender has priority in the proceeds under section 9-322(c)(2) because its security interest in the proceeds is perfected and the proceeds are cash proceeds. If the secured party does not satisfy all the conditions of section 9-322(c)(2), section 9-322(a) determines priority of the proceeds security interest.

Section 9-322(d) establishes a rule for determining priority between security interests in *proceeds* of non-filing collateral when the proceeds are *filing collateral*. Filing collateral includes accounts, general intangibles, goods, payment intangibles, commercial tort claims, and nonnegotiable documents — types of collateral in which a secured party perfects a security interest by filing. The proceeds priority rule of section 9-322(c)(2), discussed in the previous paragraph, essentially limits its scope to proceeds of non-filing collateral that are themselves non-filing collateral or cash proceeds because its conditions for priority require that the proceeds are the same type as the collateral or are cash proceeds. It becomes clear that the scope of section 9-322(d) is limited to proceeds that are filing collateral when sections 9-322(d) and (e) are read together. Section 9-322(d) establishes a rule of priority for proceeds when the collateral is "chattel paper, deposit accounts, negotiable documents, instruments, investment property, or letter-of-credit rights perfected by a method other than filing," without limitation to the type of proceeds. However, section 9-322(d) is expressly subject to section 9-322(e), which commands that section 9-322(d) applies only if the proceeds of collateral "are not cash proceeds, chattel paper, negotiable documents, instruments, investment property, or letter-or-credit rights," all of which are non-filing collateral.

The priority rule of section 9-322(d) ranks conflicting security interests in proceeds according to priority in time of filing as to the proceeds. This is a first-to-file rule, not a first-to-file-or-perfect rule. For example, suppose Bank perfects a security interest in Debtor's deposit account by establishing control. Subsequently, Lender perfects a security interest in Debtor's existing and after-acquired equipment by filing a financing statement covering all equipment. Debtor uses funds in the deposit account to purchase equipment, which Bank can identify as proceeds of the deposit account. Bank perfects its proceeds security interest in the equipment by filing a financing statement covering the equipment within 20 days of Debtor's acquisition of it. Because Lender is the first party to file a financing statement against the equipment, it has priority in the equipment under section 9-322(d), which ranks conflicting security interests by time of filing. Although Bank would have priority in the equipment under the first-to-file-or-perfect rule of section 9-322(a) because it has an earlier priority date, that rule is subject to section 9-322(d). Section 9-322(c) does not apply because the proceeds (equipment) are not cash proceeds or of the same type as the collateral (deposit account).

D. Priority of Security Interest or Agricultural Lien Perfected by Financing Statement Containing Incorrect Information — Section 9-338

Section 9-338 determines the priority of a security interest or an agricultural lien against certain secured parties and purchasers when a filed financing statement contains incorrect information of the type described in section 9-516(b)(5). Section 9-516(b)(5) requires that a financing statement include the debtor's mailing address, indicate whether the debtor is an individual or an organization, and, for organization debtors, indicate the type of organization, its jurisdiction, and its identification number (hereinafter "debtor's information"). Although section 9-520(a) directs a filing officer to refuse a financing statement that omits that information, a filing officer is not authorized to determine the accuracy of information provided in a financing statement. Consequently, a filed financing statement may be effective but inaccurate.

Section 9-338(1) states that a security interest or agricultural lien perfected by a financing statement containing incorrect debtor's information is subordinate to a perfected security interest to the extent that the secured party gives value in reasonable reliance upon the incorrect information. The security interest perfected by that financing statement otherwise would have priority. Article 9 does not indicate what constitutes "reasonable reliance" on the incorrect information. However, Official Comment 2 to section 9-338 notes that a person "who has not made itself aware of the information in the filing office with respect to the debtor cannot act in 'reasonable reliance' upon incorrect information." In other words, a conflicting secured party cannot act in reasonable reliance on the incorrect information unless it sees or otherwise has knowledge of the contents of the financing statement. The relevance of the incorrect information also seems important in establishing reasonable reliance. A secured party should have to prove that the incorrect information was a factor in its decision to enter the secured transaction if the earlier perfected security interest is to be subordinated because of incorrect information in the financing statement. The comment indicates that a subsequent buyer or secured party would rely on the misinformation to its detriment on "rare occasions."

Section 9-338(2) enables a purchaser of collateral, other than a secured party, to take free of the security interest or agricultural lien that is perfected by filing a financing statement containing incorrect debtor's information.

The requirements for taking free vary depending on the type of collateral. Section 9-338(2) states that a purchaser of tangible chattel paper, tangible documents, goods, instruments, or a security certificate takes the collateral free of a security interest or agricultural lien to the extent the purchaser gives value and receives delivery of the collateral in reasonable reliance on the misinformation. A purchaser of other types of collateral takes the collateral free of a security interest or agricultural lien perfected by a financing statement containing incorrect information to the extent the purchaser gives value in reasonable reliance on the misinformation. Because the *other types* of collateral are intangible collateral, there is no delivery requirement. The *reasonable reliance* standard should be the same for purchasers as it is for secured parties because sections 9-338(1) and (2) both use the term "reasonable reliance."

Section 9-338 does not apply when a financing statement includes other types of incorrect information. Nor does it apply when the information required by section 9-516(b)(5) becomes incorrect after filing. Sections 9-506 and 9-507, discussed in Chapter 3, determine the effectiveness of a financing statement in those situations.

E. Priority of Lien Arising by Operation of Law — Section 9-333

Section 9-333 determines the priority between a security interest and a *possessory lien* arising by statute or operation of law. Section 9-333(a) adopts three requirements of a *possessory lien*: 1) it secures payment or performance of an obligation for services or materials furnished with respect to goods by a person in the ordinary course of its business; 2) it is created by statute or case law, not by Article 9; and 3) its effectiveness depends on the lienholder's possession of the goods. Statutes and case law creating liens do not always require that the lienholder retain possession of the collateral to maintain the lien. Such liens are not within the scope of section 9-333, because the effectiveness of the lien does not depend on the lienholder possessing the goods.

Section 9-333(b) awards a possessory lien priority over a security interest in the goods to the extent of the value of the services or materials furnished with respect to the goods, unless the statute that creates the lien expressly provides otherwise. This rule rejects the first-to-file-or-perfect rule; the possessory lien is superior to a security interest that the secured party perfects before the lien arises. In theory, the subordinated secured party should be in no worse position since without the materials or services furnished by the lienholder the value of the collateral is diminished, presumably by the value of the materials or services.

Checkpoints

- An unperfected security interest is always subordinate to a perfected security interest.

- A lien creditor has priority over an unperfected security interest if the lien creditor acquires its lien before the earlier of perfection of the security interest or the secured party's filing of the financing statement and satisfying the debtor's-agreement attachment requirement.

- A buyer of tangible collateral or a lessee of goods takes the collateral free of an unperfected security interest if it gives value and receives delivery of the collateral without knowledge of the security interest and before it is perfected.

- A licensee or buyer of intangible collateral takes the collateral free of an unperfected security interest if it gives value without knowledge of the security interest and before it is perfected.

- Priority among perfected security interests is determined by the first-to-file-or-perfect rule — the security interest with the earliest date of perfection or date of filing has priority.

- Priority of a security interest in proceeds of collateral generally is determined by the first-to-file-or-perfect rule.

- Special proceeds priority rules govern proceeds of non-filing collateral — collateral which typically is not perfected by filing a financing statement.

- A lien on the collateral arising by operation of law generally has priority over a security interest in the collateral.

Chapter 7

Priority Rules When the Debtor Transfers the Collateral

Roadmap

- Continuation of a security interest after the debtor transfers the collateral
- Situations in which a buyer, lessee, or licensee of the collateral can take it free of a perfected security interest
- Priority when the transferee of the collateral creates a security interest in it
- Priority when a new debtor creates a security interest in the collateral

---

A. Priority of Perfected Security Interest against a Buyer, Lessee, or Licensee of the Collateral — Sections 9-315, 9-320, 9-321

Two questions arise when a debtor transfers the property that is the collateral for a security interest. Does the security interest continue in the collateral notwithstanding the transfer? And if it continues, which interest has priority—secured party or transferee? Before exploring those concepts, a brief explanation of Article 9 terminology is helpful. Article 9 sections frequently use the word *disposition*, a term Article 9 does not define, to indicate transfer of the collateral. Disposition of the collateral can occur through sale, lease, license, or other type of transfer. Because the most frequent disposition of collateral is by sale, many of the examples will involve sale of the collateral.

1. Continuation of the Security Interest or Agricultural Lien after Disposition of the Collateral— Section 9-315

The general rule of Article 9 is that a security interest or agricultural lien survives disposition of the collateral. Section 9-315(a)(1) states that a security interest or agricultural lien continues in the collateral notwithstanding disposition of the collateral unless the secured party authorizes the disposition free of the security interest or another section of the UCC adopts a contrary rule. Notice that the security interest continues whether it is perfected or unperfected. Although the section establishes continuation notwithstanding transfer, it provides two situations where the security interest does not continue: the security interest in the transferred collateral is terminated if the secured party authorizes the disposition free of the security interest, and the security interest does not continue if other sections allow a transferee to take free of the security interest.

Continuation of the security interest means that the collateral now owned by the transferee remains collateral for the security interest. It does not mean that the transferee is obligated to pay the debt secured by the collateral—the transferee is not obligated unless it agrees to be liable for the obligation. However, the secured party can repossess the collateral from the transferee if the person liable for the secured debt defaults. Remember that the transferee of the collateral is a *debtor* under the Article 9 definition of debtor. The person liable for the obligation is an *obligor* under the Article 9 definition of obligor.

The security interest or agricultural lien continues in the collateral unless the secured party authorized the disposition "free of the security interest or agricultural lien." The quoted phrase emphasizes that the security interest continues unless the secured party authorizes the disposition free and clear of the security interest. A secured party who consents to disposition of the collateral does not necessarily authorize the disposition free of the security interest. Whether an authorization is "free of the security interest or agricultural lien" is a question of fact that Article 9 leaves to the courts.

Official Comment 2 to section 9-315 indicates that the secured party can authorize the disposition in the "security agreement or otherwise." Prior texts of Article 9 included that phrase in the statute. The comment confirms that the drafters did not intend a change in meaning by moving the phrase to the comment. Consequently, an authorization contained in the security agreement, a collateral writing, or given orally should be sufficient. An authorization of the disposition free of the security interest, no matter in what medium it appears, terminates the security interest in the transferred collateral.

What constitutes an *otherwise* authorization often presents a troublesome question. Many of the cases involving *otherwise* authorizations involve situations where the transferee of the collateral argues that the authorization comes from the secured party's conduct. For example, suppose Bank has a security interest in Debtor's equipment. The security agreement prohibits sale of the collateral without first obtaining the written consent of Bank. Debtor, however, has previously sold items of collateral without first obtaining Bank's consent. Although Bank is aware of the sales, it does not rebuke Debtor nor declare a default (for failure to obtain consent) because Debtor is not otherwise in default. When Debtor subsequently defaults, Bank claims a security interest in the collateral against the buyer. The security interest continues in the collateral unless Bank's conduct constitutes an authorization free and clear of the security interest.

Courts have split on this issue, with similar facts constituting authorization in one case, but not in another. The decision frequently turns on whether the court believes that the conduct of the secured party showing authorization can supplant the parties' agreement requiring written consent to any sale. Section 1-303, which establishes a rule that express terms control over conduct but also makes conduct relevant to show a waiver of an inconsistent term, is cited as support on both sides of the issue. Courts must be mindful of the section 9-315(a) rule that the security interest continues unless the secured party authorizes the disposition free of the security interest; authorization of the disposition alone does not terminate the security interest.

Another facet of this issue involves a *conditional authorization* — a secured party authorizes the disposition on the condition that it receives all or some of the proceeds of the disposition. Does the debtor's failure to remit the proceeds to the secured party void the authorization? Like the authorization-by-conduct issue, courts have split on this issue. The drafters of Revised Article 9 recognized the split but expressly left the issue for the courts, declaring, in Official Comment 2 to section 9-315, that the free-of-the-security-interest requirement in section 9-315(a)(1) "is not intended to address the frequently litigated situation in which the effectiveness of the secured party's consent to a disposition is conditioned upon the secured party's receipt of the proceeds."

Perhaps you are thinking that the way to avoid authorization problems is to have the security agreement provide that the debtor agrees not to transfer the collateral. In section 9-401(b), Article 9 expressly provides that such a provision does not prevent the effectiveness of the transfer from the debtor to the transferee. The section establishes the same result for a provision in a security agreement that makes the transfer a default—the transfer is nevertheless effective between the transferor and transferee. A secured party cannot stop the debtor from transferring its rights in the collateral, although the transfer may place the debtor in default. However, the transferee is not automatically subordinate to the secured party simply because the debtor breached the security agreement. Article 9 determines whether the transferee's right to the collateral is superior to the security interest of the secured party.

Remember that section 9-315(a)(2), discussed in Chapter 5, attaches the security interest to any identifiable proceeds produced by the disposition of the collateral. Combining sections 9-315(a)(1) and (a)(2) results in the secured party having a security interest in the transferred collateral and in the proceeds of the transferred collateral. Consequently, if the obligor defaults, the secured party can claim the transferred collateral held by the transferee, and the proceeds of the disposition from the transferor. Additionally, the secured party can choose which source to use first—collateral or proceeds—and can use both if necessary to satisfy the obligation. The only limitation on claiming both sources is that the collateral, including the proceeds, is liable only to the extent of the secured debt. Consequently, any surplus that remains after the secured party satisfies the obligation does not belong to the secured party. If the security interest does not survive the disposition because of the secured party's authorization or a contrary UCC rule, the secured party is limited to a security interest in any identifiable proceeds of the collateral.

2. UCC Sections That Allow a Transferee to Take the Collateral Free of the Security Interest— Sections 2-403(2), 9-320, and 9-321

Several UCC sections adopt rules that allow a transferee to take the collateral free of a security interest or agricultural lien. All but one of those sections are located in Article 9. Article 2 contains the other section. These sections establish exceptions to the rule of section 9-315(a) that the security interest continues in the collateral after the disposition. The alternative for a secured party when a transferee takes the collateral free of the security interest is to claim the proceeds of the collateral.

a. Buyer of Goods—Section 9-320

Section 9-320 establishes rules allowing certain buyers to take the collateral free of the security interest in the collateral. To take the collateral free of the security interest means that the collateral is not subject to the security interest.

1. Buyer in Ordinary Course of Business — Sections 9-320(a), 1-201(b)(9)

Section 9-320(a) enables a buyer of goods in ordinary course of business to take free of a perfected security interest in the goods even if the buyer knows of the security interest, unless the buyer is buying farm products from a person engaged in farming operations. Federal law, discussed later in this chapter, protects a buyer of farm products. Although section 9-320(a) literally applies to perfected security interests, Official Comment 2 to the section notes that a buyer who takes free of a perfected security interest also takes free of an unperfected security interest. Consequently, a buyer of goods can take free of an unperfected security interest under section 9-320(a) or section 9-317(b), discussed in Chapter 6, although the sections create different conditions that a buyer must satisfy to take free of the security interest. A buyer takes the collateral free of the security interest under section 9-320(a) if the buyer: 1) is a buyer in ordinary course of business; 2) is not buying farm products from a person engaged in farming operations; and 3) the buyer's seller created the security interest in the collateral.

A. Buyer in Ordinary Course of Business Requirements — Section 1-201(b)(9)

Section 1-201(b)(9) defines *buyer in ordinary course of business* (BIOCB) as "a person that buys goods in good faith, without knowledge that the sale violates the rights of another person in the goods, and in the ordinary course from a person, other than a pawnbroker, in the business of selling goods of that kind." And if that isn't enough, section 1-201(b)(9) further defines some of those requirements! The definition begins with a person. In the UCC, *person*, defined in section 1-201(b)(27), includes an individual or an organization. Consequently, a BIOCB can be an individual, a corporation, partnership, limited liability company, consumer, or merchant.

A BIOCB must buy goods. Article 9 contains a lengthy definition of goods in section 9-102(a)(44), but generally goods are *all things that are moveable when a security interest attaches.* The definition excludes property that is an account, chattel paper, document, instrument, commercial tort claim, general intangible, investment property, letter-of-credit right, letter of credit, money, or oil, gas, or other minerals before extraction.

Section 1-201(b)(9) states the BIOCB may *buy* with "cash, by exchange of other property, or on secured or unsecured credit...." The essence of this requirement is that a BIOCB buys the goods with something like new value. New value is important to the secured party because a security interest automatically attaches to proceeds of collateral and if the buyer takes free of the security interest, the proceeds become the only collateral. Section 1-201(b)(9) expressly denies BIOCB status to a person who acquires goods as security for or in total or partial satisfaction of a money debt. For example, a buyer who buys inventory collateral in exchange for cancelling a debt the seller owes the buyer cannot be a BIOCB.

The BIOCB must buy in *good faith*. Section 1-201(b)(20) defines good faith as "honesty in fact and the observance of reasonable commercial standards of fair dealing." *Honesty in fact* is a subjective standard sometimes referred to as the "empty head, pure heart" test. *The observance of reasonable commercial standards of fair dealing* is an objective standard whereby a buyer's conduct is judged against the standards of the business, industry, or trade.

The BIOCB must be without knowledge that the sale violates the rights of another person in the goods. In the UCC, *knowledge*, defined in section 1-202(b), means actual knowledge. The knowledge that disqualifies a buyer from BIOCB status is knowledge that the sale violates the rights of a person with a security interest in the goods. The rights that a sale of collateral likely violates are the terms in the security agreement that prohibit sale of the collateral, or prohibit sale without first obtaining the secured party's consent. A typical buyer will not know that the sale violates a secured party's rights in the goods because a buyer rarely sees a copy of the security agreement, even if it knows that a security interest covers the goods. Knowledge that the sale violates the rights of the secured party is distinct from knowledge of the security interest. Section 9-320(a) declares that a BIOCB takes free of the security interest even if the buyer knows of its existence. Consequently, a buyer can be a BIOCB and take free of the security interest if it merely knows that a security interest covers the goods or knows that a financing statement covering the goods is filed against the debtor.

A BIOCB must buy *in the ordinary course*. Section 1-201(b)(9) explains the requirement by declaring that a buyer "buys goods in the ordinary course if the sale to the person comports with the usual or customary practices in the kind of business in which the seller is engaged or with the seller's own usual or customary practices." Those guidelines indicate that buying in "ordinary course" views the sale from the seller's perspective. A sale is in the ordinary course if it comports with the customary business practice for the type of business in which the seller is engaged, even if the sale is not within seller's usual practice. Additionally, a sale comporting with seller's customary practices is "in the ordinary course," even if the sale does not comport with the industry practice.

A BIOCB must buy goods from a person that is *in the business of selling goods of that kind*. Realistically, this requirement limits the BIOCB to a buyer of inventory because a seller in the business of selling goods of the kind sold to the buyer is selling goods it holds for resale. That fits the Article 9 definition of inventory in section 9-102(a)(48). The section expressly excludes a pawnbroker from being the type of seller that enables BIOCB status.

Finally, a BIOCB must take possession of the goods, or have a right to recover the goods from the seller under Article 2. The purpose of this provision is to limit buyer in ordinary course of business status to buyers that have a right to possession of the goods as against the seller. Possession by a buyer in ordinary course of business should include possession by buyer's agents or transferees.

A buyer satisfying all the requisites of section 1-201(b)(9) is a BIOCB. The good news for buyers is that a buyer of inventory in the typical sale transaction unquestionably will satisfy the BIOCB requirements. However, a BIOCB must also satisfy the requisites of section 9-320(a): not buying farm products from a person engaged in farming operations, and the buyer's seller creates the security interest. Additionally, section 9-320(e) prevents the application of 9-320(a) against a secured party that has possession of the collateral.

B. The "Buyer's Seller" Requirement — Sections 9-320(a)

Section 9-320(a) enables a BIOCB to take the collateral free of a security interest *created by the buyer's seller*. This requirement means that the seller to the BIOCB must have created the security interest that conflicts with the BIOCB. For example, suppose Green buys a computer from Computer Systems Inc. (CSI), a seller of computers. CSI previously granted a security interest in all its inventory of computers to Bank. Green can take free of Bank's security interest, the security interest created by Green's seller — CSI.

C. Buyers of Farm Products from a Person Engaged in Farming Operations — The Food Security Act

Many have criticized section 9-320(a)'s exclusion of buyers of farm products from its protection. Congress addressed this matter in the Food Security Act (FSA) of 1985 (7 U.S.C. 1631) and enacted law giving certain buyers of farm products the same protection as other section 9-320(a) buyers. The FSA enables a buyer in the ordinary course of business buying a farm product from a seller engaged in farming operations to take free of a security interest created by the seller, even though the security interest is perfected and the buyer knows of it. "Buyer in the ordinary course of business" as defined in the FSA has an important difference from the UCC: under the FSA a buyer can qualify as a *buyer in the ordinary course of business* regardless of whether the buyer knows that the sale violates the rights of another person in the collateral.

The FSA provides two exceptions to its protection of a buyer. One exception pertains to buyers in states that establish a central filing system for security interests in farm products in accordance with the FSA requirements. Only a few states have done so. The second exception provides that the buyer takes the collateral subject to the security interest if, within one year prior to the sale, the buyer receives written notice of any payment obligations the secured party imposes on the buyer for release of the security interest, and the buyer fails to perform the payment obligation. This allows the secured party to notify a potential buyer that payment for the farm products should be made to the secured party. The FSA authorizes the secured party to compel the debtor/farmer to furnish the secured party with a list of buyers to whom the debtor may sell the farm product. Because any notice the secured party sends is effective for one year, the secured party can send yearly notices to the listed buyers for as long as the security interest is effective. The FSA levies a penalty on a debtor for selling a farm product to a buyer not included on the list. However, if the buyer does not receive the written notice, it nevertheless takes free of the security interest regardless of the debtor's failure to comply.

2. Buyer of Consumer Goods — Section 9-320(b)

Section 9-320(b) permits a buyer of consumer goods to take free of a perfected security interest if the buyer satisfies the requirements of the section. The section looks inviting to a buyer who is purchasing consumer goods, but its protection is more illusory than real because of the consumer goods requirement. The section applies only when the seller of the goods uses them primarily for personal, family, or household purposes. That is the section 9-102(a)(23) definition of consumer goods. Consequently, a buyer of goods from a seller that is not making a consumer use of the goods cannot take free of the security interest regardless of the buyer's intended use of the goods. This rule applies when a consumer sells to a consumer — such as a "garage sale" or a "classified ad" sale.

Section 9-320(b) establishes other requirements in addition to the seller's use. The buyer must buy: 1) without knowledge of the security interest; 2) for value; 3) primarily for personal, family, or household purposes; and 4) before the secured party files a financing statement covering the goods. The fourth requirement identifies the type of security interest usually involved in the priority conflict governed by section 9-320(b) — a purchase-money security interest in consumer goods. A purchase-money security interest in consumer goods is automatically perfected without filing under section 9-309(1) (except for goods covered by a certificate-of-title statute). Consequently, a buyer may be able to buy before a secured party files a financing statement because a secured party might never file a financing statement. However, a secured party who wants protection against the section 9-320(b) buyer can file a financing statement covering the goods and protect its right to follow the goods into the hands of a buyer from the debtor. Section 9-320(e) prevents the application of section 9-320(b) against a secured party that has possession of the collateral.

3. Buyers of Oil, Gas, or Minerals — Section 9-320(d)

Section 9-320(d) protects a buyer of minerals in specific situations. A buyer in ordinary course of business buying oil, gas, or other minerals at the well-head or minehead or after extraction takes free of an interest in such property "arising out of an encumbrance." An *encumbrance*, section 9-102(a)(32), is a right in real property, such as a mortgage, other than an ownership interest. Consequently, a qualifying buyer takes free of a person with a mortgage on the real property that encumbers minerals on the property. Section 1-201(b)(9) establishes the requisites of a buyer in ordinary course of business. The section expressly includes a seller of oil, gas, or other minerals at the wellhead or mine-head as a person in the business of selling goods of that kind. Although Official Comment 7 to section 9-320 declares that a buyer of minerals takes free of a security interest, section 9-320(d) literally allows a buyer to take free of "an interest arising out of an encumbrance." Because encumbrance is a right in real property, an Article 9 security interest is not an encumbrance.

b. Licensees and Lessees — Section 9-321

Section 9-321 adopts rules allowing licensees of general intangibles and lessees of goods in ordinary course of business to take their interests free of security interests. The rules operate virtually the same as section 9-320(a) with respect to buyers in ordinary course of business.

Section 9-321(a) defines a licensee in the ordinary course of business as "a person that becomes a licensee of a general intangible in good faith, without knowledge that the license violates the rights of another person in the general intangible, and in the ordinary course from a person in the business of licensing general intangibles of that kind." This definition is very similar to the definition of buyer in ordinary course of business, and much of the previous discussion of a BIOCB is relevant. The section further defines *ordinary course* as a license that "comports with the usual or customary practices in the kind of business in which the licensor is engaged or with the licensor's own usual or customary practices." This definition views ordinary course from the licensor's position. Ordinary course is satisfied if the license comports with either the industry practice or the licensor's practice.

Section 9-321(b) provides that a licensee in ordinary course of business takes its rights under a *nonexclusive license* free of a security interest in a general intangible created by the licensor, although the security interest is perfected and the licensee knows of its existence. The rule operates only as to a nonexclusive licensee. Consequently, an exclusive licensee is not protected by 9-321(b) and takes the license subject to a security interest in the general intangible unless the secured party authorizes the transfer free of the security interest. The difference between a nonexclusive license and an exclusive license is that the exclusive license gives the licensee the exclusive right to perform the licensed act and prohibits the licensor from granting that right to anyone else. In the nonexclusive license, the licensor can license many licensees to perform the licensed act.

A similar rule exists for a lessee in ordinary course of business. Section 9-321(c) provides that a lessee in ordinary course of business takes its leasehold interest free of a security interest in the goods created by the lessor, even if the security interest is perfected and the lessee knows of its existence. The definition of *lessee in the ordinary course*, section 2A-103(1)(o), is essentially the same as the definition of *buyer in the ordinary course.*

c. Entrusting of Collateral — Section 2-403(2)

Section 2-403(2) protects a buyer in ordinary course of business buying goods that have been entrusted to a merchant who deals in goods of that kind. *Entrusting*, defined at section 2-403(3), includes two situations. One is when a person delivers possession of goods to another person. For example, an entrusting occurs when the owner of a watch delivers it to a jeweler for the sole purpose of repairing the watch. The other is when a person acquiesces in another person's retention of possession of goods.

Section 2-403(2) declares that the entrusting of possession of goods to a merchant who deals in goods of that kind enables the merchant to transfer all rights of the entruster to a buyer in ordinary course of business. A qualifying buyer of the goods receives the rights of the entruster of the goods. Section 1-201(b)(9), discussed previously in this chapter, establishes the requirements for a buyer in ordinary course of business (BIOCB). For example, suppose the owner of a watch delivers it to a jeweler for the sole purpose of repairing it. The jeweler sells the watch to a buyer who has no knowledge that the jeweler has possession of it solely for the purpose of repair. Under section 2-403(2), the buyer acquires all the owner's rights (the entruster) in the watch, if the buyer is a BIOCB and the jeweler is a merchant who sells watches. The result is that the buyer has a superior right to the watch over the owner, regardless that the owner did not grant the jeweler the right to sell the watch.

Section 2-403(2) enables a buyer to acquire the secured party's rights in the collateral if the secured party is the *entruster* of the goods. A secured party who entrusts the collateral to a merchant who deals in goods of that kind empowers the merchant to transfer the secured party's rights to a buyer in ordinary course of business, regardless of whether the secured party authorized the sale. A buyer who acquires the secured party's rights in the collateral takes it free of the security interest. However, if the owner of the goods is the person entrusting them to the merchant, then section 2-403(2) transfers the owner's rights to the buyer. In that instance, section 9-315(a)(1) would continue the security interest in the collateral despite the disposition. It seems likely that the effect of section 2-403(2) on a security interest will be negligible because a secured party will rarely be the entruster of collateral. Entrusting occurs by delivery of the collateral to the merchant or acquiescence in the merchant's retention of possession—types of acts a secured party, who rarely has possession of the collateral or knowledge that the debtor has delivered the collateral to the merchant, is unlikely to perform.

B. Subordination of a Security Interest Created by a Transferee of Collateral—The "Double Debtor Problem"—Section 9-325

An interesting priority conflict arises when a transferee of collateral, who takes the collateral subject to a security interest created by the transferor, creates a security interest in the collateral. In essence, there are two debtors of the same collateral, each of whom creates a security interest to a different secured party. Section 9-325 establishes a specific priority rule to resolve that conflict—labeled the "double debtor problem" by Official Comment 2 to section 9-325. The rule grants priority to the secured party of the transferor if the conditions to priority are satisfied. Literally, section 9-325 subordinates a security interest created by a *debtor* to a security interest created by *another person*. The transferee of the collateral is the *debtor* under the section 9-102(a)(28) definition because it is the person with the ownership interest in the collateral. The transferor of the collateral, who was the debtor, is the *another person* of section 9-325.

Section 9-325(a) subordinates the security interest created by the debtor if: 1) the debtor acquires the collateral subject to the security interest created by the other person; 2) the security interest created by the other person is perfected when the debtor acquires the collateral; and 3) there is no period thereafter when the security interest created by the other person becomes unperfected. For example, suppose Bank perfects a security interest in Buyer's existing and after-acquired equipment in January 2006. Lender perfects a security interest in Owner's equipment in September 2006. In December 2006, Owner sells all the equipment collateral to Buyer, who takes it subject to Lender's security interest. Buyer is the *debtor* and Owner is the *another person*. Bank's security interest attaches to the transferred equipment under its after-acquired property clause. Lender's security interest continues in the equipment notwithstanding the sale. Under section 9-325, Bank's security interest is subordinate to Lender's security interest because Buyer took the equipment subject to Lender's security interest, Lender's security interest was perfected when Buyer acquired the collateral, and there is no period thereafter when Lender's security interest is unperfected. Lender has priority regardless that Bank would have priority under the first-to-file-or-perfect rule of section 9-322(a)(1). If Lender allows its perfection to lapse, section 9-325 is not applicable and priority is determined under section 9-322(a) and section 9-515(c).

Section 9-325(b) limits the subordination of the security interest created by the debtor to situations where that security interest otherwise would have priority, or where the security interest is created solely under sections 2-711(3) or 2A-508(5) for a buyer or lessee after its rightful rejection or justifiable revocation of acceptance. If the security interest created by the debtor is already subordinate under the applicable priority rule, then the other secured party does not need the aid of section 9-325.

C. Priority of a Security Interest Created by a New Debtor — Section 9-326

A debtor that grants a security interest in its property might restructure its business into a different entity or merge with another entity in a manner such that the debtor's identity ends, and the new entity becomes bound under the debtor's security agreement. The entity that becomes bound as debtor is the *new debtor*, defined in section 9-102(a)(56). The general rule is that a secured party with a perfected security interest against the original debtor will have a perfected security interest against the new debtor. For example, suppose Lender perfects a security interest in Corporation's existing and after-acquired inventory by filing a financing statement. Subsequently, Corporation merges with Newcorp and ceases to exist. Newcorp assumes Corporation's obligation to Lender, and consequently is a "new debtor." Lender has a perfected security interest in Newcorp's existing and after-acquired inventory to the extent that the security agreement and financing statement of the Lender/Corporation security interest would have been effective against Corporation had it acquired the inventory. In essence, the Lender/Corporation security agreement and financing statement now automatically attach and perfect any property of Newcorp of the type described by those records. Attachment and perfection of the security interest against the new debtor are discussed in Chapters 2 and 3, respectively.

Issues of priority arise if the new debtor grants, before or after it becomes bound as debtor, a security interest in the same type of collateral to another secured party. If the conflict involves collateral transferred by the original debtor to the new debtor, section 9-325, discussed in the preceding section, determines priority between the security interests. If the conflict involves collateral that originates with the new debtor, section 9-326 determines priority. For example, suppose Newcorp, the debtor from the previous example, grants a security interest in its existing and after-acquired inventory to Bank, who perfects by filing a financing statement before the merger with Corporation. Newcorp then becomes bound as debtor under the Lender/Corporation security agreement. Newcorp purchases inventory. Bank and Lender both have a perfected security interest in the inventory. Section 9-326 determines priority of the security interests. If the new debtor creates all the conflicting security interests, section 9-326 does not apply and the other priority rules of Article 9 determine priority.

Section 9-326(a) adopts a priority rule that subordinates a security interest that originates with the original debtor to a security interest that originates with the new debtor. Literally, section 9-326(a) is not very enlightening. It subordinates a security interest that is perfected by a financing statement effective against the new debtor solely because of section 9-508 to a security interest perfected other than by a financing statement effective solely under section 9-508. The key to the section is realizing that the security interest created by the original debtor is perfected against the new debtor by a *financing statement that is effective solely under section 9-508* because section 9-508, discussed in Chapter 3, permits the financing statement filed against the original debtor to remain effective automatically against the new debtor. The security interest originally created by the new debtor is a security interest that is perfected *other than by a filed financing statement that is effective solely under Section 9-508* because section 9-508 applies only to financing statements filed against an original debtor. A secured party with a security interest originally created by the new debtor would not perfect its security interest with a financing statement filed against the original debtor.

The original debtor could have created several security interests in the same collateral to several secured parties. All such conflicting security interests are perfected against the new debtor by financing statements effective solely under section 9-508. Section 9-326(b) declares that, with one exception, the other priority rules of Article 9 determine priority of such security interests. In essence, section 9-326(b) preserves the priority established by Article 9's other priority rules as if there were no new debtor.

The exception involves a new debtor who becomes bound as debtor under security agreements that originate with several original debtors. In this situation the new debtor has completed merger transactions with several debtors and has become bound under the security agreements of different original debtors at different times. All those secured parties are perfected by financing statements that are effective solely under section 9-508; consequently, section 9-326(a) is not applicable. Section 9-326(b) determines priority between those security interests according to priority in the time that the new debtor became bound by the security agreement of each original debtor. It awards priority to the secured party whose security agreement is the earliest security agreement under which the new debtor became bound as debtor.

A secured party who is perfected by a filed financing statement effective solely under section 9-508 can change its manner of perfection and the change affects, perhaps even improves, its priority position. Although section 9-508 continues the effectiveness of the secured party's financing statement, section 9-509(b) authorizes the secured party to file a financing statement against the new debtor when the new debtor becomes bound as debtor under the security agreement of the original debtor. Filing a financing statement against the new debtor is prudent and, as explained in Chapter 3, is necessary if the secured party wants to remain perfected in collateral the new debtor acquires more than four months after becoming bound as debtor and the difference in the names of the debtors makes the filed financing statement seriously misleading. If the secured party files a financing statement in the name of the new debtor, it is perfected *other than by a filed financing statement effective solely under section 9-508*. Consequently, the secured party can assert that section 9-326(a) gives it priority over a secured party whose filed financing statement is effective solely under section 9-508. If all secured parties that are perfected solely under section 9-508 file new financing statements against the new debtor, section 9-326(a) would not apply and the first-to-file-or-perfect rule of section 9-322(a)(1) would determine priority among them.

Checkpoints

- A security interest continues in collateral notwithstanding the debtor's disposition of the collateral unless the secured party authorizes the disposition free of the security interest or a UCC section creates a different rule.

- A buyer in the ordinary course of business takes the collateral free of a security interest created by the buyer's seller.

- A lessee in the ordinary course of business takes the collateral free of a security interest.

- A licensee in the ordinary course of business of a nonexclusive license takes the license free of a security interest.

- A secured party of a debtor that transfers the collateral has priority over a secured party of a debtor that is the transferee of the collateral if the transferee takes the collateral subject to the security interest, the security interest is perfected, and the security interest remains perfected.

- A secured party of a new debtor has priority over a secured party of an original debtor if the security interest of the secured party of the original debtor is perfected against the new debtor by the financing statement filed against the original debtor.

Chapter 8

Priority Rules for Purchase-Money Security Interests and Future Advance Security Interests

---

Roadmap

- Requisites of a purchase-money security interest
- Priority of a purchase-money security interest in inventory, livestock, software, and other goods
- Priority of a future advance security interest against a secured party, a lien creditor, or a buyer

---

A. Priority of Purchase-Money Security Interests — Sections 9-103, 9-324

Article 9 awards a dominant priority (commonly known as a *super priority*) to purchase-money security interests. A purchase-money security interest has priority under the rules of section 9-324 over a conflicting security interest in the same collateral although the other security interest otherwise would have priority under section 9-322(a)(1). The purchase-money security interest priority rules are divided by type of purchase-money collateral. Section 9-324 establishes priority rules for purchase-money security interests in inventory, livestock, software, and goods other than inventory or livestock — mainly equipment. Before examining the priority rules, a long detour into the types of transactions that qualify as purchase money is necessary.

1. Requisites of a Purchase-Money Security Interest — Section 9-103

In its simplest sense, a purchase-money security interest exists when a secured party secures the value it gives to enable the debtor to acquire goods with a security interest in the goods the debtor acquires. For example, suppose a buyer wants to buy a desk on credit for her business. The seller agrees to allow her to buy the desk by paying for it over a six-month period, if she will grant the seller a security interest in the desk to secure the purchase price. The buyer agrees. That security interest is a purchase-money security interest. A lender has a purchase-money security interest when it agrees to make the debtor a loan to enable it to purchase the collateral and takes a security interest in the collateral. A purchase-money security interest exists only in collateral consisting of goods or software in the goods.

The literal definition of purchase-money security interest in section 9-103 is somewhat complex, but in essence it is simply a security interest where goods secure the obligation incurred to obtain the goods. Section 9-103(b)(1) declares that a security interest in goods is a purchase-money security interest "to the extent that the goods are purchase-money collateral for the security interest." Goods are *purchase-money collateral*, defined in section 9-103(a)(1), if they secure "a purchase-money obligation incurred with respect to that collateral." A *purchase-money obligation*, defined in section 9-103(a)(2), is an obligation "incurred as all or part of the price of the collateral or for value given to enable the debtor to acquire rights in or the use of the collateral if the value is in fact so used." Combining those definitions results in a security interest being purchase-money when the goods secure the obligation incurred to obtain the goods. The obligation can be *the price of the collateral*, allowing a seller to have a purchase-money security interest, or *the value given to enable the debtor to acquire rights in the collateral*, allowing a lender to have a purchase-money security interest. Official Comment 3 to section 9-103 states that the purchase-money obligation includes "expenses incurred in connection with acquiring rights in the collateral, sales taxes, duties, finance charges, interest, freight charges, expenses of collection and enforcement, attorney's fees, and other similar obligations." Additionally, section 9-103(d) designates the security interest of a consignor in consigned goods as a purchase-money security interest in inventory.

Because the definition of purchase-money obligation requires that the debtor "in fact" use the value to acquire the collateral, a purchase-money lender must be careful to insure that the debtor acquires the purchase-money collateral with the value the secured party gives. For example, suppose Lender loans Debtor money to enable Debtor to purchase an automobile. Debtor uses the funds to pay off a debt and purchases the automobile using other funds. Lender has a security interest in the automobile, but it is questionable whether it is a purchase-money security interest because Debtor did not use Lender's loan to acquire the automobile. The simple solution is for the lender/secured party to make the loan proceeds payable to the seller of the goods, or at least the seller and debtor jointly.

a. Cross-Collateral Purchase-Money Security Interest in Inventory—Section 9-103(b)(2)

Section 9-102(b)(2) validates a cross-collateral purchase-money security interest in inventory. Unfortunately, the definition in section 9-102(b)(2) is not very helpful in determining the meaning of a cross-collateral purchase-money security interest. Perhaps more enlightening is the following explanation. A cross-collateral purchase-money security interest is a security interest in which the purchase-money collateral secures the obligation the debtor incurs to obtain the inventory collateral and obligations the debtor incurs to the secured party to obtain other purchase-money inventory collateral, and the purchase-money obligation is secured by the purchase-money collateral and other purchase-money collateral the debtor obtains by using value from the secured party. The benefit of the cross-collateral purchase-money security interest is that a secured party who engages in multiple purchase-money security interest transactions with the debtor is able to secure *each* purchase-money obligation with *all* the purchase-money collateral and maintains purchase-money status for the entire security interest.

For example, suppose Seller finances Debtor's purchase of an item of inventory and Debtor authenticates a security agreement that grants a security interest in that item to secure its price and any other obligations Debtor owes Seller. Seller subsequently finances Debtor's purchase of another item of inventory and Debtor again authenticates a security agreement that grants a security interest in the item to secure its price and any other obligations Debtor owes Seller. The purchase-money security interest in each item secures the item's price, and the price of the other item. To create a cross-collateral purchase-money security interest, the security agreement for each purchase-money security interest must include a future advance clause that permits the purchase-money collateral of each purchase-money security interest to secure the purchase-money obligation *and* other obligations the debtor owes to the secured party.

b. Dual-Status Purchase-Money Security Interest — Sections 9-103(e), (f)

A dual-status purchase-money security interest refers to a security interest that is part purchase-money and part non-purchase-money. It is created when the security agreement that evidences a purchase-money security interest includes a future advance clause or an after-acquired property clause, or when the debtor renews, refinances, consolidates, or restructures the purchase-money obligation. Courts have questioned whether those events transform a purchase-money security interest into a non-purchase-money security interest because the purchase-money collateral secures non-purchase-money obligations (the future advance), the purchase-money obligation is secured by non-purchase-money collateral (after-acquired property), or the refinanced obligation does not enable the debtor to acquire rights in the purchase-money collateral. Section 9-103(f) settles those disputes in favor of purchase-money status in all the previously mentioned situations, unless the security interest arises in a consumer-goods transaction, in which case Article 9 expressly leaves the answer to the courts.

Section 9-103(f) declares that purchase-money security interest status is not lost if the purchase-money collateral secures a non-purchase-money obligation, if non-purchase-money collateral secures a purchase-money obligation, or if the purchase-money obligation is renewed, refinanced, consolidated, or restructured. However, the non-purchase-money collateral and the non-purchase-money obligation do not satisfy the definition of purchase-money security interest. Consequently, those portions of the security interest do not qualify for purchase-money status. The result is that a purchase-money security interest that secures non-purchase-money obligations, such as a future advance, or includes other collateral, such as after-acquired property, is split into a purchase-money security interest portion and a non-purchase-money security interest portion — a dual-status security interest.

For example, suppose Debtor grants Lender a purchase-money security interest to secure a $10,000 purchase-money loan. Subsequently, Debtor borrows $5,000 from Lender and, because the purchase-money security agreement includes a future advance clause, the purchase-money collateral secures the $5,000 loan. The secured obligation is part purchase-money ($10,000) and part non-purchase-money ($5000). The non-purchase-money portion does not qualify for the special priority that Article 9 bestows upon a purchase-money security interest. Section 9-103(g) places the burden on the secured party of proving the extent to which the obligation is purchase-money.

When a dual-status security interest includes a purchase-money obligation and a non-purchase-money obligation, a payment by the obligor could be applied to either or both obligations. Section 9-103(e) supplies a three-tier rule for applying a debtor's payment in that situation. *First*, the payment is applied pursuant to the parties' agreement as to any "reasonable" method of application. The section does not require that the parties make the agreement in the security agreement, in writing, or concurrently with the security agreement. *Second*, in the absence of agreement, the payment is applied pursuant to "any intention of the obligor manifested at or before the time of payment." Section 9-103(e)(2) does not limit when or how the debtor can manifest its intent. Consequently, a debtor can manifest its intent at the time it makes the payment. *Third*, in the absence of agreement or the obligor's manifestation of intent, a secured party must apply a debtor's payment first to any unsecured obligations, second to purchase-money secured obligations in the order in which they were incurred, and lastly to non-purchase-money secured obligations. Official Comment 7 to section 9-103 clarifies "order in which the obligations were incurred" as meaning paying first the purchase-money obligation incurred first.

c. Dual-Status Purchase-Money Security Interests in Consumer Goods Transactions — Section 9-103(a), (b), (h)

Sections 9-103(e) (the rules for application of payments) and (f) (validation of a dual-status security interest) expressly prohibit their application to a consumer-goods transaction. A *consumer-goods transaction*, section 9-102(a)(24), has three components: an individual, using consumer goods collateral, to secure a consumer obligation. The Article 9 exclusion leaves for the courts the resolution of whether a dual-status security interest can exist in a consumer-goods transaction. They are to decide, without drawing any inference from Article 9's exclusion, whether to continue purchase-money security interest status for a consumer-goods transaction security interest with a future advance, after-acquired property, or a restructured purchase-money obligation.

A court could resolve this issue by using the definition of a purchase-money security interest in sections 9-103(a) and (b)(1). Those sections seem to allow a dual-status security interest. Section 9-103(b)(1) states that a security interest is a purchase-money security interest "to the extent" that the goods are purchase-money collateral. *To the extent* seems to allow a security interest to be purchase-money to some extent and non-purchase-money to some extent. Goods are *purchase-money collateral* when they secure a purchase-money obligation. A *purchase-money obligation* exists when a debtor incurs an obligation for the purchase price or enabling loan of the collateral. Those definitions do not prohibit the apportionment of collateral or obligation into purchase-money and non-purchase-money portions. Consequently, a security interest can be part purchase-money although the purchase-money collateral secures future advances, after-acquired property secures the purchase-money obligation, or the purchase-money obligation has been renewed, refinanced, consolidated, or restructured.

For example, suppose Debtor and Secured Party agree to extend for six months the payment of a loan now due in a purchase-money consumer-goods transaction. Although this renewal does not enable Debtor to acquire rights in the collateral, it still represents the value that enabled Debtor to acquire the collateral and *to that extent* the security interest can be deemed purchase-money.

If a court allows a dual-status purchase-money security interest in a consumer-goods transaction, a difficult problem arises when the debtor makes a payment on the debt and the parties have not agreed on how to allocate the payment between purchase-money and non-purchase-money obligations. What part of the security interest is purchase-money, and what part is non-purchase-money after the payment? A bankruptcy judge adopted the "first in first out" method of allocation. (*See* In re Conn, 16 B.R. 454 (Bankr. W.D. Ky. 1982).) However, most courts are less willing to allocate in the absence of an agreement by the parties. (*See* Coomer v. Barclay's Am. Fin., Inc., 8 B.R. 351 (Bankr. E.D. Tn 1980).) A court could utilize the allocation method of section 9-103(e)(3), regardless of the section's express statement that it does not apply to consumer-goods transactions. That limitation simply means that the allocation method is not applicable as statutory law. It does not preclude a judge from adopting the rule in a consumer goods purchase-money security interest.

2. Priority of a Purchase-Money Security Interest in Inventory — Sections 9-324(b), (c)

A perfected purchase-money security interest in inventory has priority over a conflicting security interest in the same inventory if the secured party satisfies section 9-324(b)'s requisites for priority. The conflicting security interest typically arises under an after-acquired property clause. For example, suppose Bank perfects a security interest in Debtor's existing and after-acquired inventory. Lender perfects a purchase-money security interest in an item of inventory it sells Debtor. Bank's security interest attaches the purchase-money inventory under its after-acquired property clause, and its priority date for that inventory is the filing date of the initial financing statement covering the inventory. Nevertheless, Lender has priority in the purchase-money inventory if it complies with section 9-324(b). If a purchase-money security interest does not qualify for priority because the secured party fails to comply with section 9-324(b), section 9-322 determines priority. Because section 9-103(d) designates the security interest of a consignor in a consignment transaction a purchase-money security interest in inventory, a consignor must satisfy section 9-324(b)'s requirements to have priority over a consignee's other secured creditors.

To achieve super priority, the purchase-money security interest in inventory must comply with four requirements. *First*, the purchase-money secured party must perfect its security interest before or at the time the debtor receives possession of the inventory. Because a secured party typically perfects its purchase-money security interest in inventory by filing a financing statement, the secured party must file the financing statement by the time debtor receives possession of the collateral.

The remaining three requirements apply only if the conflicting security interest is perfected by filing a financing statement. If it is perfected by any other method, the purchase-money secured party need not comply with these conditions to achieve super priority. However, it is likely a purchase-money secured party will need to comply with these requirements because most secured parties perfect security interests in inventory by filing a financing statement.

Second, the purchase-money secured party must send "an authenticated notification to the holder of the conflicting security interest." The definitions of *send* and *authenticate*, sections 9-102(a)(74) and (9), respectively, allow for a mailed or electronic notification. A conflicting secured party is entitled to this notification only if it has filed its financing statement before the purchase-money secured party files its financing statement or, if the purchase-money security interest is temporarily perfected under section 9-312(f), before the beginning of the twenty-day period of temporary perfection. (Temporary perfection, discussed in Chapter 5, pertains to security interests in negotiable documents or goods in possession of a bailee who has not issued a negotiable document.) Practically, this requires that the purchase-money secured party search the financing statement index for financing statements covering the debtor's inventory that were filed before the purchase-money secured party files its financing statement or before the beginning of the temporary perfection period, and send the authenticated notification to those filers.

Third, the holder of the conflicting security interest must receive the notification within five years before the debtor receives possession of the inventory. This requirement does not mean that the holder of the conflicting security interest must receive the notification five years in advance. It means that a notification received any time within five years before the debtor receives possession of the purchase-money inventory is sufficient. Consequently, the purchase-money secured party can comply with the notification requirement for all its purchase-money transactions involving the same type of collateral within a five-year period by sending one notification to each conflicting secured party. Official Comment 6 to section 9-324 notes that the definition of *receives*, section 1-202(e), allows a purchase-money secured party to comply with this requirement by delivering the notification to the address the conflicting secured party indicates on its filed financing statement, even if that address is incorrect.

Fourth, the notification must state that the person giving it has or expects to acquire a purchase-money security interest in inventory and describe the inventory. The notification gives the holder of a conflicting security interest knowledge of the purchase-money security interest so that any future advance the secured party might make in reliance on the after-acquired inventory is made with awareness of its likely subordination to the purchase-money security interest.

Although section 9-324(b) does not prescribe the order in which the secured party must satisfy the requirements, the secured party's first act should be to file its financing statement because the notification requirements apply only to a conflicting secured party that files a financing statement before the purchase-money secured party files. Consequently, the purchase-money secured party's filing closes the window to conflicting filings. The second, third, and fourth steps should be: search the UCC index for conflicting security interests, notify conflicting secured parties, and deliver the collateral to the debtor. Complying with the requirements in that order insures priority for a secured party that perfects the purchase-money security interest by filing.

Section 9-324(b) extends the super priority of a purchase-money security interest in inventory to particular types of proceeds of the inventory. A purchase-money security interest with priority in the inventory has priority in identifiable "cash proceeds" of the inventory the debtor receives on or before it delivers the inventory to the buyer, except as otherwise provided by section 9-327 for security interests in deposit accounts—a type of cash proceeds. Section 9-322 or a specific rule determines priority in cash proceeds the debtor receives after delivery of the inventory to the buyer. In addition, super priority continues in proceeds of inventory that are "chattel paper" or an "instrument," and in "proceeds of the chattel paper," if the purchase-money secured party satisfies the requirements for priority in that collateral established in section 9-330 (discussed in Chapter 9). A purchase-money security interest in inventory does not have super priority in any other type of proceeds, although it has a security interest in proceeds under section 9-315(a). Article 9's other priority rules, typically section 9-322, govern the priority between conflicting security interests in proceeds.

More than one purchase-money security interest can exist in the same inventory. For example, a debtor may seek a loan from a lender for part of the purchase price of the inventory and finance the balance of the purchase price from the seller of the collateral. If each creditor takes a security interest in the purchase-money collateral, each has a purchase-money security interest. Additionally, more than one lender can advance funds to enable the buyer to purchase inventory and secure the loan with a security interest in the purchase-money inventory. If more than one purchase-money security interest satisfies the section 9-324(b) requirements for priority, section 9-324(g)(1) awards priority to the purchase-money seller over the purchase-money lender. If there is no purchase-money seller, section 9-324(g)(2) allows the first-to-file-or-perfect rule of section 9-322(a) to determine priority between purchase-money lenders.

3. Priority of a Purchase-Money Security Interest in Livestock — Section 9-324(d)

A perfected purchase-money security interest in livestock that are farm products has priority over a conflicting security interest in livestock if the purchase-money secured party satisfies section 9-324(d)'s requisites for priority. Section 9-322 determines priority of a purchase-money security interest that does not qualify for super priority. The definition of *farm products*, section 9-102(a)(34), includes livestock born or unborn and aquatic goods produced in aquacultural operations, if the debtor is engaged in farming operations. The super priority of a perfected purchase-money security interest in livestock continues in all types of identifiable proceeds and in products of the livestock in their unmanufactured states, except deposit account proceeds governed by section 9-327.

The section 9-324(d) requirements for priority of a livestock purchase-money security interest are the same as those for priority of a purchase-money security interest in inventory, with one exception: the holder of the conflicting security interest must receive the authenticated notification within six months before the debtor receives possession of the livestock. This means that a single notification to the holder of a conflicting security interest preserves priority for purchase-money transactions in the same type of collateral within a six-month period. A summary of the four priority requirements follows. Review the discussion in the preceding section for a detailed explanation.

First, the purchase-money secured party must perfect its security interest at or before the time the debtor receives possession of the livestock. The remaining three requirements apply only if the conflicting security interest is perfected by filing a financing statement, the typical method of perfection. *Second*, the purchase-money secured party must send "an authenticated notification to the holder of the conflicting security interest." A conflicting secured party is entitled to this notification only if it has filed a financing statement before the purchase-money secured party files its financing statement, or before the beginning of the twenty-day period of temporary perfection if the purchase-money security interest is temporarily perfected under section 9-312(f). Temporary perfection under section 9-312(f) is for security interests in negotiable documents or goods in possession of a bailee who has not issued a negotiable document, and pertains to livestock in the possession of a person other than the debtor or the secured party. *Third*, the holder of the conflicting security interest must receive the notification within six months before the debtor receives possession of the livestock. *Fourth*, the notice must state that the person giving it has or expects to acquire a purchase-money security interest in livestock and describe the livestock.

If more than one purchase-money security interest qualifies for super priority in the livestock, the priority rules of section 9-324(g) determine priority. That section awards priority to the purchase-money seller over the purchase-money lender. If all conflicting purchase-money security interests are held by lenders, section 9-324(g)(2) allows the first-to-file-or-perfect rule of section 9-322(a) to determine priority.

4. Priority of a Purchase-Money Security Interest in Software — Section 9-324(f)

Section 9-103(c) authorizes a purchase-money security interest in software only to the extent that there is also a purchase-money security interest in goods acquired in an integrated transaction with the software, and the debtor acquired the software for the principal purpose of using it in the goods. For example, when a debtor obtains a loan that enables it to purchase goods and software that operates the goods and grants a security interest in the goods and software, the security interest is a purchase-money security interest in goods and a purchase-money security interest in software. Section 9-324(f) awards priority to a perfected purchase-money security interest in software over a conflicting security interest in the software if the purchase-money security interest in the goods acquired in the transaction with the software has priority over the conflicting security interest in the goods. Section 9-324(a) or (b) determines priority of the purchase-money security interest in the goods, depending on whether the goods are inventory or non-inventory. The super priority of a perfected purchase-money security interest in software continues in proceeds of the software to the extent that the purchase-money security interest in the goods has priority in the proceeds of the goods, subject to the section 9-327 rules for priority in a deposit account.

If more than one purchase-money security interest in software qualifies for super priority in the software, section 9-324(g) awards priority to the purchase-money seller over the purchase-money lender. If all the conflicting purchase-money security interests are held by lenders, section 9-324(g)(2) allows the first-to-file-or-perfect rule of section 9-322(a) to determine priority.

5. Priority of a Purchase-Money Security Interest in Other Goods — Section 9-324(a)

Section 9-324(a) awards super priority to a purchase-money security interest in all other types of goods if the purchase-money security interest is perfected when the debtor receives possession of the goods or within twenty days thereafter. The time-of-perfection requirement is the only requirement for super priority. Section 9-324(a) applies mainly to a purchase-money security interest in equipment. For example, suppose Bank perfects a security interest in Debtor's existing and after-acquired equipment. Lender loans Debtor money to purchase equipment, takes a security interest in the equipment purchased, and files a financing statement to perfect its purchase-money security interest five days after Debtor receives the equipment. Bank's security interest attaches the purchase-money equipment under its after-acquired property clause. Lender has priority in the purchase-money equipment because it perfected the purchase-money security interest within twenty days after Debtor received the collateral. Section 9-322 determines priority of a purchase-money security interest that does not qualify for priority due to failure to perfect timely. A purchase-money security interest that has priority in the goods also has priority over a conflicting security interest in the proceeds of the goods, except deposit account proceeds governed by section 9-327, *if* the purchase-money security interest is perfected in the proceeds. Section 9-315, discussed in Chapter 5, governs perfection of a security interest in proceeds.

If more than one purchase-money security interest qualifies for super priority in the goods, section 9-324(g)(1) awards priority to the purchase-money seller over the purchase-money lender. If all the conflicting purchase-money security interests are held by lenders, section 9-324(g)(2) allows the first-to-file-or-perfect rule of section 9-322(a) to determine priority.

B. Priority of Future Advances —
Sections 9-322(a), 9-323

Frequently, the secured party makes a loan to the debtor after the secured party gives the initial value for attachment of the security interest. Article 9 labels that transaction a *future advance*. Many, if not most, security agreements include a *future advance clause* that functions as the debtor's agreement that the collateral will secure any obligation that the debtor owes to the secured party, in addition to the initial value that the secured party gives the debtor. Section 9-204(c), discussed in Chapter 2, validates future advance clauses in security agreements. A priority issue arises if a secured party makes a future advance after another person acquires an interest in the collateral. Article 9 adopts rules for determining the priority of the future advance against the interest of a secured party, buyer, or lien creditor.

1. Priority between Security Interests —
Section 9-322(a)(1)

a. Priority Based on Earlier of Filing or Perfection —
Section 9-322(a)(1)

If a secured party makes a future advance after another security interest attaches to the collateral, the first-to-file-or-perfect rule of section 9-322(a)(1) determines the priority of the future advance, except for the relatively rare future advance covered by section 9-323(a), discussed in the next section. Although section 9-322(a) is silent regarding the specific issue of priority of a future advance, Official Comment 4 to section 9-322 and Official Comment 3 to section 9-323 indicate clearly that section 9-322(a) determines priority between a future advance and another security interest.

Under section 9-322(a)(1), the priority of a future advance dates from the earlier of the time the secured party files a financing statement covering the collateral or the secured party perfects the security interest for the initial value. Consequently, a future advance has the same priority date as the initial value and will have priority over a security interest that arises between the initial value and the future advance. For example, on May 1 Bank makes a loan to Debtor and perfects a security interest in all the equipment of the Debtor by filing a financing statement. The security agreement includes a future advance clause. On June 5 Lender makes a loan to Debtor and perfects a security interest in the same collateral as Bank by filing a financing statement. On July 10 Bank makes a loan to

Debtor under the future advance clause. Under section 9-322(a)(1), May 1 is the priority date for Bank's May 1 and July 10 advances. Lender's priority date is June 5. Bank has priority as to both advances. The secured party's knowledge or lack of knowledge of the intervening security interest is irrelevant to priority.

Future advances can be made "pursuant to commitment" or at the option of the secured party. A secured party makes an advance *pursuant to commitment*, defined in section 9-102(a)(68), when its agreement with the debtor obligates the secured party to make the future advance. For example, when a secured party promises the debtor that it will make monthly loans to the debtor to enable it to meet its payroll, the loans made for that purpose are pursuant to commitment. A secured party makes an optional advance when the secured party has discretion to make the loan. For example, after receiving the initial secured loan, the debtor applies for another loan from the secured party. The secured party can grant or refuse the debtor's loan request—the loan is optional. A secured party's future advance can have priority under section 9-322(a) regardless whether it is optional or pursuant to commitment.

b. Priority Based on Time of the Advance — Section 9-323(a)

Section 9-323(a) adopts a rule applicable to a future advance made under a security interest perfected in the manner set forth in section 9-323(a). The rule establishes the time a future advance is perfected for the purpose of determining priority of the future advance under the first-to-file-or-perfect rule of section 9-322(a)(1). The rule is somewhat difficult to untangle, so the good news is that Official Comment 3 to section 9-323 remarks that the type of advance the section covers is the "rare case."

Section 9-323(a)(1) expressly limits its rule to future advances made while the underlying security interest is perfected automatically upon attachment under section 9-309 (discussed in Chapter 5) or perfected temporarily (twenty days) under sections 9-312(e), (f), and (g) (discussed in Chapter 5). A security interest perfected in any other manner, including filing, is not within the scope of section 9-323(a) and section 9-322(a) will determine the priority of a future advance made under the security interest. Section 9-323(a)(2) adds an additional limitation that the section is inapplicable if the future advance is made pursuant to a commitment that the secured party makes before or while the security interest was perfected by a method other than those specified in section 9-323(a)(1). That pertains to the situation where a secured party commits to making a future advance while the security interest is perfected by a method other than section 9-309 or section 9-312(e), (f), or (g), but the secured party makes the advance while the security interest is perfected automatically or temporarily under those sections. In that situation, the secured party has perfected the security interest by different methods at different times. For example, a secured party with a security interest automatically perfected for twenty days could also perfect by another method to remain perfected after the lapse of twenty days.

Section 9-323(a) states that for the purpose of determining priority under section 9-322(a)(1), perfection of the security interest dates from the time the secured party makes the future advance. Because there is no financing statement covering the security interest, the priority date of the future advance (the earlier of filing or perfection) is the day the secured party makes the advance. Consequently, the advance will be subordinate to a security interest with an earlier priority date. For example, on March 1 Bank loans Debtor money and takes a temporarily perfected (twenty days) security interest in a negotiable document of title in debtor's possession under section 9-312(e). The security agreement includes a future advance clause. On March 9 Lender perfects a security interest in the same document by filing a financing statement. On March 17 Bank makes a future advance. On March 19 Bank files a financing statement describing the document as collateral. Section 9-323(a) makes March 17 the perfection date for the security interest in the future advance. Consequently, Lender's security interest has priority over Bank's March 17 advance under the first-to-file-or-perfect rule of 9-322(a)(1) because Lender's priority date is March 9, while Bank's priority date for the future advance is March 17. However, Bank has priority over Lender regarding Bank's March 1 advance under section 9-322(a)(1), because Bank's priority date for that security interest is earlier than Lender's priority date.

Section 9-323(c) creates an exception to the rule of section 9-323(a) when the security interest arises from a sale of an account, chattel paper, payment intangible, or promissory note or is a security interest of a consignor secured party. Section 9-323(a) does not apply to those security interests. Consequently, if a secured party in that transaction makes a future advance, section 9-322(a) determines priority.

c. Priority of Advance Secured Party Makes After Debtor Repays Initial Advance — Section 9-322(a)(1)

Section 9-322(a)(1) determines the priority of an optional future advance the secured party makes after the debtor repays the initial obligation. In this situation the original security interest is discharged due to payment of the obligation and thus no security interest exists before the secured party makes the future advance because there is no obligation secured. Although such an advance frequently is labeled a future advance, it actually is the advance that satisfies the value requirement for attachment of the security interest. Section

9-322(a)(1) treats this security interest the same as any security interest—priority goes to the security interest that is first to file or perfect, provided there is no period thereafter when there is neither filing nor perfection. If the secured party makes an advance pursuant to commitment after the debtor repays the initial obligation, there is a security interest at all times because the commitment furnishes the value necessary for attachment of the security interest.

The key to determining priority of the security interest is the rule that a filed financing statement remains effective for its five-year life (section 9-515) and can perfect any security interest in the collateral described in the financing statement. Recall that under section 9-513, except for a security interest in consumer goods, a secured party is not obligated to terminate a filed financing statement although there is no outstanding secured debt unless the secured party receives the debtor's authenticated demand to do so. Consequently, the financing statement establishes the priority date of a security interest created after the filing and after the initial obligation is repaid. The drafters declare their concurrence with this result in Official Comment 3 to section 9-323.

For example, on May 1 Bank makes a loan to Debtor and perfects a security interest in Debtor's accounts by filing a financing statement. Lender perfects a security interest in the same collateral on May 29. Debtor repays the loan from Bank on July 1. Bank makes Debtor another loan on August 5 and secures it with a security interest in Debtor's accounts. The previously filed financing statement perfects the security interest because the collateral is the same for both security interests. Under section 9-322(a)(1), the priority date for Bank's August 5 security interest is May 1, the earlier of filing or perfection. Bank's security interest is superior to Lender's security interest.

d. Priority of Advance Made without a Future Advance Clause— Section 9-322(a)(1)

Section 9-322(a)(1) determines the priority of a future advance the secured party makes under a new security agreement when the original security agreement does not include a future advance clause. Although that advance supplies the value for the security interest that is created with the new security agreement, nevertheless it commonly is called a future advance. The debtor must authenticate a new security agreement because the security agreement for the original security interest did not include a future advance clause. Regardless of the new security agreement, the previously filed financing statement perfects the security interest to the extent that the collateral described in the financing statement matches the collateral described in the security agreement. Consequently, the new security interest has the same priority date as the original security interest.

For example, on May 1 Bank perfects a security interest in Debtor's accounts by filing a financing statement that describes the collateral as "Debtor's existing and after-acquired accounts." The security agreement does not include a future advance clause. Lender perfects a security interest in the same collateral on May 29. On June 27 Bank makes another loan to Debtor and Debtor authenticates a new security agreement that grants a security interest in the same collateral to secure the loan. Because the collateral for both of Bank's security interests is Debtor's accounts, no new financing statement is required and Bank's May 1 financing statement perfects its June 27 security interest. Article 9 does not prevent a financing statement from perfecting more than one security interest. Bank's priority date for its June 27 security interest is May 1. Bank has priority for both security interests because the priority dates are earlier than Lender's priority date.

2. Priority of a Future Advance Against a Lien Creditor — Section 9-323(b)

Section 9-323(b) establishes rules for determining the priority between a future advance and a lien creditor. It resolves the conflict created when a secured party with a perfected security interest makes a future advance *after* a person becomes a lien creditor. Section 9-317(a)(2), discussed in Chapter 6, determines the priority of advances made *before* the lien creditor acquired its interest.

Under section 9-323(b) a security interest is subordinate to a lien creditor for advances the secured party makes more than 45 days after the person becomes a lien creditor, unless the advance is made without knowledge of the lien or pursuant to a commitment entered into without knowledge of the lien. Any advance the secured party makes within 45 days after a person becomes a lien creditor is superior to a lien creditor because the rule subordinates only the advances the secured party makes more than 45 days after the person becomes a lien creditor. This 45-day protection for advances is absolute and not dependent upon the secured party's lack of knowledge of the lien. Advances made after the 45-day period are subordinate to the lien creditor *unless* made without knowledge of the lien or made pursuant to a commitment entered into without knowledge of the lien. Consequently, even an advance made after 45 days has priority if it satisfies either condition.

An advance made after the 45-day period has priority over a lien creditor if the secured party makes it pursuant to a commitment entered into without knowledge of the lien creditor. *Pursuant to commitment*, defined in section 9-102(a)(68), essentially means the secured party has promised to make the advance. Section 9-323(b)(2) requires that the secured party make the commitment for the advance without knowledge of the lien. The secured party's knowledge of the lien when it makes the advance is inconsequential. For example, suppose Bank has a perfected security interest in Debtor's equipment. The security agreement includes a future advance clause and Bank commits to make a loan to Debtor every 60 days. Lender becomes a lien creditor as to the equipment on September 1. On November 1 Bank, with knowledge of Lender's lien, makes the committed advance. The advance, although made outside of the 45-day period and with knowledge, has priority over Lender because Bank makes it pursuant to a commitment entered into without knowledge of the lien.

Section 9-323(c) creates an exception to the rule of section 9-323(b) when the security interest arises from a sale of an account, chattel paper, payment intangible, or promissory note or is a security interest of a consignor secured party. Section 9-323(b) does not apply to those security interests. Consequently, if a secured party in that transaction makes a future advance, the lien creditor takes subject to it.

3. Priority of a Future Advance Against Buyers and Lessees of Goods — Sections 9-323(d)–(g)

Sections 9-323(d) and (e) adopt rules for determining the priority of a future advance against a buyer of goods. Sections 9-323(f) and (g) adopt the same rules when the conflicting interest is held by a lessee of goods. The sections protect buyers and lessees of goods who take the collateral subject to all advances made before they acquired their interest. A person who takes the collateral free of the security interest under sections 9-320 or 9-321 also takes free of any future advance and does not need the protection of section 9-323. The rules pertain only to advances made after acquisition of the other person's interest. I will discuss the rules in the context of buyers, but the rules for lessees are the same.

Section 9-323(d) declares that a buyer of goods, other than a buyer in ordinary course of business (who presumably needs no protection), takes free of advances made after the *earlier* of the time the secured party acquires knowledge of buyer's purchase or 45 days after the purchase. Consequently, a buyer takes free of a future advance the secured party makes more than 45 days after the buyer's purchase or after the secured party has knowledge of the buyer's purchase, whichever occurs first. The corollary of the rule is that a secured party has priority over the buyer for advances made within 45 days after the buyer's purchase if made without knowledge of the purchase. However, the 45-day period ends immediately if the secured party acquires knowledge of the purchase.

For example, suppose Bank perfects a security interest in Debtor's equipment. The security agreement includes a future advance clause. Buyer purchases an item of equipment from Debtor on October 1 but does not take free of the security interest. Bank, who has no knowledge of Buyer's purchase, makes an advance to Debtor on November 1. Buyer's rights in the equipment are subject to the advance because Bank makes it without knowledge of the purchase and within 45 days after the purchase. If Bank learns of Buyer's purchase but nevertheless makes the November 1 advance, Buyer takes free of the advance, although Buyer remains subject to the security interest for the obligation existing when Buyer purchased the equipment. If Bank makes an advance on December 1, Buyer takes free of that advance because it is made more than 45 days from Buyer's purchase, regardless of Bank's lack of knowledge of the purchase.

Section 9-323(e) creates an exception to the rule of section 9-323(d) for an advance made "pursuant to a commitment." The section declares that section 9-323(d) does not apply to an advance made pursuant to a commitment if the secured party makes the commitment without knowledge of the buyer's purchase and within 45 days after the purchase. If section 9-323(d) does not protect the buyer, the buyer takes subject to the advance under the rule of section 9-315(a)(1). The secured party's knowledge of the buyer's purchase when it makes the advance is inconsequential. Also irrelevant is the timing of the advance. The conditions of section 9-323(e) apply to the commitment, not the advance.

For example, suppose Bank perfects a security interest in Debtor's equipment on September 1. The security agreement includes a future advance clause and a commitment to make loans every 60 days. Buyer purchases an item of equipment from Debtor on October 1. Buyer does not take free of the security interest. Bank, with knowledge of Buyer's purchase, makes the committed advance on November 1. Section 9-323(d) does not apply because Bank made the advance pursuant to a commitment it made without knowledge of and before 45 days after the Buyer's purchase. Bank easily satisfies the conditions of section 9-323(e) because it made the commitment before Buyer purchased the collateral. Consequently, Buyer does not take free of the future advance, although Bank made it with knowledge of Buyer.

Section 9-323(d) literally protects only a buyer "other than a buyer in ordinary course of business" presumably because a buyer in ordinary course of business takes the goods free of a security interest, including any future advances, under section 9-320(a). (Sections 9-323(f) and 9-321(c) adopt the same rules for a lessee.) However, a buyer can be a buyer in ordinary course of business, yet not take free of a security interest under section 9-320(a) because of the requirement that the buyer's seller must create the security interest (discussed in Chapter 7). That buyer deserves section 9-323(d)'s protection from future advances, but literally does not qualify for it. It seems unlikely that the drafters intended to exclude that buyer from protection against future advances. Official Comment 6 to section 9-323 remarks that "a buyer [or lessee] in ordinary course who takes free of the security interest under Section 9-320 [or section 9-321]" is not subject to any future advances. That comment should guide the interpretation of sections 9-323(d) and (f) so that courts apply the protection of those sections to any buyer or lessee who does not take free of the security interest under sections 9-320(a) or 9-321(c).

Checkpoints

- A purchase-money security interest exists when a security interest in goods, software used in goods, or livestock secures the obligation that enabled the debtor to obtain that collateral.

- Article 9 allows a security interest, other than a consumer-goods transaction, to be part purchase-money and part non-purchase-money when the purchase-money security interest also includes after-acquired collateral, future advances, or a refinancing of the obligation.

- Courts are to decide whether a consumer-goods transaction purchase-money security interest can be part purchase-money and part non-purchase-money.

- A purchase-money security interest has priority over a conflicting security interest in the collateral if the purchase-money secured party complies with the requirements for priority in section 9-324.

- A future advance has priority over a conflicting security interest that is perfected before the secured party makes the future advance because a future advance has a priority date based on the earlier of the time of filing the financing statement or perfecting the security interest.

- A future advance has priority over a lien creditor if the secured party makes the advance within 45 days after the time the person becomes a lien creditor, without knowledge of the lien, or pursuant to a commitment entered into without knowledge of the lien and within 45 days after the time the person becomes a lien creditor.

- A future advance has priority over a buyer or lessee of goods collateral if the secured party makes the advance before the earlier of the time the secured party has knowledge of the purchase or lease or 45 days after the purchase or lease, or pursuant to a commitment entered into without knowledge of the purchase or lease and within 45 days after the purchase or lease.

Chapter 9

Priority Rules for Security Interests in Specific Collateral

Roadmap

- Specific priority rules for chattel paper, instruments, deposit accounts, set-offs, investment property, letter-of-credit rights, fixtures, crops, accessions, commingled goods, and buyers and secured parties of certificate-of-title goods

---

Although section 9-322 establishes a rule for determining priority between perfected security interests, it yields to priority rules that Article 9 adopts for security interests in specific types of collateral. There are many such rules. Read them carefully, because some have conditions to their application and if the conditions are not satisfied, section 9-322 applies.

A. Priority of a Purchaser of Chattel Paper or an Instrument — Section 9-330

Section 9-330 establishes a priority rule that determines priority between a purchaser of chattel paper who satisfies the section's requirements and a secured party with a security interest in the chattel paper. *Chattel paper*, defined in section 9-102(a)(11) and discussed in Chapters 1 and 3, typically arises in a transaction where a record embodies both a debt and a security interest in goods securing the debt. The "record" can be written or electronic. Section 9-330 also adopts a similar priority rule for a purchaser of an instrument. *Instrument* is defined in section 9-102(a)(47), and typically is a negotiable instrument, such as a promissory note.

Section 9-330 governs the priority conflict between a secured party with a security interest in the chattel paper or instrument and a subsequent purchaser of the chattel paper or instrument. Because the UCC's definition of *purchase*, section 1-201(b)(29), includes taking an interest in property by a security interest and by sale, section 9-330 determines priority whether the subsequent purchaser buys the chattel paper or instrument or takes a security interest in it. However, if the purchaser does not satisfy section 9-330's requirements for priority, Article 9's other rules determine priority between the claimants. The applicable rule is usually section 9-322(a) because it determines priority between perfected security interests and Article 9 treats a sale of chattel paper or a negotiable instrument like a security interest.

1. Priority When the Secured Party Claims a Security Interest in Chattel Paper Merely as Proceeds of Inventory — Section 9-330(a)

Section 9-330(a) determines priority between a purchaser of chattel paper and a secured party who claims a security interest in the chattel paper "merely as proceeds of inventory." Neither the section nor the comments elaborate on the phrase *merely as proceeds of inventory*. The comment, however, directs the reader to Permanent Editorial Board (PEB) Commentary No. 8 for an explanation. The PEB Commentary indicates that a secured party's claim to chattel paper is merely as proceeds of inventory when three factors are present: 1) the underlying security interest is in inventory only; 2) the chattel paper is a proceed of the inventory; and 3) the chattel paper proceed is not the basis on which the secured party gives additional value, such as a loan, to the debtor. Basically, a secured party's claim to chattel paper is merely as proceeds of inventory when the secured party has a security interest in inventory that continues in chattel paper proceeds of the inventory. A claim to chattel paper is *not* merely as proceeds of inventory when a lender takes a security interest in "inventory and chattel paper." In that situation, the secured party gives value relying on the chattel paper and the inventory as collateral, so its claim to the chattel paper is not merely as proceeds of inventory.

Section 9-330(a) grants a purchaser of chattel paper priority over a security interest in the chattel paper claimed merely as proceeds of inventory if the purchaser in *good faith* and *in the ordinary course of the purchaser's business* gives *new value* for the chattel paper, *takes possession* of it (or obtains control of electronic chattel paper), and the *chattel paper does not indicate that it has been assigned* (known as "unlegended chattel paper") to an identified assignee. The purchaser's knowledge of the conflicting security interest does not disqualify it from priority. *Unlegended*, discussed later in this section, is a word Official Comment 5 to section 9-330 uses to describe chattel paper that does not indicate it has been assigned to the secured party. For example, suppose Bank perfects a security interest in Debtor's inventory of goods. Debtor sells an item of the inventory to a buyer who signs a contract that includes buyer's agreement to pay the purchase price and grant of a security interest in the good to secure the purchase price. The contract is chattel paper, a proceed of Bank's inventory, and Bank has a security interest in it. Debtor sells the unlegended chattel paper to Purchaser who, in good faith and in the ordinary course of its business, gives new value and takes possession of the chattel paper. Section 9-330(a) grants Purchaser priority in the chattel paper regardless of whether Bank would have priority under the first-to-file-or-perfect rule.

The purchaser of chattel paper must satisfy the five requirements of section 9-330(a) to have priority. *Good faith* means the purchaser is honest in fact and observes reasonable commercial standards of fair dealing. Official Comment 6 to section 9-330 declares that good faith does not require that the purchaser search the UCC filing records for prior filed financing statements. The purchaser typically satisfies the *new value* requirement, defined in section 9-102(a)(57), by buying the chattel paper with money, although new value includes other types of transfers from the purchaser. The purchaser must purchase the chattel paper *in the ordinary course of its business*. This is not the buyer-in-ordinary-course-of-business requirement of section 1-201(b)(9). A purchaser satisfies the requirement if buying chattel paper is in the ordinary course of its business. A financial institution purchaser, such as a bank, buys the chattel paper in the ordinary course of its business. The purchaser must take *possession* of tangible chattel paper or obtain *control* of electronic chattel paper. Section 9-105, discussed in Chapter 4, establishes the requisites for control of electronic chattel paper.

The last requirement for the purchaser's priority is that the chattel paper does not indicate that it has been assigned to another person. The typical assignee is the secured party who is claiming the chattel paper as proceeds of its inventory collateral although the debtor has taken no other action of assignment. Because *assignment* includes any transfer of an interest in the collateral, a secured party with a proceeds security interest is an assignee of the chattel paper. Chattel paper might include a stamped or printed *legend* indicating that it has been assigned to another person or that another person has a security interest in it. Insertion of a legend depends on whether the inventory secured party, or other assignee, and the debtor agree to place that term in the chattel paper. If the chattel paper indicates its assignment to another person, the purchaser does not satisfy the priority requirements of section 9-330(a). Note that section 9-330(a) does not require that the purchaser have knowledge of the assignment, only that the chattel paper indicates the assignment.

2. Priority When the Secured Party Claims the Chattel Paper Other Than Merely as Proceeds of Inventory — Sections 9-330(b), (f)

Section 9-330(b) determines the priority in chattel paper between a purchaser and a secured party that claims an interest in the chattel paper "other than merely as proceeds of inventory." This category includes a secured party that perfects a security interest in the debtor's existing and after-acquired chattel paper and a secured party that claims the chattel paper as a proceed of collateral other than inventory, such as a proceed of equipment. Section 9-330(b)'s requirements for priority are nearly the same as those of section 9-330(a). The purchaser must give new value for the chattel paper, take possession of it (or obtain control of electronic chattel paper), in the ordinary course of its business, and act in good faith. These are identical to the priority requirements of section 9-330(a).

The final requirement for priority is that the purchaser must purchase the chattel paper without knowledge that its purchase violates the rights of the secured party. "Knowledge" means actual knowledge. The disqualifying knowledge is knowledge that the purchase violates a secured party's rights in the chattel paper, not knowledge of the security interest or knowledge of a filed financing statement. A sale of chattel paper would violate the rights of the secured party if the debtor agreed not to sell the chattel paper but sold it nevertheless. The purchaser's knowledge of that violation prevents it from having priority under section 9-330(b). Additionally, section 9-330(f) directs that a purchaser "has knowledge that the purchase violates the rights of the secured party" if the chattel paper indicates that it has been assigned to an identified secured party other than the purchaser. If the chattel paper contains that statement — a legend — the purchaser *has knowledge* that the purchase violates the secured party's rights regardless of whether the purchaser sees the legend or has actual knowledge of the violation.

3. Priority in Chattel Paper as Proceeds of a Purchase-Money Security Interest in Inventory — Sections 9-330(e), 9-324(b)

Under section 9-324(b), discussed in Chapter 5, the super-priority of a purchase-money security interest in inventory extends to chattel paper proceeds of the inventory, if the purchase-money secured party satisfies the requirements for priority of section 9-330(a) or (b), whichever section applies. Because the UCC definition of purchase includes taking an interest in property by a security interest, a secured party with a purchase-money security interest in inventory is also a purchaser of the chattel paper proceeds. The purchase-money secured party has priority over a conflicting security interest in the chattel paper if it satisfies the priority requirements of section 9-330. Section 9-330(e) directs that a purchase-money security interest in inventory automatically satisfies the new value requirement.

4. Proceeds of Chattel Paper — Section 9-330(c)

A purchaser who has priority in the chattel paper also has priority in the proceeds of the chattel paper in two situations under section 9-330(c). *First*, a purchaser has priority in the proceeds if it has priority under the rules of section 9-322 (discussed in Chapter 6). Under section 9-322(c), a purchaser with priority in chattel paper also has priority in cash proceeds of the chattel paper if its security interest in the proceeds is perfected. *Second*, a purchaser automatically has priority in proceeds that are the specific goods covered by the chattel paper or cash proceeds of the specific goods, regardless of whether its security interest in the proceeds is perfected. The typical proceed of chattel paper is the cash paid on the monetary obligation, although any property within the *proceeds* definition, section 9-102(a)(64), is proceeds.

The second rule noted above pertains to the situation where the transferor of the chattel paper reacquires an interest in the goods covered by the chattel paper. The reacquisition could result from the buyer of the goods exercising its contractual or statutory right to return the goods for defects. The returned goods are proceeds of the chattel paper under Article 9's definition of proceeds. Because the proceeds of the chattel paper are the specific goods covered by the chattel paper, a chattel paper purchaser has automatic priority in them under section 9-330(c)(2). If the returned goods are sold for cash, the chattel paper purchaser has priority in the cash. If the transferor reacquires an interest in the goods through repossession of the goods after the buyer's default, the specific goods are proceeds of the chattel paper and a purchaser having priority in the chattel paper also has priority in the repossessed goods.

5. Priority of a Purchaser of an Instrument — Section 9-330(d)

Section 9-330(d) grants a purchaser of an instrument priority over a secured party that has a nonpossessory security interest in the instrument if the purchaser gives value and takes possession of the instrument in good faith and is without knowledge that the purchase violates the rights of the secured party. *Instrument*, defined in section 9-102(a)(47), includes checks and promissory notes. As with purchasers of chattel paper, the purchaser of an instrument can be either a buyer of the instrument or a person with a security interest in the instrument. Section 9-330(d)'s requirements for priority are the same as those of section 9-330(b) with two changes—there is no requirement that the purchaser act in the ordinary course of its business, and the purchaser must give value, not new value.

Section 9-330(f) mandates that a purchaser of an instrument has knowledge that its purchase violates a secured party's rights if the instrument indicates that it has been assigned to an identified secured party. If the instrument includes that legend, the purchaser has knowledge that the purchase violates the secured party's rights, regardless of whether the purchaser sees the legend or has actual knowledge of the violation.

A purchaser with priority under section 9-330(d) is subject to the rights of a holder in due course of a negotiable instrument as established in section 9-331(a), discussed in the next section, and consequently can be subordinate to a holder. If a purchaser is unable to satisfy the requirements of section 9-330(d), section 9-322(a) determines priority.

Section 9-324(b) extends the super-priority of a purchase-money security interest in inventory to instrument proceeds of the inventory if the purchase-money secured party satisfies the requirements of section 9-330(d). Because the purchase-money secured party is a "purchaser" of the instrument proceeds, it has the opportunity to achieve priority over a conflicting security interest in the instrument.

B. Priority of a Purchaser of Negotiable Instruments, Negotiable Documents, and Securities — Section 9-331

A person who becomes a holder in due course of a negotiable instrument (section 3-302), a holder of a duly negotiated document of title (section 7-501), or a protected purchaser of a security (section 8-303) has priority in such property over a previously perfected security interest in such property to the extent provided in Article 3, 7, or 8, respectively. Section 9-331(a) allows the priority rules of those articles to override any applicable priority rules of Article 9. Generally, Articles 3, 7, and 8 do not subordinate the holder or purchaser of the property to a prior security interest. If they do, (as in section 7-503) the security interest has priority.

Article 8 additionally protects certain interests in investment property from adverse claims and liability. Section 9-331(b) recognizes and embraces that protection by providing that Article 9 does not limit the rights of or impose liability on a person to the extent of such person's Article 8 protection.

Articles 3, 7, and 8 disqualify holders and purchasers of certain types of property from attaining a preferred status under those articles if such persons take their interest in the property with notice of an adverse claim or defense. For example, under section 7-501(a)(5), a document of title can be duly negotiated only to a person who is without notice of a claim to the document. A filed financing statement gives notice that the secured party named in the financing statement might be claiming an interest in the collateral indicated therein. However, section 9-331(c) declares that filing a financing statement under Article 9 does not constitute notice of a claim or defense so as to disqualify persons from preferred status under those articles.

C. Deposit Accounts, Set-Offs, and Transfers of Money — Sections 9-327, 9-340, 9-332

1. Priority of a Security Interest in a Deposit Account — Section 9-327

Section 9-327 determines the priority between conflicting security interests in a deposit account, a type of cash proceeds. *Deposit account*, defined in section 9-102(a)(29), includes a demand, time, savings, passbook or like account maintained with a bank. *Bank*, defined in section 9-102(a)(8), includes savings and loan associations and credit unions. A security interest in a deposit account can arise as the primary collateral for the security interest or as proceeds of the collateral. A security interest in a deposit account, other than a proceeds security interest, must be perfected by control. (Perfection by conrol is discussed in Chapter 4.) A security interest in a deposit account that arises as proceeds of collateral is perfected under the rule of section 9-315(d)(2), which establishes automatic perfection of a security interest in identifiable cash proceeds if the security interest in the underlying collateral was perfected.

Priority in a deposit account depends on the type of perfection and the time of perfection. Section 9-327(1) grants priority to a security interest in a deposit account perfected by control over a security interest in the deposit account perfected by any other method. This conflict usually involves a secured party with a primary interest in the deposit account perfected by control and a secured party with a proceeds security interest in the deposit account perfected as proceeds of collateral. For example, Lender perfects a security interest in Debtor's equipment by filing a financing statement. Subsequently, Creditor perfects a security interest in Debtor's checking and savings accounts with Last-Bank by establishing control. Debtor sells an item of equipment for cash and deposits the cash in its checking account with LastBank. Creditor has priority under section 9-327(1) regardless of the fact that Lender has an earlier priority date under section 9-322(a). Section 9-327 supplants the first-to-file-or-perfect rule of section 9-322(a).

Section 9-327 provides two rules to determine priority between security interests perfected by control. *First*, except as provided in the second rule, security interests perfected by control rank according to priority in time of establishing control. Priority goes to the secured party who establishes control first. *Second*, a bank with a security interest in its customer's deposit account (control is automatic under section 9-104(a)(1)) has priority over all security interests perfected by control, except for a secured party that establishes control by becoming the customer of the bank. A secured party that establishes control of the deposit account by becoming the customer of the bank that maintains the account (section 9-104(a)(3)) has priority over the security interest of the bank.

Section 9-327 does not determine priority between security interests in a deposit account if none of the security interests is perfected by control. This situation occurs when the conflict is between security interests attaching the deposit account as proceeds of collateral. In that case, the first-to-file-or-perfect rule of section 9-322(a) determines priority. However, it is possible that a secured party with a security interest in a deposit account as proceeds of collateral could establish control of the deposit account so that section 9-327 will determine its priority.

2. Priority of a Bank's Right to Set-Off and Recoupment against a Deposit Account — Section 9-340

A bank that maintains a deposit account for its customer generally has either (or both) a contractual right or common law right to set-off any debt the customer owes the bank against any debt the bank owes the customer. *Bank*, defined in section 9-102(a)(8), includes savings and loan associations and credit unions. The debt a customer owes the bank typically consists of money the customer borrows from the bank, the customer's overdrafts the bank pays, and service fees and charges pertaining to account maintenance. The debt a bank owes its customer typically consists of the money in the deposit account. A customer depositing money with its bank creates a debtor-creditor relationship because the customer loans the bank money by making deposits to the account and the bank agrees to repay the customer upon its demand (such as by writing a check) or at a specified time (such as with a certificate of deposit). A conflict can exist between a bank exercising its set-off right against its customer's deposit account and a secured party with a security interest in the deposit account.

With one exception, section 9-340(a) makes a bank's right of set-off or recoupment in its customer's deposit account effective against a secured party that has a security interest in the deposit account. The set-off is effective against a secured party regardless of whether its security interest is created before the creation of the debt that the customer owes its bank. Additionally, section 9-340(b) maintains the superiority of a bank's set-off right over a security interest in the deposit account regardless of whether the bank also has a security interest in its customer's deposit account.

The exception to the superiority of a bank's set-off right functions when a secured party establishes control by becoming the bank's customer of the debtor's deposit account. In that situation, section 9-340(c) states that a bank's exercise of its set-off right is ineffective against such secured party. A secured party who is concerned about its security interest being subordinate to a bank's set-off rights should establish control of the deposit account by becoming the bank's customer of the account. However, the exception of section 9-340(c) applies only against a bank's *set-off* rights, leaving intact its *recoupment* rights. The difference between set-off and recoupment, neither being defined in Article 9, is that a recoupment right arises from the same transaction that creates the other party's claim, while set-off can arise out of a transaction independent of the other party's claim. Consequently, recoupment in a deposit account situation pertains to charges originating from the deposit account transaction, such as account maintenance charges.

3. Priority of a Transferee of Money or Funds from a Deposit Account—Section 9-332

Section 9-332 allows a transferee of money subject to a security interest or a transferee of funds from a deposit account subject to a security interest to take the money or funds free of the security interest. Section 9-332 has a significant impact on secured parties, especially with respect to deposit accounts. A secured party with a security interest in a deposit account, whether direct or as proceeds, probably believes that its right to the funds in the account has priority over a transferee of the funds. That is not the rule; the transferee has priority in the funds it receives. For example, suppose Secured Party perfects a security interest in Debtor's inventory. Debtor deposits money from the sale of inventory in its checking account with its bank. Debtor draws a check on the account payable to Creditor. Under section 9-332(b), Creditor, as transferee, takes the funds free of the security interest. Such transfers are not proceeds of the deposit account, but rather are orders from the account holder for disbursement of its funds. Consequently, any property a transferee acquires with the protected funds should not be proceeds of the collateral.

Section 9-332 disqualifies a transferee from protection if it acts in collusion with the debtor to violate the rights of the secured party. Neither the section nor the comment elaborates on the meaning of collusion. Official Comment 4, however, notes that the term is intended to be "most protective (i.e., least stringent)" with respect to the rights of the transferee. Consequently, a transferee's knowledge that the money or funds in the deposit account is subject to a security interest should not result in collusion. Collusion seems to require that the transferee and the debtor collaborate to deprive the secured party of its rights.

The method of transfering the funds is irrelevant; it can be by check, funds transfer, or debiting the debtor's account and crediting the transferee's account. However, the protected transfer is of money or funds, not a transfer of the account or of an interest in the account.

Official Comment 2 to section 9-322 notes that although Article 9 does not define *transferee*, the debtor is not a transferee. Consequently, a debtor could not use section 9-332 to extinguish a security interest by moving funds from its deposit account that is subject to a security interest to another deposit account that is not subject to a security interest. Both the section and the comment are silent as to whether "transferee" includes the holder of a conflicting security interest. If the holder of a conflicting security interest can be a transferee, then a subordinate secured party could take the funds from the deposit account free of the security interest. Although that result does not seem just, it is consistent with the words of section 9-322.

D. Priority of a Security Interest in Investment Property — Section 9-328

Section 9-328 provides priority rules for determining most conflicts between perfected security interests in investment property. *Investment property*, defined in section 9-102(a)(49), means a security, whether certificated or un-certificated, security entitlement, securities account, commodity contract, or commodity account. (Attachment and perfection of a security interest in investment property are discussed in Chapters 2 and 4, respectively.) A security interest in investment property can be perfected by control (section 9-106), by filing a financing statement (section 9-312(a)(1)), automatically upon attachment for specific security interests (section 9-309), or, in the case of certificated securities, by delivery (section 9-313(a)). Priority is determined according to the method of perfection of the security interest.

Section 9-328(1) awards priority to a security interest in investment property perfected by control over a security interest otherwise perfected. The timing of perfection or knowledge of the conflicting security interest is irrelevant to priority.

More than one secured party may establish control of the same investment property. In that situation, section 9-328(2) essentially determines priority according to the time of establishing control. The priority rules of section 9-328(2) are subject to the priority rules of sections 9-328(3) and (4), discussed in the following paragraphs. Section 9-328(2)(A) determines priority between conflicting security interests in a *security* perfected by control according to priority in the time of establishing control under section 8-106. The first security interest to establish control has priority. Section 9-328(2)(C) determines priority between security interests in a *commodity contract carried with a commodity intermediary* perfected by control according to priority in time of establishing control under section 9-106. Section 9-328(2)(B) determines priority between security interests in a *security entitlement carried in a securities account* perfected by control according to priority in time of establishing control under section 8-106(d). Because section 8-106(d) permits a secured party to establish control of a security entitlement by various methods, section 9-328(2)(B)'s rules correspond to the method of control the secured party uses. However, regardless of the control method used, section 9-328(2)(B) awards priority based on the time the secured party established control of the security entitlement.

Section 9-328(3) determines the priority between conflicting security interests perfected by control in a *security entitlement* or *securities account* when one of the security interests is held by the debtor's securities intermediary (such as a brokerage company). Section 9-328(3) awards the security interest held by the debtor's securities intermediary priority over other security interests, regardless of which secured party first established control.

Section 9-328(4) adopts the same priority rule with respect to *commodity accounts* and *commodity contracts* that section 9-328(3) adopts for security entitlements and securities accounts. When the debtor's commodity intermediary and another secured party with control both claim a security interest in a commodity account or commodity contract, the commodity intermediary has priority under section 9-328(4).

Section 9-328(6) determines priority for all types of investment property between secured parties whose security interests are granted by brokers, securities intermediaries, or commodity intermediaries and perfected by a method other than control. Section 9-328(6) states that all those security interests rank equally. Consequently, each secured party receives its pro rata share of the investment property collateral. Section 9-309 establishes perfection upon attachment of a security interest in investment property granted by a broker or securities intermediary and a security interest in a commodity contract or commodity account granted by a commodity intermediary. However, if such a secured party chooses to perfect its security interest by control, section 9-328(6) does not apply, and the applicable rule of section 9-328 determines priority.

Section 9-328(5) provides a specific rule for determining priority of a security interest in a registered form certificated security perfected by taking delivery of the security as authorized by section 9-313(a). Such a security interest has priority over a conflicting security interest perfected by a method other than control. If the conflicting security interest has been perfected by control, it has priority over the security interest perfected by delivery under the rule of section 9-328(1).

Section 9-322 determines priority between conflicting security interests in investment property that are not governed by the rules of section 9-328. Such security interests include those perfected by filing and unperfected security interests.

E. Priority of a Security Interest in a Letter-of-Credit Right — Section 9-329

A beneficiary's assignment of its right to payment or performance under a letter of credit creates a security interest in a letter-of-credit right. A security interest in a letter-of-credit right can also arise as proceeds of collateral or as a supporting obligation. Section 9-329 determines priority between conflicting security interests in a letter-of-credit right. A secured party who perfects its security interest by establishing control has priority over a secured party who perfects other than by control. Control is the only method of perfecting a security interest in a letter-of-credit right, except for a security interest arising as proceeds of collateral or as a supporting obligation of collateral. Consequently, a secured party who takes a direct interest in a letter-of-credit right and perfects by establishing control has priority over security interests perfected by a different method.

More than one secured party can perfect its security interest in a letter-of-credit right by establishing control. Additionally, a secured party whose security interest in a letter-of-credit right arises originally as proceeds or a supporting obligation can perfect its security interest by control regardless of whether it also is perfected by another manner. Section 9-329(2) states that conflicting security interests perfected by control rank according to priority in time of obtaining control. The secured party that first establishes control of the letter-of-credit right has priority.

F. Priority of a Security Interest in Fixtures and Crops against Owners and Encumbrancers — Section 9-334

1. Property That Is a Fixture

Before examining the rules for determining the priority between a secured party with a fixture security interest and the conflicting interest of an encumbrancer or owner, it is useful to explore the attributes of a fixture. Because fixture collateral generally retains its separate physical identity although it is attached to real property, determining whether the collateral for a security interest is a fixture, a good, or real property can be problematical. Correctly classifying the collateral is important because the type of property controls how a person perfects a secured interest in it. A colleague once described a fixture as "anything you cannot remove in five minutes using a screwdriver." That may be more helpful than Article 9's pronouncements on the question. Additionally, the case law of some jurisdictions has established tests for when a good is a fixture.

Article 9 lends some help in determining whether collateral is a fixture. Section 9-102(a)(41) defines *fixtures* as "goods that have become so related to particular real property that an interest in them arises under real property law." This indicates that a fixture starts out as a good, but subsequently is attached to real property. Goods that are used in real property but are not attached to the real property, such as a window air conditioner, remain goods and are not fixtures. A security interest in goods attaches and is perfected under the general rules of Article 9. Additionally, section 9-334(a) declares that an Article 9 security interest does not exist in ordinary building materials incorporated into an improvement on land. Consequently, building materials such as lumber, bricks, tile, cement, glass, and steel cannot be collateral for a security interest under Article 9 *after* such property has been incorporated into an improvement on land. Such types of property become an integral part of the real property and entirely lose their personal property characteristics. A mortgage is the appropriate security device for taking an interest in real property as collateral for a debt.

Goods that are attached to real property but are not within the above-described types of property are fixtures. They retain their personal property characteristics, but are attached to real property and an interest in the real property would include the personal property now attached to the real property. For example, a furnace begins life as a good. An owner of a building purchases it and installs it in the building, attaching it to gas and electric lines and to a chimney vent. Anyone with a property interest in the building, such as the owner or mortgagee, has an interest in the furnace. (And you could not remove it in five minutes using a screwdriver.) It is a fixture and a secured party could take a security interest in it as collateral for a debt.

Several priority rules in section 9-334 require that the fixture secured party perfect with a "fixture filing." Section 9-502(b) establishes the requirements for a *fixture filing*. A sufficient fixture filing must: satisfy all the section 9-502(a) requirements of a sufficient financing statement; indicate it covers fixtures; indicate it is to be filed in the office where a mortgage on real estate would be filed or recorded; describe the real property to which the fixture is related; and provide the name of the record owner of the real property if the debtor does not have an interest of record in it. (Chapter 3 discusses these requirements in detail.) Section 9-501(a)(1) requires that a fixture financing statement be filed in the office where a mortgage on real estate is filed or recorded.

2. Priority Rules and Remedies after Default for Fixture Security Interests — Section 9-334

Section 9-334 has seven specific priority rules relating to fixture security interests and one general rule. The rules are divided by type of security interest, type of fixture, and type of conflicting interest. The rules determine priority between fixture security interests and owners or encumbrancers of the real property. Article 9 defines *encumbrance* in section 9-102(a)(32) as a right in real property, other than an ownership interest, and includes mortgages and other liens on real property. An encumbrancer is a person who has an encumbrance. A mortgagee is an example of an encumbrancer. Priority between conflicting *security interests* in fixtures is determined by Article 9's other priority rules, generally section 9-322. Consequently, a secured party should make a general Article 9 filing, in addition to a fixture filing, to insure priority against other security interests.

Section 9-334(c) establishes a general priority rule that a security interest in fixtures is subordinate to the conflicting interest of an encumbrancer or owner, other than the debtor, except as otherwise provided in sections 9-334(d)–(h). It means that a secured party with a fixture security interest is subordinate to the owner or encumbrancer who is not also the debtor, unless the secured party satisfies the requirements for priority in those sections.

Section 9-334(d) awards priority to a purchase-money security interest in fixtures over the interest of a *prior* encumbrancer or owner if the secured party satisfies the requirements of section 9-334(d). The requirements are: 1) the interest of the encumbrancer or owner arises before the goods become fixtures; 2) the security interest is perfected by a fixture filing before the goods become fixtures or within twenty days thereafter; and 3) the debtor has an interest of record in the real estate or is in possession of the real estate. For example, suppose Bank records a mortgage on Debtor's building and land that encumbers all fixtures, present and after-acquired. Seller sells Debtor goods that are to become fixtures and takes a purchase-money security interest in the goods sold to secure the purchase price. The goods are affixed to Debtor's real property. Three days later Seller makes a fixture filing. Seller has priority in the fixtures over Bank under section 9-334(d).

Notice that the secured party's priority under section 9-334(d) depends on the debtor either being in possession of the real property or having an interest of record in it. Complying with this requirement means that the secured party must either contract with the owner of the real estate or someone who is in possession of the real estate, such as a lessee, or obtain the owner's consent to the security interest. A security interest in fixtures granted to the secured party by a debtor who is the builder of a structure on the real property does not satisfy the requirement because the debtor does not have an interest of record in the real property and is not in possession of the real property. In that situation, the owner of the real property must consent to the security interest or be the debtor authenticating the security agreement and named in the financing statement.

The priority of a purchase-money security interest is subject to the rule of section 9-334(h). Section 9-334(h) subordinates the purchase-money security interest to a "construction mortgage" if the mortgage is recorded before the goods become fixtures and the goods become fixtures before completion of construction. The section defines *construction mortgage* as a mortgage that "secures an obligation incurred for the construction of an improvement on land, including the acquisition cost of the land, if a recorded record of the mortgage so indicates." Consequently, section 9-334(h) protects a lender who advances money the debtor uses to build the structure in which the fixtures will be placed. Because the lender's advances enable the debtor to build the structure, the construction mortgage is much like a purchase-money security interest. Section 9-334(h) additionally gives construction-mortgage status to a mortgage given to "refinance a construction mortgage."

Section 9-334(e)(1) grants the fixture security interest priority over the owner or encumbrancer (including a construction mortgage) of the real property whose interest arises *subsequent* to perfection of the fixture security interest. This rule is basically a first-to-file-or-record rule—the party first to file or record has priority. Under section 9-334(e)(1), the security interest has priority in the fixture if: 1) it is perfected by a fixture filing before the interest of the encumbrancer or owner is of record; 2) it has priority over any conflicting interest of a predecessor in title of the encumbrancer or owner; and 3) the debtor has an interest of record in the real property or is in possession of the real property.

Priority under section 9-334(e)(1) requires that the security interest have priority over the interest of the predecessor in title of the conflicting encumbrancer or owner. The purpose of that requirement is to allow an encumbrancer or owner having priority over a secured party to transfer its interest free of the security interest. Otherwise, the transferee encumbrancer or owner would be subordinate to the secured party under section 9-334(e)(1) because its interest would be recorded after the fixture filing of the secured party. Essentially, the requirement creates a shelter rule for the transferee—the transfer is sheltered by the transferor's good title—regardless of whether it otherwise would be subject to the security interest.

Section 9-334(e)(2) creates a priority rule applicable to a specific type of fixture: "readily removable ... factory or office machines ... equipment that is not primarily used or leased for use in the operation of the real property; or ... readily removable replacements of domestic appliances which are consumer goods." A security interest "perfected by any method" before these goods become fixtures has priority in the fixtures over the interests of owners or encumbrancers, including a construction mortgage. Because those fixtures have characteristics of fixtures and personal property (some might be removable with a screwdriver in less than five minutes), a secured party might reasonably conclude that the collateral is an ordinary good rather than a fixture and perfect a security interest in it under the Article 9 rules for goods. To circumvent that dilemma, the security interest has priority if the secured party perfects it by any method before the goods become fixtures. Neither the section nor the comments elucidate the meaning of "readily removable." Limiting the application of the rule to situations where the fixtures are readily removable is consistent with the policy of the rule: it applies in instances where it is difficult to determine accurately whether the collateral is fixture or goods.

Section 9-334(e)(3) determines the priority between the fixture security interest and the holder of a lien obtained by legal or equitable proceedings. A lien obtained by legal or equitable proceedings is an interest in property obtained involuntarily through an attachment or levy or a lien arising as a result of a judgment. A fixture security interest perfected by any method has priority over a lien creditor who obtains its interest after the security interest is perfected.

A *manufactured home*, section 9-102(a)(53), can be a fixture. If so, the priority rules of section 9-334 determine priority between a security interest in the manufactured home and the conflicting interest of an owner or encumbrancer. Official Comment 10 to section 9-334 notes that a secured party could establish priority using any applicable priority rule of 9-334. However, section 9-334(e)(4) adopts a specific rule that grants priority to a fixture security interest in a manufactured home. Section 9-334(e)(4) applies only if the secured party perfects its security interest by complying with section 9-311(a)(2)—perfecting by complying with a statute that requires indicating the security interest on the certificate of title for the manufactured home. Many jurisdictions have laws that require the owner of a manufactured home to obtain a certificate of title for it and perfect the security interest by indicating the security interest on the certificate of title. If the governing jurisdiction has not enacted such laws, section 9-334(e)(4) is not applicable. Additionally, the security interest must be created in "a manufactured-home transaction." A *manufactured-home transaction*, section 9-102(a)(54), is a purchase-money security interest in a manufactured home or a security interest in which a manufactured home is the primary collateral, provided in both situations the manufactured home is not classified as inventory of the debtor. Consequently, a secured party can have priority whether it finances the debtor's purchase of the manufactured home or takes a security interest in an existing manufactured home. Section 9-334(e)(4) gives priority to a secured party that satisfies those requirements over the interest of the owner or encumbrancer.

Section 9-334(f) grants a security interest in fixtures priority over the conflicting interest of an encumbrancer or owner in two situations, regardless of whether the secured party perfects the security interest. *First*, section 9-334(f)(1) makes the security interest superior to the interest of the owner or encumbrancer if the owner or encumbrancer consents to or disclaims any interest in the fixture in an authenticated record. *Second*, section 9-334(f)(2) makes the security interest in the fixture superior to the interest of an encumbrancer or owner if the debtor has the right to remove the fixture from the real property.

This rule primarily applies when a debtor is a lessee of real property and has the right, under the terms of the lease or local law, to remove fixtures it attached to the leased property.

A secured party with a fixture security interest has a choice of remedies under section 9-604 if the debtor defaults. Section 9-604 permits the secured party to enforce the security interest in accordance with: 1) the general default remedies of Part 6 of Article 9 (remedies are discussed in Chapter 11), or 2) any rights with respect to the real property. Additionally, the secured party may remove the fixture from the real property if the security interest has priority over all owners and encumbrancers. A condition to the removal is that the secured party must reimburse an encumbrancer or owner of the real property, who is not also the debtor, for any physical damage to the structure, but not for any diminution in value of the real property caused by removal of the fixture. Section 9-604(b)(2) does not elaborate on the meaning of allowing the secured party to proceed "in accordance with the rights with respect to real property...." Comment 3 to the section declares that the rule "serves to overrule cases holding that a secured party's only remedy after default is the removal of the fixtures from the real property." However, section 9-604(b) apparently does not create any such rights. It simply allows the secured party to exercise what rights it has in real property.

3. Priority of a Security Interest in Crops — Section 9-334(i)

Section 9-334(i) determines priority between a security interest in crops growing on real property and a conflicting interest in the crops held by an owner or encumbrancer of the real property. The section declares that a perfected security interest in crops growing on real property has priority over the interest of an owner or encumbrancer if the debtor has an interest of record in or is in possession of the real property on which the crops are growing. There are no time-of-perfection or type-of-perfection requirements for priority.

G. Security Interest in an Accession — Section 9-335

An *accession*, section 9-102(a)(1), is a good that is physically united with another good in such a manner that the identity of the original good is not lost. A good becomes an accession after it is united with the other good. The following example from Official Comment 3 to section 9-335 helps illustrate this concept. An engine is installed in a tractor. Either the engine or the tractor could be the accession, because each is a good that is physically united with the other good, and its identity is not lost in the union of the two goods. If a secured party has a security interest in the engine, it is the accession, and the tractor is the other good. If a secured party has a security interest in the tractor, it is the accession, and the engine is the other good. The accession and the other good unite to form the *whole*.

Section 9-335(a) allows a secured party to obtain a security interest in an accession, and, if a security interest already exists in the good before it becomes an accession, the security interest continues after the good becomes an accession. Additionally, if the security interest is perfected when the good becomes an accession, section 9-335(b) declares that it remains perfected in the accession. For example, suppose a secured party has a perfected security interest in an engine. The engine is installed in a tractor and becomes an accession. The security interest in the engine continues perfected although it is now an accession. Alternatively, a person could take a security interest in an accession after it is united with another good. For example, suppose a secured party takes a security interest in the tractor's engine after it has been installed in the tractor. The accession security interest is in the engine — an accession — not in the tractor.

A security interest in an accession has several potential conflicts: more than one security interest could exist in the accession; a security interest could exist in the whole good; or a security interest could exist in the other good united with the accession. Section 9-335(c) directs that the applicable Article 9 priority rule governs priority between security interests, with one exception discussed in the next paragraph. Generally, the first-to-file-or-perfect rule of section 9-322 will determine priority. However, one of the secured parties could have a purchase-money security interest, resulting in the application of section 9-324.

Section 9-335(d) determines priority between conflicting security interests when a security interest in the accession conflicts with a security interest in the whole that is perfected by compliance with a certificate-of-title statute under section 9-311(b). In that situation, section 9-335(d) grants priority to the security interest perfected in the whole over the security interest in the accession. For example, suppose Bank has a security interest in Debtor's automobile, perfected by compliance with the applicable certificate-of-title law. Seller sells Debtor four tires for the automobile and takes a purchase-money security interest in the tires. The tires are installed on the automobile. Section 9-335(d) awards priority to Bank.

Sections 9-335(e) and (f) create a remedy after default for the accession secured party whose security interest has priority over the claims of all persons to the whole. Section 9-335(e) authorizes that secured party to remove the accession from the whole. The secured party must reimburse the owner, a secured party, or a lienholder, other than the debtor, for the cost of physical injury to the whole or to other goods united with the accession, but not for any diminution in value of the whole or the other goods caused by the absence of the accession or the necessity of replacing it.

H. Security Interest in Commingled Goods — Section 9-336

Commingled goods, defined in section 9-336(a), are goods that are physically united with other goods in such a manner that their identity is lost in the resulting product or mass. Such goods include goods that are manufactured into a product, such as flour that has become part of baked goods, and goods that are mixed into a mass, such as grain mixed with other grain of the same type. "Product or mass" is the property that results when goods are mixed so that the individual goods lose their identity.

Under section 9-336(c), a security interest in goods that are commingled with other goods continues as a security interest in the product or mass resulting from the commingling, but terminates as a security interest in the individual goods. In essence, the security interest in the goods attaches automatically to the product or mass. If a secured party perfects its security interest in the goods before the goods are commingled into the product or mass, section 9-336(d) continues the perfection into the product or mass.

Section 9-336(f) determines the priority of conflicting security interests in the product or mass *provided* those security interests attach to the product or mass through section 9-336(c). In that case, a security interest in the product or mass that is perfected through section 9-336(d) has priority over a security interest in the product or mass that is unperfected when the goods become commingled. If all conflicting security interests in the product or mass are perfected through section 9-336(d), they rank equally in proportion to the value of each secured party's collateral at the time it became commingled goods. For example, if Lender's and Bank's security interests in their original collateral were $10,000 and $5,000, respectively, when the collateral was commingled, Lender's share of the product or mass is two-thirds and Bank's share is one-third, up to the amount of their secured obligations. If, before commingling, more than one security interest exists in the same good, Official Comment 6 to section 9-335 states that the multiple security interests should be treated like a single security interest for purposes of determining their pro rata share in the product or mass. Priority among the claimants to the share is determined by Article 9's other priority rules. If a conflicting security interest in the product or mass is perfected by a method other than section 9-336(d), Article 9's other priority rules determine priority.

I. Priority for Buyer or Secured Party of Goods Covered by a Certificate of Title — Section 9-337

Section 9-337 establishes a priority rule applicable to subsequent buyers of and security interests in goods covered by a *clean* certificate of title—a certificate of title that does not indicate the current security interest. Section 9-337 applies when goods that are subject to a perfected security interest in one jurisdiction become covered by a certificate of title of another jurisdiction, but the new certificate does not indicate the security interest. (Sections 9-102(a)(10) and 9-303, discussed in Chapter 10, establish when goods "become covered by a certificate of title.") The event that activates section 9-337 is the issuance of a certificate of title by the new jurisdiction that does not show that the goods are subject to a security interest or contain a statement that the goods may be subject to security interests not shown on the certificate. The reason for the omission is irrelevant. A certificate of title that indicates only that the vehicle was previously titled or registered in another state is not a certificate that contains a statement that the goods may be subject to security interests not shown on the certificate of title.

The priority rule of section 9-337(1) protects only a *non-professional* buyer of the goods: "a buyer ... other than a person in the business of selling goods of that kind." Section 9-337(1) authorizes a buyer to take the collateral free of the security interest if the buyer gives value and receives delivery of the goods after issuance of the certificate and without knowledge of the security interest. Because a protected buyer must give value and receive delivery of the goods *after issuance of the certificate*, the buyer presumably relies on the clean certificate in making its purchase and arguably deserves to take free of the security interest. A buyer's failure to satisfy any of the requirements for priority disqualifies the buyer from section 9-337's protection and results in priority being determined by Article 9's other rules.

Section 9-337(2) adopts a similar rule for a conflicting subsequent security interest. The existing security interest is subordinate to a security interest that attaches and is perfected in accordance with the certificate-of-title laws of the new jurisdiction after issuance of a clean certificate of title if the subsequent secured party is without knowledge of the existing security interest. Like the buyer, this secured party presumably relies on the clean certificate of title because it must perfect after issuance of the certificate.

Sections 9-316(d) and (e), discussed in Chapter 10, grant temporary perfection for a perfected security interest in goods that become covered by a certificate of title in a new jurisdiction although the secured party has not complied with the perfection requirement of indicating the security interest on the new certificate. Perfection continues until the earlier of four months after the goods become covered by the new certificate or the remaining period of perfection in the other jurisdiction. A buyer or secured party fulfilling the requirements of section 9-337 has priority over that security interest notwithstanding that the security interest is temporarily perfected in the new jurisdiction. Of course, if the secured party perfects in the new jurisdiction by indicating its security interest on the certificate of title, the buyer or secured party could not satisfy the conditions for obtaining priority under section 9-337.

Checkpoints

- A purchaser of chattel paper or an instrument who satisfies the requirements of section 9-330 has priority over a prior perfected security interest in that collateral.

- A security interest in a deposit account perfected by establishing control has priority over a security interest perfected by another method; but if all conflicting security interests perfect by establishing control, priority is determined by the time and method of control.

- A bank's right of set-off in its depositor's deposit account has priority over a security interest in the deposit account, except as against a security interest perfected by the control method of becoming the bank's customer of the account.

- A transferee of funds from a deposit account takes the funds free of a security interest in the account.

- A security interest in investment property perfected by establishing control has priority over a security interest perfected by another method; but if all conflicting security interests perfect by establishing control, priority is determined by the time and method of control.

- A security interest in a letter-of-credit right perfected by establishing control has priority over a security interest perfected by another method; but if all conflicting security interests perfect by establishing control, the first to establish control has priority.

- A security interest in fixtures that satisfies the requirements of section 9-334 has priority over an encumbrancer or owner of the real property that claims an interest in the fixture.

- A security interest continues in a good that becomes an accession, and the Article 9 priority rules determine priority in an accession, unless the conflicting security interest is perfected under a certificate-of-title statute, in which case it has priority over a security interest in the accession.

- A security interest in goods that become commingled goods continues in the commingled product or mass, and all such security interests rank equally in the product or mass in proportion to the value of each party's collateral at the time it became commingled goods.

- A buyer or secured party who buys goods covered by a "clean" certificate of title can have priority over a security interest if it complies with the requirements of section 9-337.

Chapter 10

Determining the Jurisdiction That Governs the Security Interest

---

Roadmap

- Rules for determining the jurisdiction that governs a security interest that has connections with multiple jurisdictions
- Rules that determine the effect of a change in governing jurisdiction on a perfected security interest

---

A. Introduction

Security interest transactions routinely involve several states, even countries. A Delaware debtor might grant its California lender a security interest in its goods kept at its Nebraska retail outlet. That secured transaction is connected with three states, each of which has enacted Article 9. Which state's Article 9 governs the security interest? Although the UCC is designed to be uniform, and for the most part it is, many jurisdictions have enacted their unique variations, particularly with respect to perfection by filing a financing statement. Consequently, it is important that the parties, especially the secured party, know which jurisdiction's Article 9 governs the transaction.

Sections 9-301 to 9-307 supply rules for determining which jurisdiction's Article 9 governs "perfection, the effect of perfection or nonperfection, and the priority of a security interest" when a secured transaction is connected with multiple jurisdictions. Although the parties to the transaction might agree that the Article 9 of a particular jurisdiction governs the transaction, section 1-301(g) makes their agreement inoperative regarding perfection, the effect of perfection or nonperfection, and the priority of a security interest. In other words, the rules of Article 9 override any agreement the parties might have made pertaining to those aspects of a secured transaction. Because perfection, its effects, and priority all have the potential to affect the rights of persons that are not parties to the security agreement, such as other secured creditors, the UCC drafters thought it unfair that the parties could choose the law that would affect a nonparty to the agreement.

That does not leave the parties' agreement as to the governing law completely inoperative. Choice of law for other aspects of the transaction is left to section 1-301 and the agreement, if any, of the parties to the secured transaction. Aspects of a secured transaction that do not concern perfection, its effects, or priority include scope, attachment, and enforcement/default. For example, the parties to a security interest that has contacts with Delaware, California, and Nebraska could agree that Delaware's Article 9 governs all matters pertaining to the secured transaction other than perfection, effect of perfection or nonperfection, and priority. In the absence of an agreement, section 1-301(d) of Revised Article 1 directs that the forum state should apply its general conflict-of-law provisions to determine which jurisdiction's Article 9 applies. However, most jurisdictions enacting Revised Article 1 have retained the choice-of-law rule of former Article 1 (section 1-105) that directs the forum state to apply its Article 9 if the transaction bears an appropriate relation to it.

Before reviewing the choice-of-law rules of Article 9 it is helpful to consider the meaning of the phrase "perfection, the effect of perfection or nonperfection, and the priority of a security interest." Perfection refers to the rules of Article 9 that specify the action a secured party must take to protect its security interest against the claims of persons other than the debtor, and is discussed in Chapters 3–5.

The meaning of the phrase "the effect of perfection and nonperfection and the priority of a security interest" is not as clearly defined as is "perfection." The phrase "perfection and the effect of perfection and nonperfection" first appeared in Article 9 in the 1972 revisions to Article 9's choice-of-law rules. It presumably refers to determining the rights of claimants to the collateral because the effects of perfection relate to how perfection of the security interest affects other claimants to the collateral. Official Comment 1 to section 9-103 of the 1972 Article 9 declared: "when conflicting claims to collateral arise, the question depends on *perfection* of security interests and thus on the effect of perfection or non-perfection."

"[P]riority" was added to the phrase in connection with the 1994 revisions to Article 8, when jurisdiction over security interests in investment property was returned to Article 9. Priority refers to determining who, among several claimants to the collateral, is first in line to get the collateral. Official Comment 9 to section 9-103 of the 1994 Article 9, in discussing the choice-of-law rule, spoke only of "perfection and priority" of a security interest, ignoring the "effects" phrase entirely.

The drafters of Revised Article 9 provide no enlightenment. They refer to the phrase only in Official Comment 2 to section 9-301, where they label it a "broader and more precise formulation" than the 1972 formulation. Additionally, the titles of all other sections of Article 9 that pertain to choice-of-law rules (sections 9-302–9-306) are captioned "Law Governing Perfection and Priority…." They make no reference to "effects." Consequently, there is no indication that "effects of perfection or non-perfection" has a different focus than "priority." Although I am always hesitant to conclude that a UCC section contains a redundancy, that may be the case here. Courts and commentators have defined the phrase as referring to the rules that resolve competing claims to the collateral, so that is the meaning I will use. You can read the phrase, "perfection, the effect of perfection or nonperfection, and the priority of a security interest," as meaning "perfection and priority."

B. General Rule — Jurisdiction Where the Debtor Is Located Governs Perfection and Priority of a Security Interest — Section 9-301

Section 9-301(1) provides the choice-of-law rule applicable to perfection, effect of perfection or nonperfection, and priority of a security interest in most types of collateral. Specific rules (discussed later in this chapter) are provided in sections 9-302–9-306 for agricultural liens, goods covered by a certificate of title, deposit accounts, investment property, and letter-of-credit rights. The rule of 9-301(1) is fairly straightforward: perfection, effect of perfection or nonperfection, and priority of the security interest are governed by the local law of the jurisdiction where the debtor is located. Comment 3 to section 9-301 informs us that "local law" of a jurisdiction means the substantive law of the jurisdiction, exclusive of its choice-of-law rules and its Article 9 choice-of-law rules. The substantive law of a jurisdiction of course includes the Article 9 of the jurisdiction. To illustrate, assume a Kentucky creditor loans money to a debtor located in Indiana and takes a security interest in the debtor's inventory located in Indiana to secure the debt. Both Indiana and Kentucky have enacted the uniform section 9-301(1). Indiana's Article 9 governs perfection of the security interest and any priority conflicts involving the collateral because the debtor is located in Indiana.

The rule of section 9-301(1) focuses on the location of the debtor — determine where the debtor is located and apply that jurisdiction's Article 9 to perfection and priority of the security interest. Section 9-307 adopts rules for determining the debtor's location. It is especially important that a secured party determine which jurisdiction's Article 9 governs perfection because that is the jurisdiction where the secured party will file its financing statement to perfect its security interest by filing. Section 9-301(1) makes it a simple task: determine where the debtor is located and file the financing statement in that jurisdiction. The rule applies to all debtors, foreign or domestic.

1. Debtor and Collateral Not Located in the Same Jurisdiction — Section 9-301(3)(C)

To continue with the previous example, suppose the Indiana debtor keeps the inventory collateral in Kentucky, the place of its business. The collateral is in Kentucky but the debtor is in Indiana. Under section 9-301(1), Indiana's Article 9 governs *perfection* of the security interest because that is the jurisdiction where the debtor is located. However, section 9-301(3)(C) directs that the local law of the jurisdiction where the collateral is located governs the effect of perfection or nonperfection and the priority of the security interest. This rule focuses on the location of the collateral — determine where the collateral is located and apply that jurisdiction's Article 9 to issues involving the priority of the security interest.

The consequence of the debtor and collateral being located in different jurisdictions is that a single jurisdiction's Article 9 does not govern perfection and priority of the security interest. Section 9-301(1), the location-of-the-debtor rule, determines the jurisdiction that governs perfection. Section 9-301(3)(C), the location-of-the-collateral rule, determines the jurisdiction that governs priority. However, the rule of section 9-301(3)(C) applies only to security interests in negotiable documents, instruments, goods, money, or tangible chattel paper. For security interests in other collateral, the Article 9 of the debtor's location governs the perfection, the effect of perfection or nonperfection, and the priority of a security interest, except where Article 9 provides otherwise.

The UCC drafters explain the policy of section 9-301(3)(C) in Official Comment 7 to section 9-301. You UCC aficionados will want to read it. For the rest of you, the reason is connected with resolving priority between a secured party and an execution lien — the lien a holder of an unpaid judgment can obtain. Realistically, the impact of section 9-301(3)(C) is not great because most states enacted the uniform version of Article 9's priority rules, so it does not matter which jurisdiction's Article 9 governs priority.

C. Rules for Determining the Debtor's Location — Section 9-307

Location of the debtor is the base-line rule for determining which jurisdiction's Article 9 governs perfection and priority. Section 9-307 provides rules, classified by the type of debtor, for determining the location of the debtor.

1. Individuals — Section 9-307(b)(1)

An individual is a human being. A *person* is any of the types of entities listed in the section 1-201(b)(27) definition, including an individual. Section 9-307(b)(1) establishes that an individual debtor is located in the jurisdiction of the individual's principal residence. Because Article 9 does not provide any guidelines for determining an individual's principal residence, a secured party who has doubts regarding the exact jurisdiction of an individual's principal residence should perfect under the Article 9s of all possible jurisdictions. For example, suppose an individual debtor maintains a residence in Florida and lives there for eight months every year, but lives the remaining four months in her Colorado residence. Most likely, the debtor's principal residence is Florida. But there is no reason to risk the adverse effect of a court determining that the debtor's principal residence is Colorado. The secured party should proceed as though the Article 9s of both Colorado and Florida govern the transaction, and perfect in accordance with the laws of both jurisdictions.

An individual debtor who owns a business in a jurisdiction other than the jurisdiction of its residence is nevertheless located in the jurisdiction of its residence. For example, an individual whose residence is in Pennsylvania, but who operates a business as a *sole proprietor* in Ohio is located in Pennsylvania for purposes of a security interest in both his business and personal assets.

If the jurisdiction of the debtor's location does not maintain a filing, recording, or registration system as a condition to or result of perfecting a nonpossessory security interest, the debtor is located in the District of Columbia pursuant to section 9-307(c). In other words, an individual debtor is deemed located in the District of Columbia if the actual location of the debtor is in a jurisdiction that does not have a system whereby a secured party perfects its security interest by filing or recording a notice of its claim to the collateral, or the jurisdiction does not have a system that provides notice of a security interest that has been perfected. Because all States of the United States have such systems, the relevance of this rule is limited to individual debtors located in foreign countries.

2. Registered Organizations—Section 9-307(e)

The debtor in many secured transactions will be what Article 9 labels a "registered organization that is organized under the law of a State"—a registered organization. Pursuant to section 9-307(e), a registered organization is located in the state under whose law it is organized. Section 9-102(a)(70) defines a *registered organization* as "an organization organized solely under the law of a single State or the United States, and as to which the State or the United States must maintain a public record showing the organization to have been organized." The key to whether an organization is a registered organization is that the state is required to maintain a public record of the entity's organization, not that the entity is required to register or provide information about it to the state. For example, suppose ABC General Partnership is formed under the partnership laws of Kansas and pursuant thereto must file a statement of partnership with the Kansas Secretary of State. The requirement of filing the partnership statement with a public office does not make the partnership a registered organization. The partnership is a registered organization only if Kansas law requires maintenance of a public registry of partnerships. The location of a registered organization debtor should be simple to determine under this rule by checking with the secretary of state's office to determine if the debtor is organized under the law of that state.

Official Comment 11 to section 9-102 notes that examples of registered organizations include corporations, limited liability companies, and limited partnerships. Consequently, a corporate debtor is located in the jurisdiction where it is organized.

Section 9-102(a)(76) defines *State* as "a State of the United States, the District of Columbia, Puerto Rico, the United States Virgin Islands, or any territory or insular possession subject to the jurisdiction of the United States." Consequently, a foreign organization cannot be an Article 9 registered organization.

A registered organization is located in a single state only. The fact that an organization organized under the law of a state must register with the secretary of state of each state where it conducts business does not create multiple locations of the debtor, even if the secretary of state maintains a registry of corporations authorized to do business in the state. An organization can be a registered organization only of the state in which it is organized.

Section 9-307(g) provides that a debtor continues to be located in the jurisdiction originally determined under section 9-307(e) notwithstanding the occurrence of events subsequent to perfection that affect its organizational status, such as dissolution, suspension, or lapse. Consequently, a secured party need not take any additional action should one of those events occur.

It is important to note that section 9-307(b) furnishes rules to determine the location of a debtor that is an *organization*, an entity that is different from a *registered organization*. Although the section 1-201(b)(25) definition of *organization* is sufficiently broad to encompass a registered organization, Article 9 separates the two entities and adopts separate location rules for each entity. Remember the interpretation maxim: a specific statute supplants a general statute. That is the case with section 9-307. The registered organization rule of section 9-307(e) applies if the debtor is within the definitions of registered organization and organization.

3. Registered Organization under Federal Law — Section 9-307(f)

Section 9-307(f) establishes the location of a debtor that is a registered organization under federal law, including banks so organized. A registered organization under federal law includes an organization organized solely under the law of the United States, and as to which the United States must maintain a public record showing such entity's organization. Under section 9-307(f), the registered organization is located in: 1) the state that federal law so designates, if any; 2) in absence of any such designation, the state that the registered organization designates, if federal law authorizes the organization to so designate; or 3) in the absence of either designation, the District of Columbia. The debtor continues to be located in the jurisdiction originally designated under 9-307(f) notwithstanding subsequent events affecting its status such as dissolution, suspension, or lapse.

4. Foreign Bank Registered Organizations — Sections 9-307(f), (i)

Section 9-307 specifies the location of a foreign bank organization. A foreign bank is a branch or agency of a bank that is not organized under federal or state law. If all branches and agencies of such a bank are located in only one state, the bank is located in that state pursuant to section 9-307(i). If all branches and agencies are not located in only one state, section 9-307(f) establishes the location as: 1) the state that federal law so designates, if any; 2) in absence of any such designation, the state that the organization designates if federal law authorizes the organization to so designate; or 3) in the absence of either designation, the District of Columbia.

5. Other Organizations — Sections 9-307(b)(2), (b)(3)

Under the location rules of sections 9-307(b)(2) and (b)(3), a debtor that is an organization other than the types discussed previously is located in the jurisdiction of its principal place of business if it has only one place of business, or in the jurisdiction of its chief executive office if it has more than one place of business. *Organization,* defined in section 1-201(b)(25), is a person other than an individual, and *person,* section 1-201(b)(27), includes a corporation, government or governmental subdivision or agency, business trust, estate, trust, partnership or association, two or more persons having a joint or common interest, or any other legal or commercial entity. In other words, "organization" catches any type of debtor other than those specifically identified in section 9-307. Most domestic corporations, limited partnerships, and limited liability companies are registered organizations, whose location is determined pursuant to section 9-307(e). Consequently, the organization subject to section 9-307(b) is frequently a general partnership or a foreign corporation.

The location-of-debtor rules of sections 9-307(b)(2) and (b)(3) operate only if the jurisdiction of the debtor's location maintains a filing, recording, or registration system as a condition to or result of perfecting a nonpossessory security interest. If the jurisdiction does not maintain such a system, section 9-307(c) establishes the debtor's location as the District of Columbia. Because all States of the United States have such systems, the impact of this rule is on organization debtors located in foreign countries.

An organization with only one place of business is located in that jurisdiction. Official Comment 2 to section 9-307 notes that *place of business* is the place where the debtor conducts its affairs. Every organization will have a place where it conducts its business or affairs. For example, a corporation organized in Spain that has a single place of business in Spain is located in Spain under the rule of section 9-307(b)(2), provided Spain has the required filing, recording, or registration system. If it does not, the organization is located in the District of Columbia. An organization with more than one place of business, however, is located at its chief executive office under section 9-307(b)(3). Official Comment 2 defines *chief executive office* is the place from which the debtor manages the main part of its operations; the place where persons dealing with the debtor would normally look for credit information. For example, suppose a general partnership is formed in Minnesota, and it maintains places of business in Iowa, Wisconsin, and North Dakota. The partners manage the business from their offices in Rochester, Minnesota. Minnesota is the location of the chief executive office and the location of the debtor. In cases of doubt, caution should cause the secured party to operate as though the debtor is located in each jurisdiction where the debtor maintains a place of business and perfect its security interest under the law of each jurisdiction.

A foreign air carrier is not subject to the organization rules, but is located at the designated office of the agent upon which service of process may be made on behalf of the carrier pursuant to section 9-307(j).

D. Maintaining Perfection of the Security Interest after Change of Governing Jurisdiction — Sections 9-316(a), (b)

1. Temporary Automatic Perfection after Change of Governing Jurisdiction — Sections 9-316(a), (b)

Choice-of-law issues do not end once you have determined the jurisdiction that governs perfection and priority of a security interest using sections 9-301 and 9-307. The next issue is what happens when the location of the debtor changes, which necessarily causes a change in the jurisdiction that governs the security interest. The jurisdiction governing perfection, the effect of perfection or nonperfection, and priority of the security interest changes if the location of the debtor changes because the location of the debtor determines which jurisdiction's Article 9 governs a security interest. For example, suppose an individual debtor located in Pennsylvania borrows money from and grants a security interest to a Maryland secured party. Sections 9-301 and 9-307 would establish Pennsylvania as the jurisdiction whose Article 9 governs the security interest and Pennsylvania's section 9-501 will require filing in Pennsylvania. If the debtor moves to Delaware, sections 9-301 and 9-307 would establish Delaware, the location of the debtor, as the jurisdiction that governs the security interest and Delaware's section 9-501 will require filing in Delaware. Assuming that the secured party has perfected the security interest with a Pennsylvania filing, must it now file a financing statement in Delaware?

Section 9-316 provides the answer. The heading of section 9-316 is "Continued Perfection of Security Interest Following Change in Governing Jurisdiction." Its only purpose is to furnish rules that establish the effect of a change in governing law on the perfection of a security interest. Section 9-316 applies when a security interest is perfected under the law of the governing jurisdiction, subsequent events cause the location of the debtor to change, and consequently another jurisdiction's Article 9 governs the security interest. The section does not apply when an unperfected security interest exists and the location of the debtor changes. In that case the security interest remains unperfected until the secured party takes the appropriate action in the new jurisdiction. The scope of section 9-316(a) is over security interests whose governing jurisdiction is established under 9-301(a) (the baseline rule, operating in absence of a specific rule) and 9-305(c) (specific security interests in investment property discussed later in this chapter).

Before reviewing the rules of section 9-316, you should note happily that the location of most organization debtors, especially registered organization debtors, rarely changes. However, registered organization debtors frequently transfer collateral to other persons and section 9-316 applies if the security interest survives the transfer and the transferee is located in a jurisdiction different from the transferor/debtor because the transferee is now the debtor.

The situation covered by section 9-316 is illustrated best with an example. Assume that the debtor is a general partnership with its only place of business in Kentucky. A dealer sells the debtor equipment on credit and takes a security interest in the equipment. Kentucky's Article 9 governs perfection and priority of the security interest because the debtor, an organization, is located in Kentucky. The secured party perfects by filing a financing statement in Kentucky. The debtor subsequently opens a second place of business in Indiana and establishes its chief executive office in Indiana. Under section 9-307(b)(3), the debtor is located in Indiana because an organization with more than one place of business is located in the jurisdiction of its chief executive office. Consequently, Kentucky's Article 9 ceases to govern and Indiana's Article 9 now governs perfection of the security interest in the debtor's equipment. Indiana's Article 9 requires filing a financing statement in Indiana for security interests that are perfected by filing. At this point the secured party has filed a financing statement only in Kentucky.

What happens to the perfection? Does the security interest remain perfected without an Indiana filing? Does it become unperfected immediately? Under section 9-316(a) the security interest does not become unperfected immediately despite the fact that the only filing is in Kentucky and Indiana's Article 9 now governs perfection of the security interest. Section 9-316(a) provides automatic continued perfection of a security interest for a limited period of time. The security interest remains perfected temporarily after the location of the debtor changes without the secured party taking any action in the new jurisdiction to perfect the security interest.

To make section 9-316(a) easier to understand it is helpful to distinguish between the two jurisdictions involved. Because the section does not make that distinction very clear, I use the folllwing terms. The *old jurisdiction* is the jurisdiction where the debtor was located previously. The *new jurisdiction* is the jurisdiction where the debtor is located presently.

Section 9-316(a) provides that a security interest perfected pursuant to the law of the old jurisdiction (Kentucky, in our example) remains perfected despite a change of the governing jurisdiction until the *earlier* of: 1) the time perfection would have ceased under the law of the old jurisdiction; 2) the expiration of four months after a change of the debtor's location to the new jurisdiction (Indiana, in our example); or 3) the expiration of one year after a transfer of collateral to a person that thereby becomes a debtor and is located in the new jurisdiction (relevant only when the debtor transfers the collateral). The security interest remains perfected for the applicable time period although the secured party takes no action to perfect the security interest in the new jurisdiction. For example, if the four-month period applies in the previous example, the security interest automatically remains perfected in Indiana for four months after the debtor changes its location. Note that the four-month period commences on the date the debtor establishes its location in the new jurisdiction, not on the date the debtor leaves the old jurisdiction.

This temporary perfection becomes permanent perfection if the secured party perfects in the new jurisdiction within the applicable period of temporary perfection. Section 9-316(b) states that the security interest remains perfected continuously if the secured party perfects in the new jurisdiction before the temporary perfection lapses. A result of continuous perfection is that the priority date of the security interest relates back to the date of the filing in the old jurisdiction under the rule of section 9-322(a)(1). Section 9-316(a) allows a secured party time to discover the change in governing jurisdiction, ascertain which jurisdiction now governs, and perfect under the new jurisdiction's Article 9 so that the security interest remains perfected continuously.

Although the four-month period applies to many security interests perfected by filing, it does not apply when the remaining period of perfection in the old jurisdiction is less than four months. (In most jurisdictions a security interest perfected by filing remains perfected for five years pursuant to section 9-513, discussed in Chapter 3.) Under section 9-316(a), a security interest remains perfected only until the expiration of perfection in the old jurisdiction when that date is earlier than four months after the change in location. For example, suppose the secured party perfects a security interest in the debtor's equipment by filing a financing statement on March 17, 2008 in Kentucky, the location of the debtor. The debtor, on January 1, 2013, changes its location to Indiana, and consequently Indiana law governs perfection. The secured party's security interest remains perfected until March 17, 2013 not May 1, 2013 (which is four months after the change). The secured party can remain perfected continuously by perfecting under Indiana's Article 9 before March 17, 2013.

If the secured party in this example files a continuation statement (continuation statements are discussed in Chapter 3) under Kentucky's Article 9 before the debtor establishes its location in Indiana, it would have the full four months to perfect under Indiana's Article 9 because a continuation statement would have continued perfection for an additional five years in Kentucky absent the change in governing jurisdiction. The secured party can file its continuation statement in Kentucky because under section 9-515(d) the six-month window for filing such statements opens on September 17, 2012. It is not clear whether the secured party obtains the full four months of protection from filing a continuation statement under Kentucky's Article 9 after the debtor establishes its location in Indiana. When the debtor is located in Indiana, section 9-301(1) establishes the local law of Indiana as the governing law and Indiana's section 9-501(a) commands filing a continuation statement in Indiana. Consequently, filing the continuation statement in Kentucky would seem to be ineffective to give the secured party four months of temporary perfection.

The period of temporary automatic perfection in the new jurisdiction can extend up to one year after the change in the location of the debtor under section 9-316(a)(3) if the change results from a transfer of collateral by the debtor to a person located in a different jurisdiction than the original debtor. In this situation, the debtor does not change its location, instead the debtor transfers the collateral to a person who is located in a different jurisdiction. The transferee becomes the debtor under the section 9-102(a)(28) definition of *debtor*. Under 9-316(a)(3), the security interest remains automatically perfected for one year after the transfer.

However, the one-year period is limited by the remaining-period-of-perfection rule discussed previously. If the perfection would have ceased under the law of the old jurisdiction before one year after the transfer, the security interest remains perfected only until the time perfection would have ceased. The four-month rule is not applicable because it applies only in the situation where a single debtor changes its location. It is worth restating that a secured party can remain continuously perfected pursuant to section 9-316(b) by perfecting the security interest under the local law of the new jurisdiction within the applicable statutory time, whether it is one year, four months, or a shorter time. To help achieve that result, the secured party should include a provision in the security agreement requiring the debtor to notify the secured party of a change in its location.

2. Consequences of Failure to Perfect after Change of Governing Jurisdiction — The Retroactive Unperfection Rule — Section 9-316(b)

The secured party's failure to perfect the security interest in the new jurisdiction within the applicable time period has serious consequences. First, section 9-316(b) states that the security interest becomes unperfected. An unperfected security interest leaves the secured party's interest in the collateral vulnerable to other secured parties and lien creditors, including a bankruptcy trustee. There is a remedy for this consequence: a secured party whose perfection has lapsed can perfect its security interest pursuant to the law of the new jurisdiction as soon as it discovers the change in location. However, because the previous perfection lapsed, there will be a gap in perfection, and the security interest will have a new priority date that is later than its original priority date.

The second consequence is worse. Section 9-316(b) states that the now unperfected security interest "is deemed never to have been perfected as against a purchaser of the collateral for value." Official Comment 3 to section 9-316 labels this consequence, "retroactive unperfection." That aptly describes its effect. As a result of the failure to reperfect, a security interest that had been perfected and protected against other interests is now treated as though it never was perfected as against a purchaser of the collateral for value, and likely is subordinate to such purchasers. The beneficiary of this rule is a purchaser for value. Sections 1-201(b)(29) and (b)(30) define *purchase* and *purchaser* as including a buyer of the collateral and a secured party with a security interest in the collateral, but the term does not include a lien creditor. Section 1-204 defines value broadly to include any consideration and acquiring rights in satisfaction of a preexisting claim.

The following example illustrates the retroactive unperfection rule. Assume Debtor is a general partnership with its only place of business in South Dakota. Merchant sells Debtor equipment on credit, takes a security interest in the equipment, and perfects it by filing a financing statement in South Dakota on August 17, 2007. Bank perfects a security interest in the same equipment in October 2007. At this point Merchant has priority over Bank pursuant to section 9-322(a)(1). On January 1, 2009 Debtor opens a second place of business in Iowa and establishes its chief executive office in Iowa. Iowa's Article 9 governs the security interest. Merchant does not perfect its security interest under Iowa law and consequently Merchant's security interest becomes unperfected. Bank, however, perfects under Iowa law within four months of the change. The retroactive unperfection rule of section 9-316(b) combined with the priority rule of section 9-322(a)(1) results in Bank's security interest having priority in the equipment.

The rule of retroactive unperfection protects a purchaser for value whether the purchaser acquires its interest before or after the change in governing law. In the previous example, the purchaser (Bank) acquired its security interest in the collateral before the change in governing law. The outcome is the same if the purchaser for value acquires its interest in the collateral after the change in governing law. Continuing with that example, suppose Bank attaches and perfects its security interest under Iowa law on March 1, 2009 during the four months of temporary perfection for Merchant. Merchant fails to perfect its security interest under Iowa law. Bank's security interest has priority over Merchant's security interest under the retroactive unperfection rule of section 9-316(b) and the priority rule of section 9-322(a). Merchant's perfection would have been continuous and it would have had priority over Bank if it had perfected its security interest under Iowa law within the four-month period.

E. Rules for Determining the Governing Jurisdiction and Effect of Change of Jurisdiction for Particular Types of Collateral

1. Goods Covered by a Certificate of Title — Sections 9-303, 9-316(d), (e)

Most jurisdictions have enacted statutes independent of Article 9 which require owners of certain types of personal property to possess a certificate of title to evidence their ownership of the property. Typically those statutes cover motor vehicles, trailers (the vessel you tow behind your car or truck), motor boats, and manufactured homes (what you might call a trailer you live in). Article 9 adopts rules for determining the jurisdiction that governs a security interest in goods covered by a certificate of title. The rules are applicable when a jurisdiction has enacted a statute that fits the Article 9 definition of *certificate of title* in section 9-102(a)(10). Under that definition, a certificate of title exists if a statute of the jurisdiction "provides for the security interest to be indicated on the certificate as a condition or result of the security interest's obtaining priority over the rights of a lien creditor with respect to the collateral." The definition establishes a certificate of title in two different situations. In one situation, the jurisdiction's law requires that a secured party perfect its security interest in the goods by indicating its security interest on the certificate—a condition of perfection. In the other situation, the jurisdiction's law requires perfection of the security interest by another method, such as filing a financing statement, but the security interest is indicated on the certificate as a consequence of perfection—a result of perfection. Most jurisdictions have statutes that fit the Article 9 definition. Jurisdictions that have enacted such statutes also enact statutory procedures that enable the secured party to have its security interest indicated on the certificate. In a jurisdiction without such a statute, the goods are ordinary goods.

a. Rules for Determining the Governing Jurisdiction— Section 9-303

There is a familiar solution to resolving choice-of-law issues for certificate-of-title goods. Section 9-303(c) states that perfection, the effect of perfection or nonperfection, and the priority of a security interest in certificate-of-title goods are governed by the local law of the jurisdiction whose certificate covers the goods. A jurisdiction's law governs from the time the goods become covered by its certificate until the goods cease to be covered by its certificate.

Section 9-303(b) establishes when goods become covered and when they cease to be covered. A certificate of title covers a good when a valid application for the certificate and the applicable fee are delivered to the appropriate authority for receiving the application. Because actual issuance of the certificate typically occurs after a party applies for it, section 9-303(b) allows the collateral to become covered by a certificate of title before the certificate is issued. A good ceases to be covered by a certificate of title at the earlier of the time it becomes covered by a certificate of title of another jurisdiction or the time the certificate ceases to be effective under the law of the issuing jurisdiction. This automatic cessation of coverage ensures that the goods are never covered by more than one certificate of title for Article 9 purposes. For example, suppose a certificate of title issued by New York covers the debtor's vehicle. The debtor subsequently moves to Connecticut and obtains a certificate of title for the vehicle from Connecticut without surrendering the New York certificate of title. Under section 9-303(b), the law of Connecticut governs perfection and priority of the security interest as soon as the collateral becomes covered by the Connecticut certificate and New York ceases to govern although the New York certificate of title might still be effective under the law of New York.

Section 9-303(a) provides that a certificate of title of a jurisdiction can cover a good even if the debtor or the good is not located in the jurisdiction whose certificate covers the good. For example, suppose an interstate trucking company is a registered organization located in Ohio, with its chief executive office in Michigan, and it obtains Michigan certificates of title for its trucks. The trucks are covered by the Michigan certificates of title, and thus Michigan's local law governs perfection and priority of any security interest in the trucks notwithstanding that the debtor is located in Ohio.

Official Comment 5 to section 9-303 helps avoid a potential choice-of-law conflict in the situation where a person sells a good covered by a certificate of title to a person in the business of selling such goods, and that person grants a security interest in it. For example, suppose the State of Utah issues Owner a certificate of title for a vehicle. Owner takes the vehicle to Nevada and trades (sells) it to Dealer, a person in the business of selling vehicles. Dealer retains the vehicle's certificate of title that Owner assigned to Dealer. Lender has a security interest in dealer's inventory, including after-acquired inventory, which attaches to the vehicle. Does section 9-303, goods covered by a certificate of title, or section 9-301, ordinary goods (the vehicle is inventory, an ordinary good), govern perfection and priority of the security interest? Official Comment 5 indicates that the rules of Article 9 classify the vehicle as an ordinary good, thus section 9-301 determines which jurisdiction governs perfection and priority of the security interest.

b. Effect of Change of Governing Jurisdiction — Sections 9-316(d), (e)

Sections 9-316 (d) and (e) establish rules that determine the effect of a change in the governing jurisdiction on the perfection of a security interest in a good covered by a certificate of title. Typically, the governing jurisdiction changes because the debtor moves the good from one jurisdiction to another and the good becomes covered by a certificate of title in the new jurisdiction. The rules operate when a good subject to a security interest "perfected by any method" in the old jurisdiction become covered by a certificate of title of a new jurisdiction. *Perfected by any method* means what it says—the security interest in the good now covered by a certificate of title can be perfected originally by any Article 9 method.

Section 9-316(d) grants continued perfection of a perfected security interest after a change of the governing jurisdiction without requiring that the secured party take action to perfect in the new jurisdiction. It declares that a security interest in a good covered by a certificate of title of the new jurisdiction and previously perfected in the old jurisdiction by any method remains perfected until perfection would have ceased under the law of the old jurisdiction as a result of an event other than the good becoming covered by a certificate of title in the new jurisdiction. Perfection could cease, for example, because the period of perfection in the old jurisdiction expires.

For example, suppose a Washington certificate of title covers Debtor's automobile. Bank perfects a security interest in the automobile by complying with Washington's certificate of title statutes. Debtor moves to Idaho and applies for an Idaho certificate of title. Debtor's automobile becomes covered by an Idaho certificate of title pursuant to section 9-303(b) when Debtor tenders the application and the fee to the proper office. Nevertheless, section 9-316(d) directs that the security interest remains perfected in Idaho without action until perfection would cease under Washington law. Suppose Creditor acquires a judicial lien on Debtor's automobile seven months after the move. If Bank's security interest is still perfected under Washington law, it is superior to Creditor's judicial lien pursuant to the priority rule of section 9-317(a).

Section 9-316(e) creates an exception to section 9-316(d)'s grant of continued perfection. The exception protects purchasers for value and also includes a retroactive unperfection rule. A security interest perfected under section 9-316(d) becomes unperfected as against a purchaser for value and is deemed never to have been perfected against such purchaser unless the secured party perfects the security interest before the *earlier* of the time the security interest would have become unperfected under the law of the old jurisdiction or the expiration of four months after the good becomes covered by the certificate of title of the new jurisdiction. Note that the four-month period commences when the goods become covered by the new certificate of title, not when the purchaser acquires its interest. Recall that a *purchaser* for value includes a buyer of the collateral and a secured party with a security interest in the collateral, but not a lien creditor. If the secured party perfects in the new jurisdiction during the allotted time, it maintains continuous perfection and section 9-316(e) has no effect.

For example, suppose a Washington certificate of title covers Debtor's automobile. Bank perfects a security interest in the automobile by complying with Washington's certificate-of-title statutes on July 1, 2007. Debtor moves to Idaho and applies for an Idaho certificate of title on November 11, 2008 by tendering the application and fee to the proper office. At that point, Idaho law governs perfection of the security interest because the automobile becomes covered by an Idaho certificate of title. On January 30, 2009, while Bank's security interest remains perfected, Creditor perfects a security interest in the automobile by complying with Idaho's certificate-of-title statute. Creditor is a purchaser for value. Bank's security interest becomes unperfected as against Creditor on March 11, 2009 unless Bank perfects by complying with Idaho's certificate-of-title statute or, atypically, by possessing the automobile pursuant to section 9-313(b). (A security interest in goods covered by a certificate of title can be perfected by possession in the limited situations noted in Official Comment 7 to section 9-311 — essentially limited to when a debtor defaults.) If Bank fails to perfect in the allotted time, the retroactive unperfection rule of section 9-316(e) deems the security interest never to have been perfected against Creditor, and Creditor's security interest is superior to Bank's security interest under section 9-322(a)(1). This result can occur regardless of whether the purchaser for value acquires its interest in the collateral before or after the change in governing law.

2. Deposit Accounts—Sections 9-304, 9-316(f), (g)

A *deposit account* is defined in section 9-102(a)(29) as a "demand, time, savings, passbook, or similar account maintained with a bank," and can include a certificate of deposit. *Bank*, defined in section 9-102(a)(8), includes banks, savings and loan associations, and credit unions. Attachment and perfection of a security interest in a deposit account are discussed in Chapters 2 and 4, respectively.

a. Rules for Determining the Governing Jurisdiction—Section 9-304

Section 9-304(a) provides that the local law of a "bank's jurisdiction" governs perfection, the effect of perfection or nonperfection, and the priority of a security interest in a deposit account. Note that the law of the bank's jurisdiction governs regardless of whether the bank is a party to the secured transaction.

A bank's jurisdiction is established in section 9-304(b) pursuant to five hierarchical rules. The rules apply in the order of their hierarchy. If a superior rule establishes the bank's jurisdiction, the subordinate rules for fixing jurisdiction are not applicable. *First*, if a deposit account agreement between the bank and customer expressly provides that a particular jurisdiction is the bank's jurisdiction for purposes of Part 3 of Article 9 (the perfection and priority sections), Article 9, or the Uniform Commercial Code, that jurisdiction is the bank's jurisdiction. Section 4-104(a)(5) defines *customer* as the person having an account with the bank. The flexibility of this rule allows the parties to choose a particular jurisdiction to govern some or all aspects of a security interest or to choose a jurisdiction to govern secured transactions and a different jurisdiction to govern other transactions within the UCC. *Second*, if a deposit account agreement between the bank and its customer expressly provides that the law of a particular jurisdiction governs the agreement, that jurisdiction is the bank's jurisdiction. *Third*, if a deposit account agreement between the bank and its customer expressly provides that the deposit account is maintained at an office in a particular jurisdiction, that jurisdiction is the bank's jurisdiction. Under this rule, there is no agreement as to the governing jurisdiction, only an agreement as to the office where the account is maintained. *Fourth*, the bank's jurisdiction is the jurisdiction of the office identified in an account statement for the deposit account as the office serving the customer's account. *Fifth*, the bank's jurisdiction is the jurisdiction of the bank's chief executive office.

b. Effect of Change of Governing Jurisdiction — Sections 9-316(f), (g)

Sections 9-316(f) and (g) provide rules for determining whether a security interest in a deposit account remains perfected when a bank changes its jurisdiction. These rules are similar to the four-months-or-expiration-of-perfection rules that apply to goods under section 9-316(a). Section 9-316(f) provides that a security interest perfected under the law of the bank's jurisdiction remains perfected despite a change of the bank's jurisdiction until the earlier of the time perfection would have ceased under the law of the old jurisdiction or the expiration of four months after a change to the new jurisdiction. Section 9-316(g) states that a secured party can remain perfected continuously by perfecting under the Article 9 of the new jurisdiction before the expiration of the earliest applicable time. Maintaining perfection in the new jurisdiction might not require action because a secured party frequently perfects its security interest in a deposit account by establishing control and the control agreement should be effective regardless of the bank's jurisdiction. Consequently, section 9-316(g) mainly affects secured parties whose security interest in the deposit account arises as a proceed of collateral and is perfected by filing a financing statement.

A secured party who fails to maintain perfection faces severe consequences. *First*, the security interest becomes unperfected pursuant to section 9-316(g). An unperfected security interest is vulnerable to other security interests, a bankruptcy trustee, and other lien creditors. A secured party whose perfection has lapsed should perfect under the law of the new jurisdiction as soon it discovers the change of governing jurisdiction. However, there will be a gap in perfection and the security interest will have a new priority date. *Second*, the retroactive unperfection rule applies and the security interest is deemed never to have been perfected as against a purchaser of the collateral for value pursuant to section 9-316(g). That enables a purchaser for value who was previously subordinate to the security interest to have priority under the priority rules of section 9-317.

3. Letter-of-Credit Rights — Sections 9-306, 9-308(d), 9-316(f), (g)

A letter of credit is an undertaking by the issuer of the letter at the request of the obligor that the issuer will honor a demand for payment made by a third party, the beneficiary of the letter, of an obligation incurred by the obligor to the beneficiary in a separate transaction. A letter-of-credit right is the beneficiary's right to payment or performance under a letter of credit. The beneficiary (who would be the debtor of the security interest) can grant a security interest in its letter-of-credit right as collateral for its obligation owed to the secured party.

a. Rules for Determining the Governing Jurisdiction — Section 9-306

Establishing the jurisdiction that governs perfection, the effect of perfection or nonperfection, and the priority of a security interest in a letter-of-credit right depends on whether the letter-of-credit right is the principal collateral or exists as a supporting obligation to the principal collateral. Section 9-102(a)(77) provides that a letter-of-credit right is a *supporting obligation* when it supports "the payment or performance of an account, chattel paper, a document, a general intangible, an instrument, or investment property." Because Article 9 adopts the policy that a supporting obligation is an incident of the collateral it supports, attachment and perfection of a security interest in a supporting obligation are automatic upon attachment and perfection of a security interest in the principal collateral. Similarly, section 9-306(c) allows the jurisdiction that governs a security interest in the principal collateral to govern a security interest in a letter-of-credit right as a supporting obligation. It declares that the section 9-306 choice-of-law rules for a letter-of-credit right do not apply to a security interest in a letter-of-credit right as a supporting obligation that is perfected only under the automatic perfection of section 9-308(d).

For other letter-of-credit right security interests, the rule of section 9-306(a) declares that the local law of the issuer's jurisdiction governs perfection, the effect of perfection or nonperfection, and the priority of a security interest in a letter-of-credit right, provided the issuer's jurisdiction is a state as defined by Article 9. Article 9's definition of *state*, section 9-102(a)(76), excludes any foreign country. Additionally, if the issuer has designated a person to pay in its place, a nominated person, the local law of the nominated person's jurisdiction governs perfection, the effect of perfection or nonperfection, and the priority of a security interest in a letter-of-credit right, provided the nominated person's jurisdiction is a state as defined by Article 9. The security interest with respect to the issuer is independent of the security interest with respect to the nominated person, if such person exists. Consequently, the jurisdiction of each person governs the applicable security interest. However, the presence of an issuer and a nominated person should not complicate choice-of-law issues because Article 9 requires a secured party to perfect a security interest in a letter-of-credit right by control, except for a security interest in a letter-of-credit right as a supporting obligation, and the control agreement should be effective regardless of the jurisdiction.

Sections 5-116(a) and (b) establish the location of an issuer or nominated person. Section 5-116 allows the parties to establish the jurisdiction by agreement in an authenticated record or by agreement in the letter of credit, confirmation, or other undertaking (a statement of the person's obligation). Absent such agreement, an issuer or nominated person is located at the address indicated in the person's undertaking. Section 5-116(b) further provides that all branches of a bank (a bank is frequently the issuer or nominated person of a letter of credit) are considered separate entities, located at the address indicated in the bank's undertaking. If the issuer or nominated person is located in a jurisdiction that is not a state, section 9-306 is not applicable and section 9-301 determines the governing law for such person. Under section 9-301, perfection and priority of a security interest in a letter-of-credit right are governed by the jurisdiction where the debtor is located as determined by section 9-307.

b. Effect of Change of Governing Jurisdiction — Sections 9-316(f), (g)

Sections 9-316(f) and (g) provide rules pertaining to a change of jurisdiction of an issuer or nominated person. These same sections apply to deposit accounts. Section 9-316(f) provides that a security interest in a letter-of-credit right perfected under the law of the issuer's or nominated person's jurisdiction remains perfected despite a change of governing jurisdiction until the earlier of the time perfection would have ceased under the law of the old jurisdiction or the expiration of four months after the change to the new jurisdiction. Section 9-316(g) declares that a secured party remains perfected continuously if it perfects under the Article 9 of the new jurisdiction before the expiration of the earliest applicable time. Maintaining perfection in the new jurisdiction might not require action because a secured party perfects its security interest in a letter-of-credit right by establishing control and the control agreement should be effective regardless of the jurisdiction. Consequently, section 9-316(g) mainly affects secured parties whose security interest in the letter-of-credit right arises as a proceed of collateral and is perfected by filing a financing statement.

Section 9-316(g) establishes those familiar serious consequences for a secured party who fails to perfect in the new jurisdiction before the expiration of the earliest time. *First*, the security interest becomes unperfected and consequently is vulnerable to other security interests, a bankruptcy trustee, and other lien creditors. *Second*, the security interest is deemed never to have been perfected as against a purchaser of the collateral for value. Consequently, a secured party whose interest was previously superior to such purchaser could become subordinate under section 9-317 because its security interest is deemed never to have been perfected. A *purchaser* for value includes a buyer of the collateral and a secured party with a security interest in the collateral, but not a lien creditor.

4. Investment Property—Sections 9-305, 9-316(f), (g)

Investment property, defined in section 9-102(a)(49), includes a certificated or uncertificated security, security entitlement, securities account, and commodity contract or commodity account. The particular types of investment property are defined in either section 8-102(a) (Article 8 covers "Investment Securities") or 9-102(a). Attachment and perfection of a security interest in investment property are discussed in Chapters 2 and 4, respectively.

a. Rules for Determining the Governing Jurisdiction—Section 9-305

The type of investment property that serves as the collateral for the security interest determines which jurisdiction's laws govern perfection, the effect of perfection or nonperfection, and priority. Sections 9-305(a) and (b) establish the rules for determining the governing jurisdiction. Those rules, however, are subject to section 9-305(c), which establishes the governing jurisdiction for security interests in investment property perfected by filing or perfected automatically.

Section 9-305(a)(1) establishes the governing jurisdiction when the security interest covers a certificated security held directly by the debtor. A certificated security is a security that is represented by a certificate—it is tangible. The local law of the jurisdiction where the certificated security is located governs perfection, the effect of perfection or nonperfection, and the priority of a security interest in a certificated security. For example, suppose an Arkansas debtor creates a security interest in its 100 shares of ABC Corporation stock held directly by the debtor and located in its safe deposit box in an Oklahoma bank. The secured creditor is located in Texas. Oklahoma law governs perfection and priority of the security because the certificate is located in Oklahoma.

Section 9-305(a)(2) establishes the jurisdiction governing a security interest in an uncertificated security. An uncertificated security is a security that is not represented by a certificate. The local law of the "issuer's jurisdiction," established by section 8-110(d), governs perfection, the effect of perfection or nonperfection, and the priority of a security interest in an uncertificated security. Section 8-110(d) provides that the issuer's jurisdiction is either the jurisdiction in which the issuer is organized or, if permitted by the law of that jurisdiction, the jurisdiction the issuer specifies as its jurisdiction.

Under section 9-305(a)(3), the local law of the securities intermediary's jurisdiction, as determined by section 8-110(e), governs perfection, the effect of perfection or nonperfection, and the priority of security interests in security entitlements or securities accounts. A *security entitlement* is the rights and property interest of an entitlement holder with respect to a financial asset. A *securities account* is an account to which a financial asset is or may be credited under an agreement allowing the account holder to exercise the rights that comprise the financial asset. A securities intermediary is generally the person who maintains the securities account for the entitlement holder and who owes certain duties (specified in Article 8 part 5) to the entitlement holder. For example, suppose Green instructs her broker to purchase 100 shares of ABC Corporation for her securities account with her broker. When Green's broker purchases the shares and credits them to her securities account, she holds a security entitlement with respect to 100 shares of ABC, although she will not hold the shares in her name. They will be held in the name of Green's broker, a securities intermediary. The broker is obligated under Article 8 to allow Green, the entitlement holder, to exercise the ownership rights of the shares.

Section 8-110(e) provides five hierarchical rules for establishing the securities intermediary's jurisdiction. The rules apply in the order of their hierarchy. If a superior rule establishes the jurisdiction, the subordinate rules are not applicable. *First*, if a securities account agreement between the securities intermediary and its entitlement holder expressly provides that a particular jurisdiction is the securities intermediary's jurisdiction for purposes of Part 1 of Article 8, Article 8, or the UCC, that jurisdiction is the securities intermediary's jurisdiction. The flexibility of this rule allows the parties to choose a particular jurisdiction to govern some or all aspects of a security interest or to choose a jurisdiction to govern secured transactions and a different jurisdiction to govern other transactions within the UCC. *Second*, if a securities account agreement between the securities intermediary and the entitlement holder expressly provides that a particular jurisdiction governs the agreement, that jurisdiction is the securities intermediary's jurisdiction. *Third*, if a securities account agreement expressly provides that the securities account is maintained at an office in a particular jurisdiction, that jurisdiction is the securities intermediary's jurisdiction. *Fourth*, the securities intermediary's jurisdiction is the jurisdiction of the office identified in the account statement as the office serving the entitlement holder's account. *Fifth*, the securities intermediary's juris-diction is the jurisdiction in which the intermediary's chief executive office is located.

Section 9-305(a)(4) establishes the commodity intermediary's jurisdiction as the jurisdiction that governs perfection, the effect of perfection or nonperfection, and the priority of a security interest in a commodity contract or commodity ac-count. *Commodity account, commodity contract,* and *commodity intermediary* are defined in sections 9-102(a)(14), (15), and (17), respectively. Section 9-305(b) pro-vides five hierarchical rules for identifying the location of the commodity inter-mediary's jurisdiction. These rules are the same as the rules for determining the location of the securities intermediary's jurisdiction discussed in the immediately preceding paragraph. When a superior rule establishes the jurisdiction, the sub-ordinate rules are not applicable. *First*, if a commodity account agreement be-tween the commodity intermediary and commodity customer expressly provides that a particular jurisdiction is the commodity intermediary's jurisdiction for purposes of Part 3 of Article 9, Article 9, or the UCC, that jurisdiction is the com-modity intermediary's jurisdiction. *Second*, if a commodity account agreement between the commodity intermediary and the commodity customer expressly provides that a particular jurisdiction governs the agreement, that jurisdiction is the commodity intermediary's jurisdiction. *Third*, if a commodity account agree-ment expressly provides that the commodity account is maintained at an office in a particular jurisdiction, that jurisdiction is the commodity intermediary's ju-risdiction. *Fourth*, the commodity intermediary's jurisdiction is the jurisdiction of the office identified in an account statement as the office serving the com-modity customer's account. *Fifth*, the commodity intermediary's jurisdiction is the jurisdiction in which the intermediary's chief executive office is located.

As noted previously, section 9-305(c) creates an exception to all the above rules. It is not, however, an exception that swallows the rule. Section 9-305(c) states that the jurisdiction in which the debtor is located governs perfection of security interests in investment property in three situations: 1) security inter-ests in investment property perfected by filing; 2) security interests in invest-ment property created by a broker or securities intermediary that are automatically perfected in accordance with section 9-309(10); and 3) security interests in commodity contracts or commodity accounts created by a com-modity intermediary that are automatically perfected in accordance with sec-tion 9-309(11). Section 9-307, discussed previously in this chapter, establishes the debtor's location. Notice that section 9-305(c) establishes only the jurisdiction that governs perfection; it does not establish the jurisdiction that governs pri-ority of the security interest. Accordingly, the provisions of 9-305(a) and (b) continue to establish the jurisdiction governing priority.

b. Effect of Change of Governing Jurisdiction — Sections 9-316(f), (g)

Section 9-316(f) provides that a security interest in investment property perfected pursuant to the law of the jurisdiction established under section 9-305(a) or (b) remains perfected despite a change of the governing jurisdiction until the earlier of the time perfection would have ceased under the law of the old jurisdiction or the expiration of four months after the change in governing jurisdiction. However, sections 9-316(f) and (g) do not apply to security interests whose governing jurisdiction is established as the debtor's location in accordance with section 9-305(c). Continued perfection after change of the governing jurisdiction of those security interests is determined by sections 9-316(a) and (b) discussed previously in this chapter. Section 9-316(g) provides that a secured party maintains continuous perfection by perfecting under the Article 9 of the new jurisdiction before the expiration of the earliest applicable time.

A secured party who fails to maintain perfection faces the familiar consequences. *First*, the security interest becomes unperfected pursuant to section 9-316(g). *Second*, the retroactive unperfection rule of section 9-316(g) deems the security interest never to have been perfected against a purchaser of the collateral for value. A secured party whose interest was previously superior to a purchaser could become subordinate under the rules of section 9-317.

5. Rules for Determining the Governing Jurisdiction for Timber to Be Cut, As-Extracted Collateral, Fixtures, and Possessory Security Interests — Sections 9-301(2), (3)(A), (B) and (4)

The governing jurisdiction for a security interest in timber to be cut or in fixtures to be perfected by a fixture filing, is the jurisdiction where the collateral is located. (*Fixtures* and *fixture filing* are defined in sections 9-102(a)(41) and (40), respectively, and discussed in Chapter 9.) Under sections 9-301(3)(A) and (B), the local law of the jurisdiction where the collateral is located governs perfection, the effect of perfection or nonperfection, and the priority of a security interest in those types of collateral.

For a security interest in as-extracted collateral, the local law of the jurisdiction where the wellhead or minehead is located governs perfection, the effect of perfection or nonperfection, and the priority of a security interest under the rule of section 9-301(4). Section 9-102(a)(6) defines *as-extracted collateral* as oil, gas, or other minerals subject to a security interest that attaches as they are extracted, and accounts arising from their sale at the wellhead or minehead.

Under section 9-301(2), the local law of the jurisdiction where the collateral is located governs perfection, the effect of perfection or nonperfection, and the priority in a security interest the secured party perfects by taking possession of the collateral—a possessory security interest.

a. Change of Governing Jurisdiction of Possessory Security Interest—Section 9-316(c)

Section 9-316(c) states that a security interest perfected by possession remains continuously perfected after the collateral is moved from one jurisdiction to another jurisdiction, provided the security interest is perfected under the law of the new jurisdiction. This is an obvious rule that hardly need be stated. If a security interest is perfected by possession, then the collateral changes jurisdiction only if the secured party or its possession agent moves the collateral to another jurisdiction. Additionally, Article 9's rules for perfection by possession are likely to be uniform in all jurisdictions adopting Article 9. Consequently, if a secured party in possession of the collateral changes the location of the collateral, the security interest will be perfected under the Article 9 of the new jurisdiction and the perfection will be continuous. If possession of the collateral does not perfect the security interest under the law of the new jurisdiction, the security interest becomes unperfected immediately and stays unperfected until the secured party perfects under the Article 9 of the new jurisdiction.

6. Rules for Determining the Governing Jurisdiction of an Agricultural Lien—Section 9-302

The governing jurisdiction of an agricultural lien is the jurisdiction where the farm products subject to the lien are located. Under section 9-302, the local law of the jurisdiction where the farm products are located governs perfection, the effect of perfection or nonperfection, and the priority of an agricultural lien on farm products.

There are no Article 9 rules addressing the question of whether an agricultural lien remains perfected after a change of governing jurisdiction. Official Comment 7 to section 9-316 declares that section 9-316 does not apply to agricultural liens. This means that the rules relating to the effect of a change of governing jurisdiction are inapplicable to agricultural liens. Although the official comments are not law, the absence of any Article 9 section covering the issue indicates strongly that comment 7 is accurate. Without the temporary perfection of section 9-316, an agricultural lien becomes unperfected immediately if the location of the farm products changes and remains unperfected until the holder of the lien perfects under the Article 9 of the new jurisdiction.

However, Official Comment 3 to section 9-316 proclaims that the retroactive unperfection rule of section 9-316(b) applies to agricultural liens. But section 9-316(b) applies to security interests described in section 9-316(a) which expressly covers only security interests whose governing jurisdiction is determined under sections 9-301(1) and 9-305(c). Section 9-302 establishes the choice of law for an agricultural lien. Courts will have to resolve the question by deciding whether to apply the express words of section 9-316 or its official comment.

Checkpoints

- Article 9 adopts rules that establish the jurisdiction that governs perfection, the effects of perfection or nonperfection, and the priority of a security interest.

- The rules are divided by the type of collateral, with the most common rule being that the jurisdiction where the debtor is located governs perfection, the effects of perfection or nonperfection, and the priority of a security interest.

- Article 9 adopts rules that establish where debtors are located.

- When there is a change in the governing jurisdiction, such as when the location of the debtor changes, Article 9 allows a perfected security interest to remain perfected in the new jurisdiction for a limited time period without requiring that the secured party perfect the security interest in the new jurisdiction.

- If the secured party has not perfected its security interest in the new jurisdiction before the period of temporary perfection lapses, the security interest becomes unperfected and is deemed never to have been perfected against a purchaser for value.

Chapter 11

Default

Roadmap

- The meaning of default
- Non-Article 9 remedies for default
- Article 9 remedies for default — collection, repossession, disposition, and acceptance of the collateral
- Parties who can redeem the collateral
- Consequences of the failure of the secured party to comply with the Article 9 default requirements

---

A. Introduction

Article 9 Part 6 provides rights and remedies for a secured party after a default occurs. It also places duties on the secured party exercising its rights. Additionally, a secured party can have rights and duties beyond those provided by Article 9 because section 9-601(a) preserves any rights and duties of a secured party created in the security agreement. This chapter focuses on the Article 9 rights, remedies, and duties. Because agricultural liens usually receive the same treatment as security interests, agricultural liens are discussed only when Article 9 provides a separate rule.

The Article 9 rights exist for any secured party whose security interest is in default; they are not restricted to use by the secured party having priority over all other interests in the collateral. A subordinate secured party's exercise of its rights does not itself constitute conversion or create liability to a senior secured party. However, there are several reasons why a senior secured party need not be concerned by the acts of a junior secured party. First, if the debtor also defaults to the senior secured party, that secured party can exercise its default rights and preempt the junior secured party from taking action against the collateral. Second, as discussed later in this chapter, Article 9 generally maintains the senior secured party's rights in the collateral despite the disposition of the collateral by the junior secured party.

Although the debtor and the obligor of a secured transaction are frequently the same person, they can be different persons. Article 9 defines *debtor* as the person with an interest in the collateral and *obligor* as the person owing performance of the obligation. However, in this chapter, "debtor" means the person with an interest in the collateral and the person who is obligated to perform. The Article 9 terms are used when the sections of Part 6 distinguish between those parties.

B. The Meaning of Default — Section 9-601

Section 9-601(a) confers the rights of Article 9 Part 6 on the secured party "after default." However, Article 9 does not define the events that constitute default under a security interest. As Official Comment 3 to section 9-601 remarks, the agreement of the debtor and secured party determine the circumstances that result in default. The rule is different for an agricultural lien. Section 9-606 states that default in an agricultural lien occurs when the secured party can enforce the lien under the provisions of the statute creating it.

Typical acts of default for a security interest include: debtor's failure to pay the obligation secured; debtor's transfer of the collateral without secured party's consent; destruction of the collateral; attachment of another security interest or lien to the collateral; debtor's failure to maintain the collateral; debtor's failure to insure the collateral; change in debtor's location; change in debtor's organizational structure; and debtor's death. If the debtor is to repay the obligation in installments, the secured party typically includes an *acceleration clause* in the security agreement or loan agreement. An acceleration clause enables a secured party to declare the entire unpaid balance immediately due upon the occurrence of a default, allowing the secured party to use its remedies to recover the entire obligation, not merely the installment in default.

Another typical acceleration clause permits a secured party to accelerate payment "when the secured party deems itself insecure." Section 1-309 validates such a clause but authorizes its use only when the secured party in "good faith believes that the prospect of payment or performance is impaired." The UCC defines *good faith* in section 1-201(b)(20) as "honesty in fact and the observance of reasonable commercial standards of fair dealing."

C. Non-Article 9 Remedies upon Default

After the debtor defaults under the security agreement, section 9-601(a) expressly allows the secured party to use remedies other than those provided by Article 9. The main Article 9 remedies are disposition of the collateral, acceptance of collateral in satisfaction of the obligation, and collection of right to payment collateral. Non-Article 9 remedies include any remedies the parties have provided in the security agreement and any available legal remedies. A secured party's decision to use a non-Article 9 remedy does not foreclose its right to use Article 9's remedies. Section 9-601(c) declares that the remedies are cumulative and can be exercised simultaneously. For example, a secured party could sue the debtor personally (a non-Article 9 remedy) and at the same time repossess the collateral (an Article 9 remedy).

1. Personal Judgment

A frequently used remedy is the secured party's suit seeking a personal judgment against the debtor for the unpaid obligation. It is an efficient remedy when the value of the collateral is less than the amount of the debt, because disposition of the collateral will leave an unpaid balance and the secured party likely would sue the debtor to recover the deficiency. Consequently, the secured party could decide to forego repossession and disposition of the collateral and go directly to a suit against the debtor on the obligation.

Of course, obtaining a judgment does not always result in the debtor's immediate payment of the judgment debt, and a secured party who has become a judgment creditor may be forced to levy on the assets of the debtor to obtain payment of the judgment. If the levy covers the collateral for the security interest, section 9-601(e) directs that the lien on the collateral created by the levy relates back to the earlier of the date of perfection of the security interest or the date of the filing of the financing statement covering the collateral. This insures that the secured party does not lose its Article 9 priority date for the collateral. If the levy arises from a judgment on an agricultural lien, the lien relates back to the earlier of perfection, filing, or any priority date provided by the statute creating the lien.

2. Foreclosure

Foreclosure of the security interest is a remedy created by the statutory law of a jurisdiction. In the typical foreclosure action, the secured party can obtain a judgment ordering sale of the property and a judgment against the debtor personally. It is an attractive remedy because the secured party obtains two remedies in one action. Typically, the sheriff, not the secured party, performs the sale under the oversight of the court, and the Article 9 requirements for disposition after default do not apply.

D. Rights and Remedies Provided by Article 9

1. Collection and Enforcement of Receivables, Deposit Accounts, and Supporting Obligations — Sections 9-607, 9-608

a. Security Interests in Receivables and Supporting Obligation

When the collateral is a right to payment (commonly labeled a *receivable*), such as an account, chattel paper, or an instrument, or a supporting obligation, section 9-607 authorizes a secured party after a default to: 1) notify the account debtor or other obligor to make payment or render performance to the secured party (an account debtor has the right under section 9-406 to request proof of the secured party's right to payment); 2) take any proceeds of the collateral to which the secured party is entitled under section 9-315; 3) enforce the obligations owed by the account debtor or other obligor; and 4) exercise any rights of the debtor with respect to the obligation and any property that secures the obligation. These self-help rights do not depend on judicial authorization but exist automatically following default unless the parties have agreed otherwise. A secured party also retains its right to dispose of these types of collateral pursuant to section 9-610, discussed later in this chapter.

The scope of section 9-607 is security interests in accounts, chattel paper, instruments, general intangibles, payment intangibles, and supporting obligations. An *account debtor* is the person obligated on an account, chattel paper or general intangible. Section 9-607 uses the phrase "other person obligated on collateral" to signify the obligor of collateral other than an account, chattel paper, or general intangible, for example, a promissory note.

Essentially, section 9-607 allows the secured party to step into the shoes of its debtor and take whatever rights the debtor had in the collateral. Typically, the secured party would require the account debtor to make any payment to it. Additionally, if the debtor has a cause of action against the account debtor as a result of the account debtor's default, the secured party has the right to bring the action after the debtor defaults. If the collateral for the security interest is a debtor's right to payment and the right to payment is secured by a mortgage on real property, the secured party can exercise the debtor's rights in the mortgage after default. Section 9-607 authorizes the secured party to enforce the rights of its debtor; it does not create additional rights.

When exercising the section 9-607(a) rights of collection or enforcement, section 9-607(c) requires that the secured party proceed in a commercially reasonable manner if it has recourse rights against the debtor or a secondary obligor or is entitled to charge back uncollected collateral against the debtor or a secondary obligor. Article 9 imposes this duty because the collection process can affect the proceeds obtained and the proceeds affect the deficiency liability of the debtor or a secondary obligor. Failure to act in a commercially reasonable manner leaves the secured party subject to liability under section 9-625 and affects its right to recover a deficiency under section 9-626. The meaning of *commercially reasonable* is discussed later in this chapter.

b. Security Interest in a Deposit Account

When the collateral is a deposit account, the secured party's rights after default include obtaining the balance of the account if the secured party perfected its security interest in the deposit account by establishing control. Control is the only method of perfecting a security interest in a deposit account, except for a security interest in a deposit account arising as proceeds of collateral. Section 9-607(a)(4) authorizes a secured party to apply the balance of the account to or for its benefit if it established control by being the bank where the debtor maintains the deposit account. Section 9-607(a)(5) authorizes a secured party to instruct the bank to pay the balance of the account to or for its benefit if it established control through an agreement with the bank or by becoming the bank's customer with respect to the deposit account. These rights supplement the collection and enforcement rights discussed previously.

c. Application of Proceeds from Collection or Enforcement — Section 9-608

Section 9-608 provides rules for distributing the proceeds a secured party receives from exercising its section 9-607 collection or enforcement rights. The section applies when the security interest secures payment or performance of an *obligation*. Consequently, a secured party with a security interest arising from a sale of receivables is not subject to section 9-608 because that security interest does not secure an obligation. Section 9-608(a) commands that the secured party apply the proceeds *first* to its reasonable expenses of collection and enforcement, including reasonable legal expenses and attorney's fees to the extent provided by the agreement and not prohibited by law; *second* to payment of the obligation secured; and *third* any remainder to the debtor unless the secured party receives, before it completes distribution of the proceeds, an authenticated demand from a subordinate security party or other lienholder for any surplus proceeds. Section 9-608(a)(2) authorizes, but does not require, the secured party to request proof of the subordinate person's right to the surplus proceeds. If requested, the holder of the subordinate interest must furnish reasonable proof of its interest within a reasonable time or the secured party need not pay the surplus to such person. If the security interest results from a sale of receivables, the debtor is not entitled to any surplus.

2. Taking Possession of Collateral after Default — Section 9-609

After default, section 9-609 authorizes a secured party to take possession of the collateral, to disable and dispose of the collateral on the debtor's premises, or to require the debtor to make the collateral available to the secured party at a designated place. Exercise of these remedies does not depend on agreement by the debtor; a secured party can employ them unless it has agreed otherwise. A secured party who obtains possession of the collateral after default is subject to the duties section 9-207 imposes on a secured party that possesses the collateral.

The remedy a secured party most commonly uses is taking possession of the collateral — repossession. Section 9-609(b) authorizes a secured party to repossess collateral with or without judicial process. Judicial process repossession is accomplished through the court and generally is the result of bringing an action seeking possession of the property or seeking a pre-judgment seizure of the collateral in an action for liability on the obligation. A court officer, typically a sheriff, performs the repossession. The statutes and case law of the applicable jurisdiction, not Article 9, govern the process.

Repossession without judicial process is the aptly named self-help repossession — repossession accomplished by the secured party without the authority of the court. It is fodder for fiction and nonfiction. Section 9-609(b)(2) validates a secured party's self-help repossession, provided the secured party can accomplish it without breaching the peace, a term Article 9 does not define or explain. Courts determine what acts breach the peace.

Self-help repossession is an easier, quicker, and less costly method of obtaining possession of the collateral than judicial process repossession. The simplest way to repossess goods without breaching the peace is to obtain the debtor's consent to the repossession at the time the collateral is repossessed.

If the debtor consents at that time, the repossession will not breach the peace. A debtor's consent to repossession contained in the security agreement, while advisable, does not achieve the same protection as obtaining the debtor's consent immediately before repossessing. A debtor who consents to repossession in the security agreement might nevertheless object to the actual repossession in a manner that causes a breach of the peace. The issue is whether the repossession breaches the peace, not whether the debtor consented to the repossession in the security agreement. To insure that the repossession does not breach the peace, the secured party should obtain the debtor's permission at the time it attempts to repossess. Unfortunately, a debtor in default frequently will not give permission for the repossession but instead will object loudly.

That leaves the question of what acts breach the peace. In general, breach of the peace in a repossession involves acts tending to violate the public peace and order, acts that produce violent resistance, and acts of forcible repossession of the collateral. There is no definitive test for this question of fact. However, because numerous cases discuss the issue it is possible to identify acts to avoid and acts that are permissible. The majority of cases discussing the issue involve repossession of a motor vehicle, the easiest type of collateral to self-help repossess. Courts have rejected a claim of breach of the peace when the secured party enters the debtor's property and repossesses a motor vehicle parked in the debtor's driveway and also when the secured party repossesses a motor vehicle parked on a public street. Generally, however, the unauthorized entry by the secured party into the debtor's residence or place of business results in a breach of the peace, even if the security agreement authorizes such entry. Courts have found unauthorized entry when the collateral is located in a garage with closed or locked doors, although repossession of a car in a garage with the doors open has been upheld.

Repossession in the face of protest from the debtor usually constitutes breach of the peace. A majority of courts find that oral protests alone are sufficient to constitute a breach of the peace, whether the repossession is from a residence, a driveway, or a public street. A few courts require more than a verbal protest before finding a breach of the peace. Requiring more than a verbal objection seems unadvisable. A disagreement over repossession should not have to reach the assault stage before a breach of the peace occurs. In fact, secured parties should advise the repossession agent to halt the repossession if the debtor objects. Courts attribute the acts of the repossession agent to the secured party. But the secured party should always employ a repossession agent—the repo man—to repossess the collateral; it can be a dangerous activity!

Occasionally, the secured party engages the services of a law enforcement officer to be present during self-help repossession. Superficially, it seems like a good idea because the law enforcement officer can help preserve the peace and prevent a breach of the peace. However, the presence of the officer likely chills the objection of the debtor and the debtor has the power—perhaps the right— to object even if it is in default. Official Comment 3 to section 9-609 notes that the section does not authorize a secured party to use law enforcement personnel except in a judicial process repossession. Courts have held that a breach of the peace occurs when the secured party uses a law enforcement officer in a self-help repossession regardless of whether there is an objection from the debtor. *See* First & Farmers Bank v. Henderson, 763 S.W.2d 137 (Ky. App. 1988).

In cases where debtors allege breach of the peace, they generally sue for conversion of the collateral and seek punitive damages. Section 9-625(b), discussed later in this chapter, makes a secured party liable for damages caused by its failure to comply with Article 9. A self-help repossession that breaches the peace does not comply with section 9-609(b)(2). Official Comment 3 to 9-625 notes that principles of tort law supplement section 9-625; thus, conversion damages are an appropriate measure of damages for a repossession that breaches the peace.

Section 9-609 provides other means for the secured party to obtain possession of the collateral. Section 9-609(c) authorizes the secured party to require the debtor to gather the collateral and make it available to the secured party at a place the secured party designates that is reasonably convenient to both parties. This remedy is particularly beneficial when the collateral is located in various places and it would be expensive and time-consuming for the secured party to repossess each item of collateral. Of course, if the debtor fails to comply with the secured party's demand, the secured party that wants possession of the collateral must repossess it, with or without judicial process.

Section 9-609(a)(2) provides a remedy that applies to equipment collateral. It empowers a secured party to render equipment collateral unusable and then dispose of it on the debtor's premises. This remedy can be effective for equipment that is difficult to repossess or store, although the remedy exists for any type of equipment collateral. It may be more convenient and economical for the secured party to disable the collateral, which may help maintain its value, and sell it directly from the debtor's premises. Although this remedy seems well suited to other types of collateral, Article 9 restricts its use to equipment collateral.

3. Disposition of Collateral after Default — Section 9-610

Section 9-610(a) permits a secured party to sell, lease, license, or otherwise dispose of the collateral after default. A significant feature of this remedy is that the secured party disposes of the collateral without judicial involvement. The court does not hold, approve, or oversee a section 9-610 disposition. The secured party may dispose of the collateral in a public or private disposition, in a single unit or separate parcels, when and where it chooses, and on terms it chooses. This freedom theoretically helps produce a higher disposition price, but the freedom is not unlimited. Section 9-610(b) adopts the requirement that the secured party must act in a commercially reasonable manner. "Every aspect of a disposition of collateral, including the method, manner, time, place and other terms, must be commercially reasonable." Section 9-611 adds the requirement that the secured party send reasonable notification of the disposition to designated persons. Section 9-602(7) commands that neither the debtor nor the obligor may waive this duty of the secured party. However, section 9-603 permits the parties to the security interest to agree on standards by which to measure the secured party's fulfillment of the duty to act commercially reasonable, provided "the standards are not manifestly unreasonable." That allows the debtor and secured party to agree on action of the secured party that would satisfy the duty. A secured party who fails to comply with Article 9's requirements for disposition faces liability for loss caused by its failure and restriction of its right to recover a deficiency against the obligor.

Section 9-610(a) authorizes the secured party to dispose of the collateral in its present condition or after any commercially reasonable preparation or processing. This seems to give the secured party complete discretion as to whether it will incur cost to prepare the collateral for disposition or dispose of it as is. However, a secured party's discretion whether to dispose of the collateral without post-default preparation is limited by the commercially reasonable requirement. Official Comment 4 to section 9-610 notes that determining commercial reasonableness requires balancing the costs and probable benefits of preparation against the fact that the secured party incurs the costs at its risk, speculating that the preparation costs will increase the disposition proceeds. Consequently, a secured party fails to act commercially reasonable if it does not take steps to prepare the collateral for disposition when it is clear that the benefits outweigh the risk.

a. Commercially Reasonable Disposition — Sections 9-610(b), 9-627

Article 9 does not define "commercially reasonable," and it offers little to supplement its proclamation that every aspect of the secured party's disposition must be commercially reasonable. There is no doubt that the drafters of

Article 9 purposefully left the standard flexible to allow the secured party latitude in disposing of the collateral, anticipating that it would result in greater proceeds to the benefit of all parties. Consequently, a general guideline for commercial reasonableness is that a secured party should act to maximize the proceeds of the disposition.

Section 9-627(b) lists three types of dispositions it declares are "made in a commercially reasonable manner": 1) a disposition in the usual manner in a recognized market; 2) a disposition at the price current in a recognized market at the time of disposition; or 3) a disposition otherwise in conformity with reasonable commercial practices among dealers in the type of property of the kind involved. Official Comment 4 to section 9-627 notes that "recognized market" is limited to markets of standardized price quotations for essentially fungible property, such as stock exchanges. Courts have adopted that standard. Many secured parties believe that the ubiquitous used car auctions are a recognized market. Courts have disagreed consistently with that proposition.

Section 9-627(c) also aids a secured party in making a commercially reasonable disposition by directing that a disposition is commercially reasonable when approved in a judicial proceeding, by a bona fide creditors' committee, by a representative of creditors, or by an assignee for the benefit of creditors. This allows a secured party to obtain approval that establishes a commercially reasonable disposition before conducting the disposition. Although such approval would entail cost and time, it might appeal to a secured party who has a contentious relationship with the debtor. Pre-disposition approval precludes later battles over the commercial reasonableness of the disposition. This approval is also available when a secured party employs the collection or enforcement remedy of section 9-607 or when a secured party accepts the collateral in total or partial satisfaction of the obligation (discussed later in this chapter).

1. Disposition Price

The disposition price is an important and litigious element of commercial reasonableness. Because most dispositions do not produce fair-market-value proceeds, debtors frequently and understandably believe that the disposition should have produced greater proceeds. Section 9-627(a) helps the secured party prove that the disposition price is commercially reasonable by stating that the secured party can establish a commercially reasonable disposition despite the fact that a disposition on different terms could have produced greater proceeds. That does not mean a court will not review the disposition price, only that a low price relative to the value of the collateral does not preclude proving commercial reasonableness. In fact, as Official Comment 2 to section

9-627 observes, a low disposition price should cause a court to scrutinize carefully the other aspects of the disposition. Some courts have held that a disposition price greatly disproportionate to the fair market value of the collateral raises a presumption that the disposition was not commercially reasonable. Section 9-627(a), however, is the only guidance Article 9 gives on whether the disposition price is commercially reasonable. The issue is decided on a case-by-case basis, with courts carefully reviewing the efforts a secured party makes to dispose of the collateral.

2. Public or Private Disposition

Section 9-610(b) authorizes a secured party to dispose of collateral in a public or private disposition, provided the chosen method is commercially reasonable. Article 9 does not define public or private. However, Official Comment 7 to section 9-610 describes a *public disposition* as one where "the price is determined after the public has had a meaningful opportunity for competitive bidding," and requires "that some form of advertisement or public notice must precede the sale ... and that the public must have access to the sale." Most courts follow the comment's guideline and require that a public disposition be open to the public, not just a limited segment of the public. "Dealers' only" auctions do not satisfy that requirement and most courts hold that such auctions are private dispositions. To prove that a public disposition is commercially reasonable, a secured party must show it gave sufficient notice of the sale to the public. Typically, notice is accomplished by advertising the sale. In a private disposition, solicitation of more than one potential buyer is important in establishing commercial reasonableness. Whether public or private, every aspect of the disposition must be commercially reasonable.

Section 9-610(c)(1) authorizes a secured party to purchase the collateral at a public disposition. However, the secured party can purchase the collateral through a private disposition only if the collateral is of a kind customarily sold on a recognized market or the subject of widely distributed price quotations, such as a stock exchange.

3. Time of Disposition

The time of the disposition is an aspect of a commercially reasonable disposition. As with other aspects of the disposition, Article 9 provides no guidance as to what is a commercially reasonable time. Factors that determine whether the time of the disposition is commercially reasonable include the type of collateral and the time of year.

In two situations involving security interests in consumer goods, sections 9-620(e) and (f) combine to require that the secured party dispose of the collateral within 90 days of taking possession of it or within any longer period agreed to after default by the debtor and any secondary obligor. However, section 9-624(b) allows the debtor to waive the mandatory-disposition requirement by entering into an authenticated agreement after default. A provision in the security agreement that the debtor waives the 90-day requirement does not result in a waiver because it is not a post-default agreement.

Section 9-620(e)(1) requires disposition in a purchase-money security interest in consumer goods when 60 percent of the "cash price" has been paid. Section 9-620(e)(2) does the same in a non-purchase-money security interest in consumer goods when 60 percent of the "principal amount of the obligation secured" has been paid. Although "cash price" is not defined, it should mean the cash price of the goods regardless of the amount of the obligation secured. The amount of the obligation secured typically would include interest charged on the cash price. If the drafters intended cash price to mean the obligation secured, they would have used words that convey such meaning. The meaning of *principal amount of the obligation secured* should be interpreted similarly as meaning the amount borrowed exclusive of interest.

4. Other Factors

Courts generally review all the circumstances of the disposition to determine whether it is commercially reasonable. Previous paragraphs have discussed preparation of the collateral, price obtained, time of the disposition, and public or private disposition. Lists of factors compiled by courts and commentators are numerous and include the above aspects as well as: 1) whether the disposition was in the wholesale or retail market; 2) disposition by unit or in parcels; 3) publicity for the sale; and 4) length of time of holding collateral prior to sale. As with all factors, the inquiry is whether the actions of the secured party further the goal to maximize the proceeds of the disposition.

b. Notification of Disposition — Section 9-611

With few exceptions, section 9-611(b) requires that a secured party disposing of the collateral under section 9-610 send "a reasonable authenticated notification of disposition." The importance of the notification is that it allows the debtor and other secured parties to monitor the disposition, perhaps even purchase the collateral, and allows other secured parties to exercise their right to demand any surplus proceeds. According to Official Comment 2 to section 9-611, the notification must be reasonable as to manner, content, and time. Sections 9-611 to 9-614 elaborate on time and content. A secured party who does not comply with this duty is liable for loss caused and the failure could limit the recovery of a deficiency. Although the duty to send notification is not expressly a component of a commercially reasonable disposition, courts frequently discuss it as though it were part of commercial reasonableness. Regardless of where it fits, failure to comply with the duty has the same effect as a failure to make a commercially reasonable disposition.

Section 9-611(d) excuses the secured party from the notification requirement for collateral that is: 1) perishable, such as fruits and vegetables; 2) that threatens to decline speedily in value, such as collateral that will become obsolete; or 3) of a type customarily sold on a recognized market. Remember that "recognized market" applies to markets with standardized price quotations.

Section 9-605 relieves a secured party from its duty of sending notification to an unknown debtor or secondary obligor and to the secured party or lienholder of an unknown debtor. This section operates primarily when the secured party is unaware the original debtor has transferred the collateral to another debtor.

Although section 9-611(b) does not expressly require a written notification, it does command the secured party to send an authenticated notification. *Authenticate*, section 9-102(a)(7), means to sign, adopt a symbol, or encrypt a record, all of which require a paper or electronic record. The instrument of notification must be electronic or written to satisfy the authenticate requirement. An oral notification should not be sufficient.

Subsection 9-611(b) requires that the secured party send notification, not that the addressee receive it. *Send*, section 9-102(a)(74)(A), means "to deposit in the mail, deliver for transmission, or transmit by any other usual means of communication with postage or cost of transmission provided for, addressed to any address reasonable under the circumstances." Consequently, the secured party can prove that it satisfied the requirement by proving that it sent the notification. However, the secured party should consider using certified mail or obtaining electronic confirmation of receipt to prove it sent a notification because the lack of receipt of notification by the debtor can be evidence that the notice was not sent or at least not sent reasonably.

1. Persons the Secured Party Must Notify — Section 9-611(c)

Section 9-611(c) establishes the persons to whom a secured party must send the notification. For all security interests the secured party must send notification to the debtor and to any secondary obligor. If the security interest is in consumer goods, section 9-611(c) does not require notification to any additional persons. For security interests in other types of collateral, the secured party must send the notification to other persons, secured parties, and lienholders as designated by section 9-611(c)(3), discussed below.

Section 9-624(a) validates a waiver of notification by a debtor or a secondary obligor if it is made in an authenticated agreement entered into after default. Consequently, a waiver of notice included in a security agreement or any other pre-default agreement is not effective. Requiring an "authenticated" agreement precludes an oral waiver of notification. Section 9-624 adopts no process through which other secured parties or lienholders can waive their right to notification.

Section 9-611(c)(1) compels the secured party to send notification of the disposition to the debtor. Recall that the debtor might not be the obligor of the defaulted obligation. Article 9's definition of *debtor* includes persons having an interest in the collateral other than a security interest or lien, regardless of whether the person is also the obligor. The obligor is the person that owes payment or performance of the secured obligation.

Section 9-611(c)(2) requires that the secured party send notification of the disposition to any secondary obligor. A *secondary obligor*, section 9-102(a)(71), is an obligor whose obligation is secondary or who has a right of recourse against the debtor, the obligor, or the property of either. Examples of secondary obligors include sureties, accommodation parties, and guarantors.

Section 9-611(c)(3) describes three groups of other persons to whom the secured party must send notification of disposition for security interests in any type of collateral except consumer goods. One group is persons from whom the secured party has received, before the notification date, an authenticated notification of a claim to the collateral. Section 9-611(a)(1) defines *notification date* as the earlier of the date on which the secured party sends its authenticated notification or the date the debtor and any secondary obligor waive the right to notification. Essentially, the secured party must send its notification to anyone from whom it has received notification before the secured party sends its notification or obtains a waiver of its duty to send the notification.

The second group is any secured party or lienholder that perfects an interest in the collateral by filing a financing statement that identifies the collateral, is indexed under the debtor's name, and is filed in the proper office for filing at least ten days before the notification date. To identify these persons the secured party must search the UCC financing statement index in the proper filing office for financing statements that were filed under the debtor's name on or before the tenth day before the notification date. The secured party must notify all persons the search discloses. For example, a secured party that sends notification on May 22 (the notification date) must search the UCC index in the proper jurisdiction in the name of the debtor and send notification to all secured parties and lienholders who had filed against the debtor as of May 12. These notification parameters limit the persons to whom the secured party must send the notification. A secured party is not required to send notification to a person who files after the ten-day cutoff, a person who files in a jurisdiction that is not the jurisdiction that governs filing on the tenth day although it was proper at the time of filing, or a person who files against a debtor who is not the debtor on the tenth day although the person was the debtor at the time of filing.

Section 9-611(e) creates a safe harbor for the secured party that insures its compliance with its duty to send notification to secured parties and lienholders in the second group of persons to be notified. The section authorizes the secured party to request that the filing office of the jurisdiction that governs perfection perform a financing statement search under the debtor's name to identify the persons to whom the secured party must send notification under section 9-611(c)(3)(B). If the secured party sends an authenticated notification to each person the search identifies, section 9-611(e) directs that the secured party "complies" with the 9-611(c)(3)(B) requirement of notification. Consequently, a secured party complies even if the filing office neglects to discover a person with a right to notification or a person properly files a financing statement between the time the filing office responds and ten days before the notification date. Additionally, in the unlikely event that the filing office does not respond before the notification date, section 9-611(e) nevertheless directs that the secured party "complies" with section 9-611(c)(3)(B) although it does not send notification to other secured parties and lienholders that qualify for notification. To qualify for the safe harbor, the secured party must request the search in a commercially reasonable manner "not later than 20 days or earlier than 30 days before the notification date."

The third group of persons the secured party must notify is secured parties that perfect a security interest under section 9-311(a) at least ten days before the notification date. Because security interests perfected under section 9-311(a) are perfected in accordance with a federal or state statute, treaty, or regulation, a jurisdiction's financing statement index will not reveal them. To identify persons in this group, the secured party must search the record system applicable to the type of security interest. For example, if a security interest is perfected by indicating the security interest on the certificate of title, the secured party must examine the certificate of title and send notification to any person that listed its security interest on the certificate of title on or before ten days before the notification date.

2. Requisites of a Reasonable Notification—
Sections 9-612–9-614

Section 9-611(b) requires that the secured party send "reasonable" notification of the disposition. The components of a reasonable notification are the timeliness, contents, and manner of the notification. Section 9-612 pertains to the timeliness of the notification and sections 9-613 and 9-614 pertain to the contents of the notification. Manner is mentioned only in Official Comment 2 to section 9-611, which remarks that the notification "must be reasonable as to the manner in which it is sent...."

Section 9-612(a) provides a general statement declaring that whether the notification is sent within a reasonable time of the disposition is a question of fact. Because a purpose of the notification is to allow the debtor, any secondary obligor, and other secured parties and lienholders to protect their rights in the collateral, notice must be sent to those persons in advance of the disposition. The question is, how much in advance? Section 9-612(b) provides a safe harbor for sending notification for all security interests except consumer transactions. It declares that a notification is sent within a reasonable time if the secured party sends it after default and at least ten days before the earliest time for the disposition designated in the notification.

Section 9-612 provides no safe harbor or any other statement regarding the notification time for a consumer transaction. A *consumer transaction*, section 9-102(a)(26), is when an individual incurs an obligation primarily for personal, family, or household purposes and secures the obligation with a security interest in collateral primarily used for personal, family, or household purposes. Official Comment 2 to section 9-612 imparts some guidance on what is a reasonable time: "A notification that is sent so near to the disposition date that a notified person could not be expected to act on or take account of the notification would be unreasonable." Courts have validated a notification sent eight days before the disposition but invalidated a notification sent three days before the disposition. It seems likely that sending the notification ten days before a consumer transaction disposition would be reasonable. Anything less does not seem sufficient to allow a consumer to act upon the information included in the notification.

Sections 9-613 and 9-614 establish the information that must be included in a notification. Both sections also establish a safe harbor for compliance by providing a form notification and stating that a completed form provides "sufficient information." "Reasonable" notification is the literal requirement of section 9-611(b), but there is no indication that "sufficient" means anything different from "reasonable." As with all safe harbors, a secured party should choose to sail in the safe harbor.

Section 9-613 adopts content requirements for a sufficient notification of a disposition of collateral for all security interests except consumer-goods transactions. A sufficient notification under section 9-613(1) must describe the debtor and the secured party, describe the collateral, state the method of intended disposition (public or private sale, lease, license, etc.), inform the debtor it is entitled to an accounting of the unpaid debt along with any charge for the accounting, and state the time and place of a public disposition or the time after which any other disposition will be made. The safe harbor form is supplied in section 9-613(5).

A notification that fails to include all the section 9-613(1) information might yet be sufficient. Section 9-613(2) states that it is "a question of fact" whether a notification that lacks any of the required information is sufficient nevertheless. Additionally, section 9-613(3)(B) validates a notification that provides "substantially the information specified," although it includes "minor errors that are not seriously misleading." Finally, a notification that includes additional information not required by section 9-613(1) is not insufficient under the rule of section 9-613(3)(A) if it provides "substantially the information specified." A secured party that uses the safe harbor form avoids these problems.

Additional information is required for a notification of a consumer-goods transaction disposition. Section 9-614 states that a sufficient notification of disposition in a consumer-goods transaction must include the information specified in section 9-613(1) and: 1) a description of any liability for a deficiency of the person to whom the notification is sent; 2) a telephone number from which the redemption amount can be obtained; and 3) a telephone number or mailing address from which additional information about the disposition and the obligation is available. The safe harbor form is supplied in section 9-614(3).

Section 9-614 does not include a provision that grants sufficiency to a notification that contains an error in the information required, even if it is a minor error. Official Comment 2 to section 9-614 declares a notification is "insufficient as a matter of law" if the secured party fails to comply with the information requirements of section 9-614(1). However, if the secured party uses the section 9-614(3) form but includes additional information at the end of the form, section 9-614(5) awards sufficiency although the additional information includes errors, unless the errors are "misleading with respect to rights arising under this article." The moral is, use the safe-harbor form and include no additional information.

c. Proceeds of Disposition—Application, Surplus and Deficiency—Sections 9-615, 9-616

A secured party that disposes of collateral under section 9-610 must apply the cash proceeds of the disposition in accordance with section 9-615(a). Noncash proceeds must be applied in a commercially reasonable manner. Although section 9-615(a) adopts an order for distributing the proceeds of the disposition, a disposition frequently does not generate enough proceeds to pay the total obligation owed to the secured party disposing of the collateral.

Section 9-615(a) commands that the secured party apply the proceeds *first* to its reasonable expenses of retaking, holding, preparing for disposition, processing, and disposing of the collateral, including reasonable attorney's fees and legal expenses to the extent provided by the agreement and not prohibited by law; *second* to payment of the obligation secured; *third* to any subordinate security interests or lienholders if the secured party receives, before it completes distribution of the proceeds, an authenticated demand from a subordinate security interest or lienholder for any surplus proceeds, and if a consignor has an interest in the collateral, the subordinate security interest or lienholder is superior to the consignor; and *fourth* to a consignor if the secured party receives, before the secured party completes distribution of the proceeds, an authenticated demand from the consignor. (Consignments are discussed in Chapter 1.) Section 9-615(b) authorizes, but does not require, the secured party to request proof of the subordinate person's interest in the surplus and until such person furnishes reasonable proof of its interest, the secured party need not comply with the demand. If there are no subordinate interests and no consignor with a right to payment, section 9-615(d)(1) compels the secured party to distribute any remaining proceeds to the debtor. The debtor is not entitled to any proceeds if the underlying secured transaction is a sale of accounts, chattel paper, payment intangibles, or promissory notes.

When a junior secured party disposes of the collateral, section 9-615(g) protects the cash proceeds it receives from the claim of a senior secured party. The conditions to this protection are that the secured party acts in good faith and is without knowledge that its receipt violates the rights of a senior security interest. If those conditions are met, the secured party: 1) takes the disposition proceeds free of the senior security interest or lien; 2) is not obligated to distribute the proceeds to any senior secured party or lienholder; and 3) is not obligated to pay any surplus to the senior security interest or lienholder. Official Comment 5 to section 9-610 declares that it is unlikely the disposition would ever violate the rights of the senior secured party because the junior secured party's disposition does not discharge or otherwise affect the rights to the collateral of the senior secured party. If there is no violation of rights, there can be no knowledge of a violation.

Protecting the junior secured party's right to the disposition proceeds results in no harm to a senior secured party or lienholder because the disposition does not affect their rights in the collateral. Unfortunately, Article 9 does not express that principle in a code section; however, the drafters express it in Official Comment 5 to UCC section 9-610. Additionally, section 9-617(a) states that a disposition after default "discharges the security interest under which the disposition is made … and any subordinate security interest or other subordinate lien." The clear implication is that senior interests remain intact.

Frequently, the proceeds of the disposition do not exceed the total of the expenses the secured party incurs plus the amount of the secured obligation. A deficiency exists in that situation—the expenses and obligation exceed the proceeds. Section 9-615(d)(2) makes the obligor liable for the deficiency, except where the underlying transaction is a sale of accounts, chattel paper, payment intangibles, or promissory notes in which there is no true obligation. Unless the obligor voluntarily pays the amount of the deficiency, the secured party must bring an action to obtain a judgment against the obligor for the deficiency. The action to recover a deficiency is discussed later in this chapter.

Section 9-615(f) establishes a rule that can affect a deficiency or surplus when the disposition transferee is the secured party, a person related to the secured party, or a secondary obligor. Sections 9-102(a)(62) and (63) define *person related to* a secured party to include a spouse, family members, and relatives, and officers, directors, and persons controlling organizations, and the spouses of such persons. In these situations, the transferee may lack the incentive to pay market value for the collateral because it can purchase the collateral at a low price while knowing that the secured party can recover the deficiency from the obligor. Additionally, the transferee has little incentive to create or increase a surplus because it will inure to the benefit of the debtor only. Consequently, a greater deficiency (or lesser surplus) may result although the disposition is commercially reasonable and the secured party complies with Article 9's notification requirements.

Section 9-615(f) applies when one of the specified persons acquires the collateral at the disposition and the proceeds of the disposition are significantly below the range of proceeds that a commercially reasonable disposition to another person would have produced. The later requirement insures that purchase by one of the specified persons does not alone activate the section. Section 9-626(a)(5) requires that the obligor or the debtor establish that the proceeds are significantly below what otherwise would have resulted. However, Article 9 provides no guidance on the meaning of "significantly below." If the obligor (or debtor) carries its burden, the amount of the deficiency (or surplus) is based on the proceeds that would have been produced in a commercially reasonable disposition to a transferee other than the secured party, related person, or a secondary obligor. Although the rebuttable presumption rule of section 9-626, discussed later in this chapter, could be used to calculate the amount of proceeds, neither section 9-615(f) or 9-626(a) expressly commands its use. If the debtor does not establish that the proceeds are significantly below what otherwise would have resulted, the secured party calculates the deficiency or surplus based on the actual proceeds.

d. Explanation of Deficiency or Surplus for Consumer-Goods Transaction — Section 9-616

Section 9-616 obligates a secured party to send an "explanation" of the amount of the surplus or deficiency in a consumer-goods transaction when a consumer obligor is liable for a deficiency or the debtor is entitled to a surplus. The surplus explanation goes to the debtor, and the deficiency explanation goes to the consumer obligor. However, a deficiency explanation is not required even if a deficiency exists if the secured party sends the consumer obligor a record waiving its right to a deficiency within fourteen days of its receipt of a request for an explanation from a consumer obligor. A consumer obligor is an individual who incurred the obligation primarily for personal, family or household purposes. There is no requirement that a secured party send an explanation for other types of security interests.

If an explanation is required, a secured party must send it before or with the accounting and payment of a surplus or before or with the first demand for payment of a deficiency. However, if the debtor or consumer obligor requests an explanation, the secured party must send it within fourteen days after it receives the request or, with respect to a consumer obligor, send a record waiving its claim for the deficiency within fourteen days after it receives the request. A *request*, defined in section 9-616(a)(2), is a record, written or electronic, authenticated by the debtor or consumer obligor, sent after disposition of the collateral, and requesting that the secured party provide an explanation.

The explanation must be written and contain specific information, some of which the secured party must provide in a prescribed order. Section 9-616(a)(1) defines *explanation* as a writing that contains: 1) the amount of the surplus or deficiency; 2) an explanation of how the surplus or deficiency was calculated; 3) a statement, if applicable, that future debits, credits, charges, and expenses may affect the amount; and 4) a telephone number or mailing address from which additional information concerning the transaction is available. Section 9-616(c) establishes the specific information required for the calculation of the deficiency or surplus and the order in which the information must appear. That information and the order in which it appears are mandatory. Section 9-616(c) requires: 1) the aggregate obligation as of a date section 9-616(c)(1) specifies, including any rebate of interest; 2) the amount of proceeds of the disposition; 3) the amount of the obligation after deducting proceeds; 4) the amount and type of expenses; 5) the amount and type of any credits; and 6) the amount of surplus or deficiency. Unfortunately, section 9-616 does not provide a safe-harbor form.

Section 9-616(d) provides a small window for errors in the explanation. An explanation is "sufficient," meaning it satisfies section 9-616(a), if it substantially complies with the section's requirements, even if it contains minor errors, provided the errors are not seriously misleading to the recipient. Because the explanation is for consumer obligors and debtors—persons with a need for full and accurate information—one should not expect a court to be generous with its mercy.

Section 9-625(e) establishes statutory damages recoverable by a debtor or a consumer obligor when a secured party fails to comply with the explanation requirement, in addition to recovery of the actual damages the person suffers. A secured party that waives its right to a deficiency but fails to send the required record of waiver within the specified time is liable for any loss its failure causes the obligor, plus $500 statutory damages. A secured party that fails to send the explanation within the specified time is liable for any loss its failure causes, plus $500 statutory damages if its noncompliance is "part of a pattern, or consistent with a practice, of noncompliance." The damages apply to a secured party whose practice or pattern is to fail to send an explanation with its demand for payment of a deficiency.

e. Effect of Disposition, Rights of Transferee, and Warranty— Sections 9-617, 9-610(d)–(f)

Section 9-617(a) establishes the rights in the collateral after its disposition of the transferee, the debtor, the secured party disposing of the collateral, and the holder of any subordinate security interest or other lien. Noticeably absent from that list is the senior security interest or lien. The omission of a rule regarding senior security interests is the drafters' tacit declaration that the disposition of collateral under a subordinate security interest does not affect the rights of a senior security interest. Official Comment 5 to section 9-610 declares: "[T]he junior's disposition does not of itself discharge the senior's security interest. See Section 9-617. Unless the senior secured party has authorized the sale free and clear of its security interest, the senior's security interest ordinarily will survive the disposition of the junior and continue under section 9-315(a)." Consequently, a senior secured party retains it rights in the collateral against the transferee after a junior secured party disposes of collateral, except in the unlikely situation where the transferee takes the collateral free of the security interest under an Article 9 rule, such as section 9-317 or section 9-320.

Section 9-617(a)(1) states that a transferee for value of collateral after default obtains all the debtor's rights in the collateral. Additionally, sections 9-617(a)(2) and (a)(3) discharge the security interest of the secured party making the disposition and any subordinate security interest or subordinate lien. Consequently, after disposition of the collateral only the transferee and senior interests have rights in the collateral. However, section 9-617(b) requires that the transferee must act in good faith to take free of the rights and interests of the debtor, the secured party, and subordinate parties. *Good faith* means the transferee is honest in fact and observes reasonable commercial standards of fair dealing. Section 9-617(c) levies a substantial cost on a transferee not acting in good faith — such transferee takes the collateral subject to the rights of the debtor, the interest of the secured party disposing of the collateral, and all subordinate security interests or other liens.

Section 9-617(b) further protects a transferee in good faith by declaring that it takes the collateral free of the rights and interests of the debtor, secured party, and subordinate interests, even if the secured party disposing of the collateral fails to comply with Article 9's commercially reasonable disposition and notice requirements or the requirements imposed in any judicial proceeding. The secured party's failure to comply with Article 9's requirements results in liability for any loss its failure causes and could affect the secured party's recovery of a deficiency. However, it does not limit the rights of a good faith transferee.

Section 9-610(d) adds a warranty of title to the rights of a transferee. It provides that a contract for disposition by sale, lease, license, or other method includes any warranty of "title, possession, quiet enjoyment, and the like" that would arise by operation of law in a voluntary disposition of the kind of property involved. These warranties relate to ownership rights, not to the quality of the property. The typical warranties arising by operation of law in a voluntary transfer are implied warranties — warranties that arise automatically because of the transfer, not from words or conduct. Such warranties include not only the Articles 2 and 2A warranties relating to title and infringement (sections 2-312 and 2A-211, respectively), but also any warranties arising outside of the UCC. The warranties of Articles 2 and 2A benefit a transferee because they include a warranty that the transfer is free of any security interest, encumbrance, claim, or interest in the goods. Consequently, a junior secured party disposing of collateral breaches the warranty if a senior security interest survives the disposition. Breach of the warranty gives the transferee a claim against the secured party disposing of the collateral; however, it does not affect the rights of the senior secured party in the collateral.

The benefits of the section 9-610(d) warranty are diminished by section 9-610(e), which authorizes the secured party to disclaim or modify the warranty. The secured party can disclaim or modify the warranty in two ways: 1) in the same manner authorized by the law creating the warranty, for example the Article 2 disclaimer section; or 2) by including an express disclaimer or modification of the warranty in the record evidencing the contract for disposition that the secured party communicates to the transferee. *Communicate*, defined in section 9-102(a)(18), allows for sending a written record or transmitting a record, by any means agreed, such as electronically. Section 9-610(f) provides wording that is sufficient to disclaim a warranty: "There is no warranty relating to title, possession, quiet enjoyment, or the like in this disposition."

Because the transferee of a default disposition may know that the disposition results from a default in performance, the secured party might argue the warranty of title is disclaimed under the rule of section 2-312(2) — circumstances giving the buyer reason to know that the secured party purports to transfer only the rights it has, not good title. The drafters attempt to rebut that argument by expressing their opinion, in Official Comment 5 to section 2-312, that section 9-610 dispositions should not be treated like typical default sales which engage the disclaimer-by-circumstances rule of section 2-312(2), but should require disclaimer by the provisions of section 9-610(e) or, as they imply, by specific disclaimer language under section 2-312(2).

4. Acceptance of Collateral in Full or Partial Satisfaction of the Obligation — Sections 9-620–9-622

A remedy available to many secured parties as an alternative to disposing of the collateral is to accept the collateral in full or partial satisfaction of the obligation secured. Accepting the collateral in full or partial satisfaction of the obligation transfers the debtor's rights in the collateral to the secured party and terminates subordinate security interests or other subordinate liens. Essentially, the secured party becomes the owner of the collateral, buying it with the obligation the collateral secures. For example, suppose a security interest in an item of equipment secures a $13,000 obligation. After default, the secured party can propose to accept the collateral in full (or partial) payment of the obligation. Typically, the secured party initiates the proposal, although the debtor may propose that the secured party accept the collateral in full or partial satisfaction of the obligation. The effect of acceptance is the same — all or part of the obligation is discharged.

The benefits to the secured party of acceptance of the collateral include: after acceptance it can, if it desires, dispose of the collateral unrestricted by the disposition requirements of Article 9; it retains any surplus from a sale; and, in a proposal for a partial satisfaction of the obligation, the acceptance establishes the deficiency amount. The cost to the secured party is that it relinquishes its right to recover some or all of any deficiency, depending on whether it proposes a full or partial acceptance. Consequently, the secured party incurs the risk that a disposition after acceptance will not produce sufficient proceeds to repay its expenses and the obligation secured. To reduce that risk, a secured party should consider proposing acceptance of the collateral when it can accurately predict the amount of proceeds a disposition will produce.

The benefits to the obligor of acceptance of collateral are that there is no deficiency or the deficiency is determined by the parties' agreement and there are no expenses of a disposition to devour the proceeds. If the debtor is not also the obligor, the benefit to a debtor is slight: freedom from monitoring the disposition of collateral. The costs to the debtor include relinquishing its right to a commercially reasonable disposition of the collateral and relinquishing its right to a possible surplus from the disposition. Nevertheless, the debtor may agree to acceptance because its property is liable for the obligation and the secured party can repossess and dispose of the property.

The problem for all parties is that they must base their decision on projected proceeds. Although it is possible to predict accurately the amount of proceeds a disposition of some types of collateral will produce — a promissory note, for example — in many instances it is a gamble.

For most security interests, a secured party has the option of accepting the collateral in either full or partial satisfaction of the obligation. However, section 9-620(g) does not authorize a secured party to accept the collateral in partial satisfaction of the obligation if the underlying security interest is a consumer transaction.

A secured party is completely disqualified from accepting the collateral in full or partial satisfaction of the obligation in two situations involving consumer-goods security interests. Section 9-620(e) compels the secured party to dispose of the collateral within a mandatory time if: 1) 60 percent of the "cash price" has been paid in a purchase-money security interest in consumer goods; or 2) 60 percent of the "principal amount of the obligation secured" has been paid in a non-purchase-money security interest in consumer goods. Although "cash price" is not defined, it should mean the cash price of the goods regardless of the amount of the obligation secured. The amount of the obligation secured typically would include interest charged on the cash price. If the drafters intended cash price to mean the total obligation secured, they would have used words to convey that meaning. The meaning of "principal amount of the obligation secured" should be interpreted similarly, as meaning the amount borrowed exclusive of interest. In those situations, the secured party must dispose of the collateral within 90 days of taking possession or any longer period agreed to by the debtor and any secondary obligor in a post-default authenticated agreement. However, section 9-624(b) authorizes the debtor to waive the mandatory disposition requirement in a post-default authenticated agreement.

Some courts found a *constructive* acceptance of collateral in satisfaction of the obligation when the secured party disposed of the collateral after holding it, in the opinion of the court, for an unreasonable length of time. Revised Article 9 precludes that result. Section 9-620(b)(1) declares that an acceptance of collateral is "ineffective unless the secured party consents to the acceptance in an authenticated record or sends a proposal to the debtor...." Consequently, a secured party's failure to dispose of the collateral timely cannot alone cause an acceptance in satisfaction of the obligation, although it could constitute a failure to make a commercially reasonable disposition.

a. Conditions to Acceptance of Collateral in Satisfaction of Obligation — Section 9-620

Section 9-620(a) imposes four conditions to a secured party's acceptance of collateral in full or partial satisfaction of an obligation. *First*, the debtor consents to the acceptance in the manner specified in section 9-620(c). *Second*, the secured party does not receive a timely notification of objection to its proposed acceptance from a person having the right to object. *Third*, if the collateral is consumer goods, the debtor is not in possession of the collateral when it consents. *Fourth*, if the collateral is consumer goods, section 9-620(e) does not require mandatory disposition of the collateral, unless waived under section 9-624(b). These conditions must be satisfied whether the secured party or the debtor proposes the acceptance because section 9-620(b) declares that a purported acceptance is ineffective unless the section 9-620(a) conditions are met.

1. Debtor's Consent

Section 9-620(c) authorizes the debtor's consent to acceptance through affirmative agreement or, for a proposal for a full-satisfaction acceptance, from failing to object to the secured party's proposal. A debtor consents through affirmative agreement under section 9-620(c)(1) if it agrees to the proposal in a record it authenticates after default. The meanings of *authenticate* and *record* allow a written or electronic consent.

A debtor consents through failing to object to a proposal only when the proposal is for acceptance in full satisfaction of the obligation. Section 9-620(c)(2) establishes three requirements for the consent. *First*, the secured party must send the debtor, after default, a proposal of its acceptance. *Second*, the proposal must offer either unconditional acceptance by the secured party in full satisfaction of the obligation or acceptance in full satisfaction subject only to a condition that any collateral not in the possession of the secured party be preserved or maintained. In other words, the only condition authorized by section 9-620(c)(2) is that any collateral not in the possession of the secured party be preserved or maintained until the secured party is able to take possession. *Third*, the secured party does not receive, within twenty days after the secured party sends the proposal, a notification of objection authenticated by the debtor. In essence, section 9-620(c)(2) places a duty on the debtor to object if it does not agree to the proposal. The time requirement is strict and short: the secured party must receive the debtor's objection within twenty days of the date it sends its proposal. A debtor consents if it does not object. Because the notification of objection must be *authenticated*, it can be written or electronic, but not oral.

Section 9-620 adopts no requirements for the contents of the proposal a secured party uses to inform the debtor of its proposal to accept the collateral. *Proposal*, defined in section 9-102(a)(66), requires a record, authenticated by the secured party, containing the terms on which the secured party is offering to accept the collateral. The only guidance as to the content of the proposal comes from Official Comment 4 to section 9-620, which states that the proposal for acceptance should include the amount or the means of calculating the amount of the obligation to be satisfied, any right to withdraw the proposal, and any conditions to the offer of acceptance. However, Official Comment 11 notes that the UCC's duty to act in good faith (section 1-304) applies to a proposal and illustrates bad faith with an example where a secured party proposes to accept collateral worth $1000 in full satisfaction of a $100 obligation.

2. Objection by Other Persons

The second condition imposed by section 9-620(a) is that the secured party does not receive timely objection to its proposal from a person having a right to object. Persons having a right to object to the secured party's proposal must act within the time section 9-620(d) allots. To prevent acceptance of the collateral, the secured party must receive an authenticated notification of objection from such persons within twenty days after the secured party sends its proposal to them. For example, a secured party who sends its proposal on June 1 must receive the objection on or before June 21.

Two categories of persons have the right to object: 1) persons specified by section 9-621 to whom the secured party must send its proposal, and 2) any person, other than the debtor, having a subordinate interest in the collateral. These persons have the right to object whether the proposal is for a full or partial satisfaction of the obligation. Persons with subordinate interests might object because the secured party's acceptance of the collateral terminates their interests in the collateral and deprives them of the right to use it to satisfy their debts. A senior secured party does not have the same incentive to object because the secured party's acceptance of the collateral does not affect the rights of the senior secured party. Nevertheless, a senior secured party might object if the debtor is in default to it and the senior secured party wants to use the collateral (either by disposing of it or accepting it) to satisfy its debt.

The first category consists of three groups that section 9-621(a) designates as persons to whom the secured party must send its proposal of acceptance. Additionally, the secured party must send its proposal to any secondary obligor when the proposal is for a partial satisfaction. The proposal sent to these persons is the same proposal the secured party sends to the debtor and the discussion of the proposal in the previous paragraphs is relevant here.

The first group is persons from whom the secured party receives, before the debtor consents to the acceptance, an authenticated notification of a claim of interest in the collateral. The notification of claim can be written or electronic, but the secured party has no duty to send the proposal to these persons until it receives the authenticated notification.

The second group is any secured party or lienholder that perfects an interest in the collateral by filing a financing statement that identifies the collateral, is indexed under the debtor's name, and is filed in the proper office at least ten days before the debtor consents to the acceptance proposal. To identify these persons, the secured party must search the UCC financing statement index in the proper filing office for financing statements that were filed under the debtor's name on or before the tenth day before the debtor consented. Because a secured party might not know the consent date beforehand, the one way to comply with this requirement is for the secured party to search the UCC index after the debtor consents and send its proposal to anyone that filed a financing statement at least ten days before the date of consent. Under this method, note that the secured party will receive the debtor's consent before it sends its proposal to others and commences their objection period.

The third group is secured parties that perfect a security interest under section 9-311(a) at least ten days before the date the debtor consents. Because security interests perfected under section 9-311(a) are perfected in accordance with a federal or state statute, treaty, or regulation, the UCC financing statement index will not reveal them. To identify persons in this group, the secured party must search the record system applicable to the type of security interest. For example, if a security interest is perfected by indicating the security interest on the certificate of title, the secured party must examine the certificate of title and send notification to any person whose security interest was listed on the certificate of title on or before ten days before the date of consent.

The second category of persons having a right to object are persons to whom the secured party need not send its notification of proposal but who nevertheless have a right to object to the proposal. These persons are not within the three groups section 9-621 designates. Their interest in the collateral is perfected by: 1) a method other than filing a financing statement or under section 9-311; 2) a filing in the name of a different debtor—for example as a consequence of a transfer of collateral; or 3) a filing in a different filing office—for example as a consequence of a change in governing jurisdiction. It is unlikely they will object because they probably do not know of the secured party's proposal. However, they have a right to object. To be effective, the secured party must receive their authenticated notification of objection within twenty days after the secured party sends its last notification of proposal to the persons designated by section 9-621.

It is possible that there are no persons to whom a secured party must send its proposal under section 9-621 and consequently, the secured party will send it proposal to the debtor only. Nevertheless, there could be persons who claim an interest in the collateral and they have a right to object to the proposal. These persons are the same persons identified in the previous paragraph. The secured party must receive their authenticated notification of objection before the debtor consents to the acceptance.

3. Conditions Pertaining to Consumer Goods

The third and fourth conditions imposed by section 9-620(a) apply only when the collateral for the security interest is consumer goods. In that case, section 9-620(a)(3) requires that the debtor not be in possession of the collateral at the time it consents to the acceptance. This does not mean that the secured party must be in possession of the collateral, only that the debtor is not in possession at the time of consent. Lastly, section 9-620(4) declares that the secured party cannot accept the collateral in satisfaction of the obligation if the mandatory disposition requirement of section 9-620(e) applies, unless the debtor waives its right to mandatory disposition. The details of mandatory disposition are discussed in section D.4. of this chapter.

Fulfillment of the four conditions results in an effective acceptance of collateral. Although section 9-620 does not use the words *effective acceptance*, Official Comment 3 to section 9-620 and Official Comment 2 to section 9-622 both use that term and leave no doubt that acceptance is not effective unless it satisfies the four conditions of section 9-620(a).

b. Effect of Accepting Collateral in Satisfaction of Obligation — Section 9-622

Section 9-622 establishes four effects of an effective acceptance: 1) it discharges the obligation to the extent agreed; 2) it transfers all the debtor's rights in the collateral to the secured party; 3) it discharges the security interest of the secured party accepting the collateral and any other subordinate security interest or subordinate lien; and 4) it terminates any other subordinate interest. Notice that section 9-622 is silent regarding the effect of an acceptance on a senior secured party or a senior lienholder. The indisputable result of that omission is that a secured party's acceptance of the collateral does not affect a senior interest. That is consistent with the effect on a senior secured party of the disposition of collateral by a junior secured party. Consequently, a senior secured party could enforce its security interest in the collateral after the junior secured party accepted it in full or partial satisfaction of the obligation.

Section 9-622(b) declares that subordinate interests in the collateral are terminated or discharged under section 9-622(a) "even if the secured party fails to comply with this article." Official Comment 2 to section 9-622 indicates that the quoted phrase pertains to the secured party's failure to comply with the procedural aspects of accepting the collateral, not the non-occurrence of one of the four conditions to an effective acceptance established in section 9-620(a). Non-occurrence of one of those conditions prevents an effective acceptance, and the comment states that the effects of section 9-622(a) result from an *effective acceptance*. Consequently, if the four conditions of section 9-620(a) are satisfied, an effective acceptance results and a subordinate interest is discharged even if the secured party fails, for example, to send a required notification of its proposal to a subordinate interest. However, failing to send a notification could result in liability to the subordinate interest because section 9-625 makes a secured party liable for any loss caused by its failure to comply with Article 9.

5. Right to Redeem the Collateral — Section 9-623

Section 9-623(a) grants the debtor, any secondary obligor, or other secured party or lienholder, the right to redeem the collateral from the secured party that is exercising its rights in the collateral after a default by the debtor. Redemption allows the debtor or other authorized party to obtain possession of the property in exchange for paying the obligation. The person that redeems the property can use it to satisfy any obligation the obligor owes it. Except in a consumer-goods transaction, section 9-624(c) permits the debtor or a secondary obligor to authenticate a post-default waiver of its right to redeem. Section 9-602(11) otherwise prohibits a waiver by the debtor or an obligor of this right.

Section 9-623(c) declares that a person can exercise its right to redeem until the secured party collects the collateral, disposes of the collateral or enters into a contract to dispose of it, or accepts the collateral in full or partial satisfaction of the obligation. Consequently, a person can redeem although the secured party has accelerated payment of the obligation, repossessed or filed an action for repossession of the collateral, sent notification of a disposition, scheduled a time for disposition, or sent notification of a proposal to accept collateral in satisfaction of the obligation.

To redeem the collateral, section 9-623(b) requires that the person tender fulfillment of all obligations secured by the collateral owed to the secured party, including expenses and fees the secured party could recover under section 9-615(a)(1). Tendering fulfillment means the person must be ready, willing, and able to pay the obligation, not merely promise to pay it. Additionally, if the secured party accelerates the balance due after the debtor defaults, the obligation secured is the accelerated balance, not just the installments in default. Nothing prevents the secured party from agreeing to allow the debtor to reinstate its performance of the credit agreement by paying any missed installments and fees. However, none of the authorized persons has the right to demand reinstatement of the agreement unless the contract provides such a right. Their only right is to redeem the collateral.

6. Secured Party's Failure to Comply with Article 9 — Sections 9-625, 9-626, 9-628

a. Basic Remedies — Section 9-625

A secured party employing Article 9's remedies after a debtor defaults is subject to requirements that it proceed in good faith and in a commercially reasonable manner and that it send any required notifications. Section 9-625 provides two basic remedies when the secured party is not complying with Article 9's requirements — an injured person can apply to the court for judicial oversight of the transaction and can seek recovery of loss caused by the secured party's noncompliance.

Seeking judicial oversight likely will require that the person who believes the secured party is not complying with Article 9 commence a lawsuit, because a secured party typically exercises its remedies without employing judicial process. Additionally, that person must act timely, since the time between repossession of the collateral and exercise of rights may be short. An example of a situation where a person might seek judicial oversight is where the secured party has scheduled a disposition that is not commercially reasonable. The person could ask the court to enjoin the disposition or set appropriate conditions for the disposition.

Section 9-625(c)(1) authorizes the debtor, obligor, other secured party, or lienholder to recover damages for loss suffered from the secured party's failure to comply with Article 9. Loss could result from a secured party's failure to repossess collateral without breaching the peace, failure to dispose of the collateral in a commercially reasonable manner, failure to send notification of disposition or acceptance, or failure to send an explanation of a deficiency. The section expressly includes as a possible loss the debtor's inability to obtain, or the increased costs of obtaining, alternative financing. Section 1-305 establishes the UCC principle that guides remedies and declares that the remedies provided "must be liberally administered to the end that the aggrieved party may be put in as good a position as if the other party had fully performed...." For example, if the secured party does not dispose of the collateral in a commercially reasonable manner and the debtor proves that a commercially reasonable disposition would have produced $5000 additional proceeds, the debtor should recover $5000. Official Comment 3 to section 9-625 notes that the normal rules of proof apply to these remedies; consequently, the injured person must prove noncompliance by the secured party and the amount of loss it incurred.

If non-Article 9 law provides a remedy for the secured party's misconduct, such law is applicable under section 1-103(b). For example, a secured party whose repossession is wrongful may have committed the tort of conversion. An injured party could recover damages in tort for conversion or damages under Article 9 that put it in as good a position as if the secured party had properly repossessed the collateral.

When a secured party's failure to comply with Article 9 affects the deficiency produced by the disposition, section 9-625(d) essentially forces a debtor to choose between recovering its actual damages for noncompliance under section 9-625(b) or reducing or eliminating its liability for a deficiency under section 9-626. Section 9-626, discussed later in this chapter, applies to a security interest other than a consumer transaction. It establishes a formula for calculating the amount of proceeds a disposition complying with Article 9 would have produced and uses that amount to determine any deficiency or surplus. Although section 9-625(d) allows a debtor to recover damages for the loss of any surplus, it declares that a debtor whose deficiency is reduced or eliminated under section 9-626 cannot otherwise recover under section 9-625(b). Consequently, a debtor who employs the section 9-626 remedy to reduce or eliminate its deficiency cannot recover actual damages otherwise recoverable under section 9-625(b), but can recover any surplus a complying disposition would have produced.

b. Statutory Minimum Damages Applicable to Consumer Goods Security Interests — Section 9-625(c)(2)

When the security interest is a consumer-goods transaction (consumer obligation secured by consumer goods), section 9-625(c)(2) provides a minimum damage recovery for debtors and secondary obligors that suffer loss caused by the secured party's noncompliance with Article 9. Official Comment 4 to section 9-625 notes that the remedy "is designed to ensure that every noncompliance with the requirements of Part 6 [of Article 9] in a consumer-goods transaction results in liability, regardless of any injury that may have resulted." A person that was the debtor or a secondary obligor at the time the secured party failed to comply with Article 9's default obligations may recover "an amount not less than the credit service charge plus 10 percent of the principal amount of the obligation or the time-price differential plus 10 percent of the cash price."

Article 9 does not define "credit service charge" or "time-price differential," but Official Comment 4 invites courts to do so "taking into account the subsection's purpose of providing a minimum recovery in consumer-goods transactions." Generally, those terms refer to the total interest charges for the obligation. As so defined, statutory damages can be a substantial sum because they consist of the total interest charged plus ten per cent of the obligation or cash price. Because section 9-625 does not indicate that an injured person can recover section 9-625(b) actual damages and section 9-625(c)(2) minimum damages, section 9-625(c)(2) damages are the minimum an injured person can collect for a secured party's noncompliance, not an addition to section 9-625(b) damages.

Sections 9-628(d) and (e) restrict recovery of statutory minimum damages in two instances. *First*, a secured party who fails to comply with section 9-616 (the deficiency explanation requirement applicable in a consumer-goods transaction) is not liable for the minimum damages of 9-625(c)(2). However, sections 9-625(e)(5) and (e)(6) award an injured person statutory damages of $500 when the secured party fails to comply with section 9-616. Consequently, an injured person recovers its actual loss and statutory damages without a statutory minimum. *Second*, a secured party is liable for section 9-625(c)(2) minimum damages only once in connection with any one security interest. For example, a secured party who pays statutory minimum damages to the debtor is not liable for those same damages to a secondary obligor, although the secured party would remain liable for actual damages suffered by that obligor.

c. Exceptions to Liability — Section 9-628

Section 9-628 limits the persons to whom a secured party is liable for its failure to comply with Article 9. The limitations are necessary because a secured party might not know the identity of the debtor. For example, if a debtor grants a security interest to a secured party and subsequently sells the collateral, the buyer is the debtor under the definition of debtor in section 9-102(a)(28) and the original debtor is the obligor. The secured party might not know the identity of the debtor. If that debtor creates a security interest in the collateral, the secured party of the original debtor might not know the identity of the other secured party.

Sections 9-628(a) and (b) state that the secured party is not liable to the debtor, obligor, other secured party, or lienholder for its failure to comply with Article 9 or other law applicable to the secured party unless the secured party knows the identity of and how to communicate with the person and, for a secured party and lienholder, knows that such person has filed a financing statement against the debtor. Additionally, the secured party's failure to comply with Article 9 does not affect the obligor's liability for a deficiency in such cases. Sections 9-628(a) and (b) complement section 9-605 under which the secured party is relieved of its Article 9 duties to a person if the secured party does not know the identity of or how to communicate with such person. Section 9-605 relieves the secured party from Article 9 duties and section 9-628 prevents the secured party from incurring liability.

In particular situations, section 9-628(c) protects the secured party from liability for failing to comply with Article 9's specific duties applicable in a consumer-goods transaction and a consumer transaction. Those duties include section 9-614 (contents of the notification) and section 9-616 (explanation of deficiency). Section 9-628(c) applies only if the secured party has a reasonable belief that the transaction is not of either type based on a representation of the consumer debtor or obligor as to the true nature of the collateral or obligation. Apparently, the Article 9 drafters think a consumer debtor might misrepresent the type of collateral or type of obligation. For example, suppose a debtor informs a secured party that the collateral securing the debtor's obligation is equipment used in its business, when in fact the collateral is consumer goods. In that situation, a secured party is unaware that its security interest is a consumer-goods security interest and thus would not comply with the specific duties Article 9 imposes for a default in a consumer-goods security interest. Section 9-628(c) states that a secured party is not liable for loss caused nor is an obligor's liability for a deficiency affected by the secured party's act or omission arising from its reasonable belief that the transaction does not involve a consumer-type security interest based on the representations of the debtor or the obligor. However, the secured party must comply with the other duties Article 9 creates.

d. Restrictions on the Secured Party's Recovery of a Deficiency— Section 9-626

1. Security Interests Other than Consumer Transactions— Section 9-626

A deficiency exists when the proceeds of the disposition or collection are not sufficient to pay the total secured obligation plus fees and expenses recoverable under section 9-615(a)(1) or section 9-608(a)(1). Sections 9-615(d)(2) and 9-608(a)(4) declare that the obligor is liable for any deficiency. A deficiency also exists when a secured party accepts the collateral in partial satisfaction of the obligation because section 9-622(a)(1) discharges the obligation only to the extent agreed to by the debtor. To recover the deficiency, the secured party must obtain a judgment against the obligor, unless the obligor voluntarily pays the deficiency. Section 9-626 provides rules governing the recovery of a deficiency in secured transactions, other than consumer transactions, after disposition, collection, or acceptance of the collateral.

Section 9-626(a)(1) adopts a rule that initially eases the burden on the secured party seeking to recover a deficiency. It states that a secured party bringing an action for a deficiency need not prove compliance with Article 9's requirements unless the debtor or a secondary obligor "places the secured party's compliance in issue." This allows the secured party to obtain a judgment by proving it has a security interest, the obligor defaulted, the collateral was disposed of (or accepted or collected), and the amount of the resulting deficiency. However, a debtor can easily "place the secured party's compliance in issue" by answering the complaint of the secured party with an allegation that the secured party did not comply with Article 9's requirements for disposition, collection, or acceptance. In that case, section 9-626(a)(2) mandates that the secured party has the burden of establishing its compliance. If the secured party carries its burden, it recovers the deficiency. If it does not, sections 9-626(a)(3) and (4), known as the "rebuttable presumption rule," establish a person's liability for the deficiency by using a formula that determines the amount of proceeds the secured party would have received if its disposition, collection, or acceptance had complied with Article 9. This rule creates a substantial restriction on the recovery of a deficiency.

The rebuttable presumption rule calculates the amount of proceeds the secured party would have received had it complied with Article 9, subject to rebuttal by the secured party, and limits the liability for the deficiency to that amount. Section 9-626(a)(3) limits the debtor's or secondary obligor's liability for a deficiency to the amount by which the debt plus expenses exceeds the greater of the proceeds the secured party received or the amount of proceeds the secured party would have received if it had complied with Article 9. This section employs the familiar deficiency calculation: obligation + expenses – proceeds = deficiency; but adds a modification: proceeds are fixed as the greater of the actual proceeds or the proceeds a secured party would have received if it had complied with Article 9. Section 9-626(a)(4) creates the presumption by declaring that the proceeds a secured party would have received from a complying transaction equal the secured obligation plus expenses and attorney's fees, unless the secured party proves that the proceeds generated by complying with Article 9 would have been less. That is why the rule is labeled the rebuttable presumption rule—the proceeds are presumed to equal the obligation plus expenses unless the secured party rebuts the presumption by showing that the proceeds produced by its compliance with Article 9 would have been less than the debt plus expenses. If the proceeds equal the total debt, there is no deficiency.

For example, suppose a secured party receives $40,000 from its private disposition of collateral. The secured obligation plus expenses and attorney's fees is $60,000. The secured party sues the debtor seeking a deficiency judgment of $20,000. The debtor alleges the secured party did not dispose of the collateral in a commercially reasonable manner and the secured party fails to prove otherwise. Under the rebuttable presumption rule, the proceeds used to calculate the deficiency are $60,000 and there is no deficiency. If the secured party can prove that the proceeds of a commercially reasonable disposition would have been $50,000, the secured party will recover a $10,000 deficiency.

The consequence to the secured party of the rebuttable presumption rule is severe: the debtor or the secondary obligor is not liable for a deficiency even if an actual deficiency exists. It gives the secured party a powerful incentive to comply with the Article 9 requirements in exercising its remedy after default.

Although section 9-626(a)(3) determines the deficiency liability by using the greater of the presumption proceeds or the actual proceeds, it is unlikely that the actual proceeds would be the greater of the two. Consequently, in most cases where the rule functions, the proceeds will equal the debt plus expenses and the debtor or the secondary obligor will have no deficiency liability unless the secured party rebuts the presumption. If the actual proceeds equal or exceed the obligation plus expenses, and that is the only instance when they would be the greater of actual versus presumption, any litigation will likely involve a surplus.

2. Consumer Transaction Security Interest — Section 9-626

Deficiencies commonly occur in security interests involving consumer debtors and obligors. However, section 9-626(a) states that its rules pertaining to recovering a deficiency, including the rebuttable presumption rule, do not apply to consumer transactions. Section 9-626(b) declares that courts should determine the proper rule for a secured party's recovery of a deficiency in a consumer transaction when the secured party fails to comply with Article 9's requirements. Additionally, the section cautions that courts should draw no inference as to the proper rule from the limitation of section 9-626(a) to transactions other than consumer transactions. Lastly, the section states that courts can continue to apply "established approaches," meaning that a court could apply common law established prior to Revised Article 9. Consequently, a court will determine the impact of a secured party's failure to comply with Article 9 on its recovery of a deficiency in a consumer transaction.

Courts struggled with this issue under previous editions of Article 9. Article 9 has always made the obligor liable for a deficiency and always made a secured party liable for loss caused by its failure to comply with Article 9. However, prior to the adoption of section 9-626 in Revised Article 9, there was no Article 9 rule that limited the recovery of a deficiency when the secured party did not comply with Article 9. Not surprisingly, courts disagreed over the consequence of noncompliance.

Three approaches emerged from the courts. Some courts held that a secured party's failure to comply barred its recovery of a deficiency. That meant that the secured party would be unable to recover the deficiency, no matter how great or small and regardless of the type or gravity of noncompliance. Other courts set off the damages the debtor proved against the amount of the deficiency and allowed the secured party to recover the balance. This allowed the debtor to recover its actual loss by deducting it from the amount of the deficiency and allowed the secured party to recover the reduced deficiency. The third and predominant solution was a judicially created rebuttable presumption rule that operated the same as the rule of section 9-626(a). Section 9-626 invites courts to revisit the issue or continue to apply the rule of the jurisdiction to recovery of a deficiency in a consumer transaction.

Checkpoints

- The parties to the security interest agree on the acts that constitute a default in a secured transaction; Article 9 does not include any provisions that define default.

- After a default, the secured party can use the remedies of Article 9 and other legal or contractual remedies.

- The secured party's Article 9 remedies are the right to collect and enforce receivables collateral, to repossess the collateral, to dispose of the collateral, or to accept the collateral in full or partial satisfaction of the secured obligation.

- The secured party can utilize the Article 9 remedies although its security interest does not have priority over all other security interests in the collateral. However, the rights of a senior secured party to the collateral are not affected by the actions of a junior secured party.

- The secured party can repossess the collateral using judicial process or self-help repossession, provided self-help repossession does not breach the peace.

- The secured party can dispose of the collateral in any manner and on any terms, provided all aspects of the disposition are commercially reasonable, and it must send notification of the disposition to the debtor and other secured parties.

- If the proceeds of the disposition are not sufficient to pay the entire obligation, the obligor is liable for the deficiency. However, if the secured party did not comply with Article 9's requirements for disposition, the rebuttable presumption rule limits the amount of the deficiency.

- The secured party or the debtor can propose that the secured party accept the collateral in full or partial satisfaction of the secured obligation and, if the other party consents to the proposal, the obligation is discharged to the extent of the agreement.

- The debtor or other secured party can redeem the collateral from the secured party of the security interest in default by tendering payment of the unpaid obligation.

- The secured party who fails to comply with the requirements of the Article 9 remedies is liable to the debtor and other secured parties for any loss its failure causes, including, for some security interests, statutory damages and minimum damages.

Chapter 12

The Validity and Effect of an Assignment of Property — Sections 9-401–409

Roadmap

- The meanings of "assign" and "assignment"
- Validity of contractual and legal restrictions on a party's right to assign its interest in property by sale or security interest
- Effect of an assignment on the account debtor's right to assert its claims and defenses against the assignee, to modify the contract assigned, and to make payment on the obligation assigned

---

A. Introduction

Part 4 of Article 9 establishes rules governing the assignment by a party of its interest in accounts, chattel paper, general intangibles, payment intangibles, promissory notes, health-care-insurance receivables, letter-of-credit rights, and leasehold interests. Those types of property typically create a right in the owner of the property to receive payment in the future. To obtain immediate funds, the owner could assign its right as collateral for an obligation, as in a security interest, or as an absolute transfer, which also can create a security interest under sections 1-201(b)(35) and 9-109(a)(3). Part 4 adopt rules governing the rights of the parties to the assignment—the assignor and assignee—and the effect of the assignment on the person who is obligated ultimately to pay the obligation of the property that was assigned—the account debtor or obligor.

Assignment and *assign* are terms that Article 9 uses repeatedly in Part 4 but does not define. Official Comment 26 to section 9-102 notes that those terms generally refer to the transfer of a right to payment, transfer of a claim, or transfer of a lien. The comment also observes that the terms may refer to the transfer of the outright ownership interest or the transfer of a limited interest such as a security interest. Consequently, an assignment can refer to a sale of the types of property listed above or the creation of a security interest in such property. Under section 9-109(a)(3), a sale of an account, chattel paper, payment intangible, or promissory note is treated as a security interest.

For example, suppose a buyer purchases goods on credit from a seller, promising to pay the purchase price in 30 days. The seller wants immediate cash, so it sells its right to receive payment from the buyer to a financier. The seller-financier transaction can be labeled an *assignment of an account*, and Article 9 treats the assignment as a security interest regardless that the parties did not create a security-for-loan security interest. The Article 9 definitions include the buyer as the account debtor, the seller as the debtor, and the financier as the secured party. The seller is also the assignor and the financier the assignee. Of course, Article 9 governs the transaction where the seller borrows money from the financier and grants it a security interest in the account. That security interest transaction also can be labeled *an assignment of an account*. Other parts of Article 9 govern the security interest created by the assignment. Part 4 pertains to the validity and effect of the assignment on the parties to it and on the parties to the underlying transaction.

B. Validity of Restrictions on the Assignment of an Account or Chattel Paper — Sections 9-406(d), (f)

Sections 9-406(d) and (f) invalidate legal and contractual restrictions and prohibitions of a person's right to transfer, assign, or create a security interest in an account or chattel paper. These restrictions are commonly known as *anti-assignment* clauses. An account debtor includes such restrictions in the contract when it wants to perform only to the other party to the contract, not to a person with whom it has never dealt. For example, a buyer of goods on account (an *account debtor* under section 9-102(a)(3)) who wants to deal only with its seller could include a term in the sales agreement prohibiting the seller from assigning the account. That prohibition is "ineffective" under section 9-406(d). The seller can assign its right to receive payment without incurring liability to the account debtor for breaching the agreement. Although sections 9-406(d) and (f) literally declare such restrictions *ineffective*, Official Comment 5 to section 9-406 defines ineffective as meaning the restriction "is of no effect whatsoever."

Section 9-406(d) renders anti-assignment agreements ineffective as to transfers of accounts and chattel paper whether they relate to the transfer of a true security interest or the transfer by sale that is a security interest under Article 9. Section 9-406(d)(1) invalidates restrictions on the right of the owner to create a true security interest in the property. It declares that an agreement that prohibits, restricts, or requires the consent of the account debtor to the creation, attachment, perfection, or enforcement of a security interest in an account or chattel paper is ineffective. That section also invalidates restrictions on the right of the owner to make a sale transfer of the property by rendering ineffective an agreement that prohibits, restricts, or requires the consent of the account debtor to the assignment or transfer of an account or chattel paper. Section 9-406(d)(2) invalidates an agreement that makes the owner's assignment, transfer, or creation of a security interest a default or breach or creates a claim, defense, remedy, or right to terminate. For example, an agreement might make an assignment a breach, although not prohibiting it. Such a clause is ineffective.

Restrictions on the transfer, assignment, or creation of a security interest in an account or chattel paper can arise also under a rule of law, statute, or regulation. For example, a jurisdiction could enact a statute that prohibits a person from assigning its right to lottery winnings (a type of account). Section 9-406(f) renders such legal restrictions ineffective in a transfer of an account or chattel paper. Laws are ineffective if they restrict, prohibit, or require the consent of the account debtor or governmental official to an assignment, transfer, or security interest in an account or chattel paper, or make the assignment, transfer, or security interest a default or breach, or create a claim.

The rules of sections 9-406(d) and (f) are subject to several exceptions. *First*, section 9-406(h) directs that sections 9-406(d) and (f) are subject to any law outside Article 9 that establishes a different rule for an account debtor who is an individual who incurs the obligation primarily for personal, family, or household purposes—in other words, a consumer debtor. This exclusion allows consumer protection laws that validate contractual and legal restrictions on assignments to remain effective. *Second*, neither section applies to an assignment of a health-care-insurance receivable, a type of account. Section 9-408(a), discussed later in this chapter, governs transfer restrictions on that property. *Third*, the rules of section 9-406(d) and (f) do not apply to an assignment of a leasehold interest or of a lessor's residual interest in leased goods. Sections 9-407 and 2A-303, discussed later in this chapter, govern such assignments.

C. Validity of Restrictions on the Assignment of a Promissory Note or Payment Intangible — Sections 9-406, 9-408

Sections 9-406 and 9-408 combine to invalidate terms in a promissory note or a payment intangible that restrict the right of the owner to create a security interest in such property. Remember that the sale of a promissory note or a payment intangible is a security interest under section 9-109(a). Section 9-406 invalidates restrictions to the creation of a true security interest in such property, while section 9-408 renders ineffective restrictions to the sale of such property.

Section 9-406(d)(1) renders ineffective terms that prohibit, restrict, or require the consent of the account debtor of a payment intangible or the obligor of a promissory note to the creation, attachment, perfection, or enforcement of a security interest in such property. Section 9-406(d)(2) invalidates an agreement that makes the owner's assignment, transfer, or creation of a security interest a default or breach or creates a claim, defense, remedy, or right to terminate. Both those sections are subject to any law outside Article 9 that establishes a different rule for an account debtor that is a consumer.

Section 9-408 invalidates terms restricting the sale of a promissory note or a payment intangible. Section 9-408(a) renders ineffective the terms in a promissory note or a payment intangible that: 1) restrict, prohibit, or require the consent of the obligor or account debtor to the creation, attachment, perfection, or enforcement of a security interest; or 2) make such acts a default or breach, or result in claims, defenses, or remedies. For example, if the terms of a promissory note between a debtor and a bank prohibit the bank from selling the promissory note, section 9-408(a) renders the terms ineffective and the bank can sell the note.

Restrictions on the transfer, assignment, or creation of a security interest can arise also under a rule of law, statute, or regulation. Section 9-408(c) renders any legal restriction ineffective. Laws are ineffective if they restrict, prohibit, or require the consent of a party or a governmental official to an assignment, transfer, or security interest in a promissory note or payment intangible, or make the assignment, transfer, or security interest a default or breach, or result in claims, defenses, or remedies.

Invalidating contractual and legal restrictions to allow the owner to sell a promissory note or payment intangible could affect the rights of the obligor or the account debtor of such property. To help prevent an adverse effect on those persons, section 9-408(d) establishes limitations on the effectiveness of an assignment by *sale* of such property. Section 9-408(d) operates only if the restrictions on the security interest would be effective in the absence of section 9-408.

Section 9-408(d) declares that the security interest created by the sale of the promissory note or payment intangible: 1) is not enforceable against the person obligated on the promissory note or the account debtor of the payment intangible; 2) imposes no duty on such person; 3) does not require the obligor or account debtor to render performance to or accept performance from the secured party (the assignee) or enable the secured party to enforce the security interest; 4) does not entitle the secured party to use or assign the debtor's rights under the promissory note or payment intangible; and 5) does not entitle the secured party to use, assign, possess, or have access to any trade secrets or confidential information in the promissory note or payment intangible. The effect of section 9-408(d) is that the obligor or account debtor continues its performance as though the security interest were never created, while the debtor (assignor) and secured party (assignee) act as though the restrictions on creation of the security interest did not exist.

D. Validity of Restrictions on Granting a Security Interest in a Health-Care-Insurance Receivable or General Intangible — Sections 9-408(a), (c)

Section 9-408 renders ineffective terms in a health-care-insurance receivable or a general intangible that restrict the right of the owner to create a security interest in such property. Section 9-408 does not invalidate all anti-assignment clauses, only clauses that impair creation or transfer of a security interest in such collateral. However, terms that restrict the *sale* of a health-care-insurance receivable are rendered ineffective nevertheless because a health-care-insurance receivable is a type of account, and the sale of an account creates a security interest. Sale of a general intangible does not create a security interest. *Health-care-insurance receivable*, defined in section 9-102(a)(46), is a right to payment under an insurance policy for health-care goods or services. *General intangible*, defined in section 9-102(a)(42), is any personal property that is not included within one of Article 9's other types of property. Intellectual property rights are a common type of general intangible.

Contractual and legal restrictions are invalidated by section 9-408. Section 9-408(a) renders ineffective terms that: 1) restrict, prohibit, or require the consent of the account debtor to the creation, attachment, perfection, or enforcement of a security interest; or 2) make such acts a default or result in claims, defenses, remedies, or a right of termination. Restrictions affecting a security interest in a general intangible or health-care-insurance receivable also can arise under a rule of law, statute, or regulation. Section 9-408(c) renders ineffective any such legal restrictions that impair the creation, attachment, or perfection of a security interest, make such acts a default, or result in claims, defenses, or remedies.

Invalidating contractual and legal restrictions to allow the owner to create a security interest in a general intangible or health-care-insurance receivable could affect the rights of the account debtor of such property. To help prevent an adverse effect on the account debtor, section 9-408(d) establishes limitations on the effectiveness of any security interest. The section applies only if the restrictions on the security interest would be effective in the absence of section 9-408. Section 9-408(d) declares that the security interest: 1) is not enforceable against the account debtor; 2) imposes no duty on such person; 3) does not require the account debtor to render performance to or accept performance from the secured party or enable the secured party to enforce the security interest; 4) does not entitle the secured party to use or assign the debtor's rights under the general intangible or health-care-insurance receivable; and 5) does not entitle the secured party to use, assign, possess, or have access to any trade secrets or confidential information in the general intangible or health-care-insurance receivable. The effect of the limitations is that the account debtor continues its performance as though the security interest were never created, while the debtor and secured party act as though the restrictions on creation of the security interest did not exist.

E. Validity of Restrictions on Granting a Security Interest in a Letter-of-Credit Right — Section 9-409

Terms in a letter-of-credit that restrict the right of a beneficiary of the letter to create a security interest in its letter-of-credit right are ineffective under section 9-409(a). *Letter-of-credit right*, defined in section 9-102(a)(51) and discussed in Chapter 2, is a right to payment or performance under a letter of credit. Section 9-409(a) provides that restrictive terms are ineffective to the extent they impair the creation, attachment, perfection, or enforcement of a security interest, and to the extent such actions would constitute a default or activate claims, defenses, remedies, or a right of termination. Any such terms established in a statute, rule of law, regulation, custom, or practice are ineffective under section 9-409(a).

Because invalidating contractual and legal restrictions could affect the other parties to a letter of credit, section 9-409(b) prevents a security interest in a letter-of-credit right from changing the duty of such persons, *if* the restrictions would be effective in the absence of section 9-409(a). Section 9-409(b) provides that the security interest: 1) is not enforceable against the applicant, issuer, nominated person, or transferee beneficiary of the letter-of-credit; 2) imposes no duty on such persons; and 3) does not require such persons to render performance to or accept performance from the secured party.

F. Validity of Restrictions on Assignment of Leasehold Interest — Section 9-407

Terms in a lease agreement that restrict a party's right to assign an interest in the lease or create a security interest in the lease are ineffective under section 9-407(a). In essence, the section enables a lessor or a lessee to assign or create a security interest in its lease interests unrestricted by any terms in the agreement prohibiting or conditioning such acts or making them a default. Section 9-407(a) operates similarly to transfer restrictions on a lessor's residual interest in the leased goods. The typical assignment or security interest is of the lessor's right to receive rental payments. The section pertains to a *true* lease, not a lease that is a security interest under section 1-203.

Section 9-407(a)(1) renders ineffective terms in a lease agreement that prohibit, restrict, or require a party's consent to an assignment or transfer of a party's interest in the lease or of the lessor's residual interest in the leased goods. The section also renders ineffective terms in a lease agreement that prohibit, restrict, or require a party's consent to the creation, attachment, perfection, or enforcement of a security interest in a party's interest in the lease or in the lessor's residual interest in the goods. Section 9-407(a)(2) renders ineffective terms in a lease agreement that make a party's assignment or transfer of, or the creation, attachment, perfection, or enforcement of a security interest in a party's lease interest or the lessor's residual interest a default or breach, or provide that such acts activate a claim, termination, or defense.

Section 9-407(b) creates two exceptions to the rule of section 9-407(a)(2). Restrictive terms rendered ineffective by section 9-407(a)(2) are effective nevertheless when the lessee transfers its right of possession or use of the goods in violation of the lease terms and when either party delegates "a material performance" in violation of the lease terms. These exceptions help protect the other party to the lease from being adversely affected by the assignment of the lease or creation of security interest in it. Although the section does not define material performance, section 9-407(c) declares that creation of a security interest is not a transfer that materially affects the lessee's rights, duties, burden, or risk unless there is an actual delegation of a material performance.

G. Account Debtor's Defenses and Claims — Section 9-404

An assignment of an account, chattel paper, general intangible, or payment intangible raises the question of whether the assignee is subject to the claims and defenses that the account debtor has against the assignor. Unless the account debtor has agreed otherwise, section 9-404(a)(1) makes the assignee's rights subject to: 1) all the terms of the agreement between the assignor and the account debtor (other than terms restricting assignment); and 2) any defense or claim of the account debtor in recoupment arising from the underlying agreement. The account debtor may assert its claim or defense arising from the underlying agreement against the assignee regardless of whether the claim or defense arises before or after the assignment. For example, an account debtor who discovers a breach of warranty in goods it purchased on credit from the seller after the seller assigned its right to payment to the assignee can use the breach as a defense to the assignee's demand for payment.

An account debtor also might have claims against the assignor arising from agreements other than the agreement assigned to assignee. Section 9-404(a)(2) makes the assignee's rights subject to any other claims or defenses of the account debtor that *accrue before* the account debtor receives an authenticated notification of the assignment, unless the account debtor has agreed otherwise. However, section 9-404(b) establishes an important limitation on the rights of the account debtor: it can assert the claim only to reduce the amount it owes the assignee, not to create an affirmative recovery against the assignee.

The rules of section 9-404(a) are subject to several qualifications. *First*, the section applies to claims and defenses of an *account debtor*. An *account debtor*, section 9-102(a)(3), is a person obligated on an account, chattel paper, or general intangible, which includes a payment intangible. Consequently, if the assignment is of a negotiable instrument, even when the negotiable instrument is part of the chattel paper that is assigned, section 9-404 does not apply and Article 3 determines whether the obligor of the promissory note can assert claims or defenses against the assignee. *Second*, section 9-404(e) states that section 9-404 does not apply to assignment of a health-care-insurance receivable. The account debtor of such property is protected by section 9-408(d) discussed previously. *Third*, section 9-404 is subject to other law protecting the rights of an account debtor who is an individual and who incurred the obligation primarily for a consumer purpose. *Fourth*, the Federal Trade Commission regulations (16 C.F.R. Part 433) make it an unfair practice for a seller to enter a consumer credit contract using a record that does not contain a statement that any assignee takes the contract subject to claims and defenses an account debtor could assert against the assignor. Section 9-404(d) declares that in a consumer transaction an assignee's rights under section 9-404 are subject to such rule regardless of whether the record includes the required statement. A consumer transaction exists when an individual secures an obligation it incurs primarily for personal, family, or household purposes with collateral it uses or acquires for use primarily for personal, family, or household purposes.

H. Account Debtor's Agreement to Assert No Defenses — Section 9-403

An assignee who realizes that its rights acquired in the assignment are subject to the claims and defenses of the account debtor under the rule of section 9-404 will likely require its assignor to obtain an agreement from the account debtor that it will not assert defenses and claims against an assignee. Such an agreement typically exists in the underlying contract between the account debtor and the assignor. Section 9-403(b) validates an account debtor's agreement that it will not assert against an assignee defenses and claims it may have against the assignor if the assignment transaction satisfies the requirements of section 9-403(b). If the agreement of the account debtor is enforceable under section 9-403(b), it nevertheless can assert its claims and defenses against the assignor.

Section 9-403(b) allows an assignee to enforce an account debtor's agreement to not assert defenses if the assignee takes the assignment for value, in good faith, without notice of a claim of a property or possessory right to the property assigned, and without notice of a defense or claim that could be asserted against a holder in due course of a negotiable instrument under section 3-305(a) (infancy, duress, lack of capacity, illegality of the transaction, fraud in the inducement, and discharge in insolvency proceedings — commonly known as the *real defenses*). The UCC definition of *good faith*, section 1-201(b)(20), means honesty in fact and the observance of reasonable commercial standards of fair dealing. Section 9-403(a) declares that *value* is defined by section 3-303(a) instead of section 1-204. Section 3-303(a) defines value broadly, with the principle difference from section 1-204 being that the Article 3 definition does not include as value any consideration sufficient to support a simple contract because a transfer that is issued for value also is issued for consideration under section 3-303(b).

Section 9-403 contains several qualifications to its rule. *First*, the section applies to the agreement made by an account debtor—a person obligated on an account, chattel paper, or general intangible. If the assignment is of a negotiable instrument, section 9-403 does not apply and Article 3 determines enforceability of the agreement. *Second*, section 9-403(c) declares that section 9-403(b) does not apply to defenses of a type that an obligor could assert against a holder in due course under section 3-305(b) (infancy, duress, lack of capacity, illegality of the transaction, fraud in the inducement, and discharge in insolvency proceedings). Consequently, the account debtor can assert such defenses against the assignee notwithstanding its agreement. Although section 9-403 does not apply to an assignment of a negotiable instrument, it essentially puts the assignee in the same position as a holder in due course of a negotiable instrument by utilizing the Article 3 definition of value and by allowing an account debtor to use the defenses that an obligor can assert against a holder in due course. *Third*, the Federal Trade Commission regulations (16 C.F.R. Part 433) make it an unfair practice for a seller to enter a consumer credit contract using a record that does not contain a statement that any assignee takes the contract subject to claims and defenses an account debtor could assert against the assignor. Section 9-403(d) declares that in a consumer transaction an account debtor may assert those claims and defenses against an assignee regardless of whether the record includes the required statement. *Fourth*, section 9-403 is subject to other law that establishes a different rule for an account debtor who is an individual and who incurred the obligation primarily for a consumer purpose.

I. Modification of an Assigned Contract— Section 9-405

The assignor and the account debtor might modify a contract previously assigned by the assignor. For example, suppose a contractor and owner contract for the construction of an office building. The contractor assigns to the bank its right to payment (an account) from the owner. During construction, the owner and contractor agree to several modifications to the original contract.

Sections 9-405(a) and (b) make a modification of or substitution for an assigned contract effective against the assignee provided the modification satisfies two conditions. *First*, the account debtor and assignor must modify the agreement in good faith. *Good faith*, section 1-201(b)(20), means honesty in fact and the observance of reasonable commercial standards of fair dealing. *Second*, the modification must occur before the assignor fully earns the right to payment it assigned or, if the assignor has earned the right to payment, before the account debtor receives an authenticated notification of the assignment. The account debtor's receipt of a notification terminates the right to make a modification that is effective against the assignee only when the modification occurs after the right to payment is fully earned.

Protection of the assignee comes from the declaration in section 9-405(a) that the assignee acquires rights under the modified contract. For example, if the modification increases the account debtor's payment obligations, the assignee receives that benefit. Additionally, section 9-405(a) validates an agreement between the assignor and assignee that any modification or substitution of the assigned contract is a breach, consequently making the assignor liable for any resulting damages. However, such a provision does not prevent the effectiveness of a modification that complies with the conditions of section 9-405.

Section 9-405 adopts two qualifications to its rule. *First*, the rule is subject to other law that establishes a different rule for an account debtor who is an individual that incurs the obligation primarily for personal, family, or household purposes. *Second*, section 9-405 does not apply to an assignment of a health-care-insurance receivable. Section 9-408(d) adopts protections for the account debtor of that type of assignment.

J. Discharge of the Obligation Assigned — Sections 9-406(a)–(c)

An assignor's assignment of its right to payment from an account debtor raises the question of whether the account debtor should make payment of the obligation to the assignor or the assignee. Section 9-406(a) authorizes the account debtor of an account, chattel paper, or payment intangible to discharge its obligation by paying the assignor until the account debtor receives an effective notification of the assignment. However, after the account debtor receives an effective notification of the assignment, it can discharge its obligation only by paying the assignee; payments to the assignor would have no effect on the obligation. *Receives*, section 1-202(e), requires that the notification come to the attention of the account debtor or be delivered at the account debtor's place of business or other authorized place.

Sections 9-406(a) and 9-406(b) establish several requirements for an effective notification. *First*, either the assignor or assignee must authenticate it. *Authenticate*, section 9-102(a)(7), allows for a written or an electronic notification. *Second*, the notification must indicate that the obligation has been assigned and that payment is to be made to the assignee. *Third*, the notification must reasonably identify the rights assigned.

An account debtor that receives a notification of assignment can request that the assignee supply proof of the assignment. If the account debtor requests, section 9-406(c) requires that the assignee must "seasonably furnish reasonable proof that the assignment has been made." *Seasonably*, section 1-205(b), means acting within the agreed time, or, in the absence of an agreement, within a reasonable time. A copy of the assignment agreement should satisfy the requirement of *reasonable proof*. Until the assignee complies, section 9-406(c) authorizes the account debtor to discharge its obligation by paying the assignor, regardless of the account debtor's receipt of an authenticated notification of the assignment.

Section 9-406(b) limits the effect of the notification in several situations. *First*, in a sale of a payment intangible, a notification is ineffective if the account debtor and the seller of the payment intangible agree to limit the account debtor's duty to pay a person other than the seller, and law other than Article 9 validates the limitation. *Second*, an account debtor has the option to disregard an otherwise effective notification that requests the account debtor to pay the assignee an amount less than the full amount of any installment or periodic payment due. The account debtor has this option regardless of whether the assignor assigned only part of the obligation to the assignee, assigned part to another assignee, or the account debtor knows of the partial assignment. Section 9-406(g) declares that the account debtor cannot waive or vary this option. However, the account debtor has discretion whether to exercise the option; the section does not compel the account debtor to do so.

The rules of section 9-406 are subject to any law outside Article 9 that establishes a different rule for an account debtor who is an individual and who incurs the obligation primarily for personal, family, or household purposes. Additionally, section 9-406 does not apply to an assignment of a health-care-insurance receivable. Finally, because an obligor of a promissory note is not an account debtor, section 9-406(a) does not apply and Article 3 governs discharge of the obligation.

Checkpoints

- Part 4 of Article 9 renders ineffective contractual and legal terms that restrict or prohibit a person from assigning by sale or security interest its right in accounts, chattel paper, general intangibles, payment intangibles, promissory notes, health-care-insurance receivables, letter-of-credit rights, and leasehold interests.

- The assignee is subject to the claims and defenses that the account debtor has against the assignor unless the account debtor has agreed to not assert its claims against the assignee.

- The agreement of an account debtor that it will not assert claims against the assignee is enforceable by the assignee if the assignment transaction is in good faith, for value, and without notice of certain claims and defenses.

- An account debtor can discharge the obligation assigned by paying the assignor until it receives notification of the assignment; after notification, discharge occurs only by paying the assignee.

Mastering Secured Transactions Checklist

Secured Transactions Article 9 Governs
- ❏ Article 9 governs any transaction, regardless of form, that creates a security interest in personal property or fixtures.
- ❏ A security interest exists when a secured party has an interest in the personal property or fixtures of the debtor as collateral to secure the payment or performance of an obligation owed to the secured party.
- ❏ Article 9 governs the sale of an account, chattel paper, a promissory note, and a payment intangible, as well as a security interest in such property.
- ❏ Other transactions Article 9 governs include: a transaction structured as a lease of goods that nevertheless is a security interest under section 1-203(b); a consignment; and an agricultural lien.

Attachment of a Security Interest
- ❏ The requirements for an attached and enforceable security interest are: the secured party gives value to the debtor; the debtor has rights in the collateral; and the debtor indicates its agreement to give a security interest in the collateral.
- ❏ The most common method by which the debtor indicates its agreement to give a security interest is by authenticating a security agreement—a record (written or electronic) that creates a security interest and includes a description of the collateral; other methods of indicating agreement include establishing control or taking possession of the collateral.
- ❏ Attachment of a security interest in proceeds of the collateral is automatic.
- ❏ A security agreement can include an after-acquired property clause that enables the security interest to attach property the debtor acquires after the security interest attaches to the original collateral.
- ❏ A security agreement can include a future advance clause that enables the security interest to secure existing and future obligations the debtor owes the secured party in addition to the initial value the secured party gives the debtor.

Perfection of a Security Interest

❏ Most security interests are perfected by filing a financing statement—a written or electronic document.

❏ A financing statement must include the names of the debtor and the secured party, mailing addresses of the debtor and the secured party, information about the organizational status and jurisdiction of the debtor, and indicate the collateral.

❏ The financing statement must be filed in the office designated by the jurisdiction that governs perfection of the security interest.

❏ Most financing statements are effective for five years from the date of filing and the effectiveness of a financing statement can be continued for five-year periods by filing a continuation statement before the financing statement lapses.

❏ If a financing statement lapses, the security interest becomes unperfected and is deemed never to have been perfected against a purchaser for value.

❏ Events that occur after a financing statement is filed, such as the debtor sells the collateral, changes it name, or merges with another entity, do not render the financing statement ineffective as to existing collateral, but can affect the security interest in collateral the debtor acquires more than four months after the event.

❏ Less common methods of perfection are applicable to certain types of collateral and include: taking possession of the collateral; establishing control; complying with federal or state law; automatic perfection; and temporary automatic perfection.

❏ A security interest in proceeds of collateral is perfected automatically for twenty days after it attaches if the security interest in the original collateral was perfected, and it remains perfected thereafter if the security interest satisfies the conditions for automatic perfection or the secured party otherwise perfects the security interest.

Priority of a Security Interest

❏ An unperfected security interest is always subordinate to a perfected security interest, and also is subordinate to a lien creditor, buyer, lessee, or licensee who satisfies the conditions for priority that Article 9 establishes.

❏ A security interest continues in collateral notwithstanding the debtor's disposition of the collateral unless the secured party authorizes the disposition free of the security interest or a UCC section provides otherwise.

❏ A buyer of goods in the ordinary course of business takes the goods free of a security interest created by the buyer's seller. Similar rules enable lessees and licensees to take the collateral free of a security interest.

❏ The general rule for determining priority between perfected security interests is the first-to-file-or-perfect rule—the security interest with the earliest date of filing or perfection has priority over other security interests in the same collateral.

❏ A purchase-money security interest has priority over a conflicting security interest in the collateral if the purchase-money secured party complies with the requirements for priority in section 9-324.

❏ A future advance security interest has priority over the interests of a lien creditor or a buyer in the collateral if it satisfies the time and lack of knowledge conditions for priority.

❏ Specific priority rules determine priority between conflicting security interests in certain types of collateral.

Jurisdiction that Governs the Security Interest

❏ Article 9 adopts rules that establish the jurisdiction that governs perfection, the effects of perfection or nonperfection, and the priority of a security interest.

❏ When there is a change in the governing jurisdiction, such as when the location of the debtor changes, a perfected security interest remains perfected temporarily in the new jurisdiction without requiring that the secured party perfect the security interest in the new jurisdiction.

❏ When the period of temporary perfection lapses, the security interest becomes unperfected and is deemed never to have been perfected against a purchaser for value unless the secured party perfects the security interest in the new jurisdiction before the temporary perfection lapses.

Default

❏ The parties to the security interest agree on the acts that constitute a default in a secured transaction; Article 9 does not define default.

❏ After a default a secured party can utilize the Article 9 remedies regardless whether its security interest has priority over all other security interests in the collateral; however, the rights in the collateral of a senior secured party are not affected by the actions of a junior secured party.

❏ The secured party can require the account debtor or obligor of receivables collateral to pay the obligation directly to the secured party.

❏ The secured party can choose to repossess the collateral using judicial process or self-help repossession, provided self-help repossession does not breach the peace.

❏ The secured party can dispose of the collateral in any manner and on any terms, provided all aspects of the disposition are commercially reasonable, and it must send reasonable notification of the disposition to the debtor and other secured parties.

❏ The secured party or the debtor can propose that the secured party accept the collateral in full or partial satisfaction of the secured obligation and, if the other party agrees, the obligation is discharged to the extent of the parties' agreement.

❏ A secured party who fails to comply with the statutory requirements of an Article 9 remedy is liable to the debtor for any loss its failure causes, including, for some security interests, statutory damages and minimum damages.

❏ The secured party's failure may result in limiting the obligor's liability for a deficiency under the rebuttable presumption rule.

Assignments of Property

❏ Article 9 renders ineffective contractual and legal terms that restrict or prohibit a person from assigning, by sale or security interest, its rights in accounts, chattel paper, general intangibles, payment intangibles, promissory notes, health-care-insurance receivables, letter-of-credit rights, and lease interests.

❏ The assignee of the property assigned is subject to the claims and defenses that the account debtor or obligor has against the assignor, unless the account debtor or obligor has agreed that it will not assert its claims against the assignee.

Index